FUNDAMENTALS OF
PROGRAMMING USING JAVA

FUNDAMENTALS OF PROGRAMMING USING JAVA

Kagiso Molefe
Nchimunya Phiri

Kruger Brentt
Publishers
2026

Kruger Brentt Publishers UK. LTD.
Company Number 9728962

Regd. Office: 68 St Margarets Road, Edgware, Middlesex HA8 9UU

ISBN: 978-1-78715-644-9

For information on all our publications visit our website at http://krugerbrentt.com/

PREFACE

Java has emerged as one of the most versatile and widely used programming languages, offering platform independence, object-oriented capabilities, and robust performance. It is extensively used in software development, web applications, mobile apps, enterprise systems, and emerging technologies such as IoT and cloud computing. Understanding Java programming fundamentals is essential for students, aspiring programmers, and professionals who wish to develop reliable, efficient, and scalable software solutions.

This book, Fundamentals of Programming Using Java, provides a comprehensive introduction to the principles, concepts, and practices of Java programming. It is designed to guide beginners as well as intermediate learners through the essentials of programming, helping them develop strong logical thinking and problem-solving skills while mastering the Java language.

The book begins with the basics of programming, including data types, variables, operators, control structures, and input/output operations. It then introduces object-oriented programming concepts such as classes, objects, inheritance, polymorphism, and encapsulation, emphasizing their practical applications in software development. Detailed explanations, examples, and illustrations help readers understand both the syntax and semantics of Java.

Subsequent chapters cover advanced topics including exception handling, file input/output, collections, multi-threading, and graphical user interfaces (GUI). The book also introduces basic concepts of software development methodology, debugging, and testing, providing readers with a holistic approach to programming. Practical exercises and examples throughout the text reinforce understanding and encourage hands-on learning.

Special attention is given to problem-solving techniques, algorithm development, and writing clean, efficient, and maintainable code. By combining theory, practical applications, and real-world examples, this book prepares readers to build a strong foundation in programming and equips them with skills necessary to tackle complex software projects.

Fundamentals of Programming Using Java serves as an essential resource for students, educators, and professionals seeking to master Java programming. By integrating foundational concepts with practical exercises and modern programming techniques, this book enables learners to confidently develop robust applications and adapt to evolving software development environments.

Kagiso Molefe

Nchimunya Phiri

CONTENTS

Chapter 1 THE MENTAL LANDSCAPE: AN INTRODUCTION

At the commencement of a journey, it is prudent to possess a mental representation of the landscape you will traverse. An intellectual journey, such as acquiring the skill to write computer programs, holds the same validity. In this instance, it is essential to understand the fundamentals of computers and their operational mechanisms. It is essential to understand the concept of a computer program and the process of its creation. As you will be developing applications in the Java programming language, it is essential to acquire knowledge about the language itself and the contemporary computer environment for which Java is intended.

While perusing this chapter, do not be concerned if you cannot comprehend every item. It would be infeasible for you to comprehend all the particulars from the succinct summaries in this chapter. Focus on acquiring sufficient knowledge of the overarching concepts to orient yourself in anticipation of the remainder of the book. The majority of the content in this chapter will be explored in far greater depth later in the book.

1.1 THE FETCH AND EXECUTE CYCLE: HOW TO USE MACHINE LANGUAGE AND EXECUTE CYCLE: MACHINE LANGUAGE

Computers are very complicated machines with lots of different parts. But the whole computer is made up of one part that does the real computing. You could call it the brain. This is the CPU, which stands for "Central Processing Unit." These days, the central processing unit (CPU) is a single "chip" about the size of an inch square. The CPU's job is to carry out programs.

A program is just a clear list of steps that a computer is supposed to follow automatically. Machine language is a very simple code that tells computers what to do. Every kind of computer has its own language called "machine language." A program can only be run directly by the computer if it is written in that language. (It can run programs written in other languages as long as they are first turned into machine language.)

It is saved in the computer's main memory, which is also known as the RAM or random access memory, and the CPU runs programs from that memory. RAM can hold more than just the program. It can also hold data that the software is using or processing. There is a list of places in main memory. There are numbers for these places, and the number that comes after a place's name is its address. A computer's memory holds millions of pieces of information, and an address lets you find the one you need.. When the CPU needs to access the program instruction or data in a particular location, it sends the address of that information as a signal to the memory; the memory responds by sending back the value contained in the specified location. The CPU can also store information in memory by specifying the information to be stored and the address of the location where it is to be stored.

On the level of machine language, the operation of the CPU is fairly straightforward (although it is very complicated in detail). The CPU executes a program that is stored as a sequence of machine language instructions in main memory. It does this by repeatedly reading, or *fetching* , an instruction from memory and then carrying out, or *executing* , that instruction. This process—fetch an instruction, execute it, fetch another instruction, execute it, and so on forever—is called the *fetch-and-execute cycle.* With one exception, which will be covered in the next section, this is all that the CPU ever does. (This is all really somewhat more complicated in modern computers. A typical processing chip these days contains several CPU "cores," which allows it to execute several instructions simultaneously. And access to main memory is speeded up by memory "caches," which can be more quickly accessed than main memory and which are meant to hold data and instructions that the CPU is likely to need soon. However, these complications don't change the basic operation.)

A CPU contains an *Arithmetic Logic Unit*, or ALU, which is the part of the processor that carries out operations such as addition and subtraction. It also holds a small number of *registers*, which are small memory units capable of holding a single number. A typical CPU might have 16 or 32 "general purpose" registers, which hold data values that are immediately accessible for processing, and many machine language instructions refer to these registers. For example, there might be an instruction that takes two numbers from two specified registers, adds those numbers (using the ALU), and stores the result back into a register. And there might be instructions for copying a data value from main memory into a register, or from a register into main memory.

The CPU also includes special purpose registers. The most important of these is the program counter , or PC. The CPU uses the PC to keep track of where it is in the program it is executing. The PC simply stores the memory address of the next instruction that the CPU should execute. At the beginning of each fetch-and-execute cycle, the CPU checks the PC to see which instruction it should fetch. During the course of the fetch-and-execute cycle, the number in the PC is updated to indicate the instruction that is to be executed in the next cycle. Usually, but not always, this is just the instruction that sequentially follows the current instruction in the program. Some machine language instructions modify the value that is stored in the PC. This makes it possible for the computer to "jump" from one point in the program to another point, which is essential for implementing the program features known as loops and branches that are discussed in Section 1.4.

A computer executes machine language programs mechanically—that is without under- standing them or thinking about them—simply because of the way it is physically put together. This is not an easy concept. A computer is a machine built of millions of tiny switches called *transistors*, which have the property that they can be wired together in such a way that an output from one switch can turn another switch on or off. As a computer computes, these switches turn each other on or off in a pattern determined both by the way they are wired together and by the program that the computer is executing.

Machine language instructions are expressed as binary numbers. A binary number is made up of just two possible digits, zero and one. Each zero or one is called a *bit*. So, a machine language instruction is just a sequence of zeros and ones. Each particular sequence encodes some particular instruction. The data that the computer manipulates is also encoded as binary numbers. In modern computers, each memory location holds a *byte*, which is a sequence of eight bits. A machine language instruction or a piece of data generally consists of several bytes, stored in consecutive memory locations. For example, when a CPU reads an instruction from memory, it might actually read four or eight bytes from four or eight memory locations; the memory address of the instruction is the address of the first of those bytes.

A computer can work directly with binary numbers because switches can readily represent such numbers: Turn the switch on to represent a one; turn it off to represent a zero. Machine language instructions are stored in memory as patterns of switches turned on or off. When a machine language instruction is loaded into the CPU, all that happens is that certain switches are turned on or off in the pattern that encodes that instruction. The CPU is built to respond to this pattern by executing the instruction it encodes; it does this simply because of the way all the other switches in the CPU are wired together.

So, you should understand this much about how computers work: Main memory holds machine language programs and data. These are encoded as binary numbers. The CPU fetches machine language instructions from memory one after another and executes them. Each instruction makes the CPU perform some very small task, such as adding two numbers or moving data to or from memory. The CPU does all this mechanically, without thinking about or understanding what it does—and therefore the program it executes must be perfect, complete in all details, and unambiguous because the CPU can do nothing but execute it exactly as written. Here is a schematic view of this first-stage understanding of the computer:

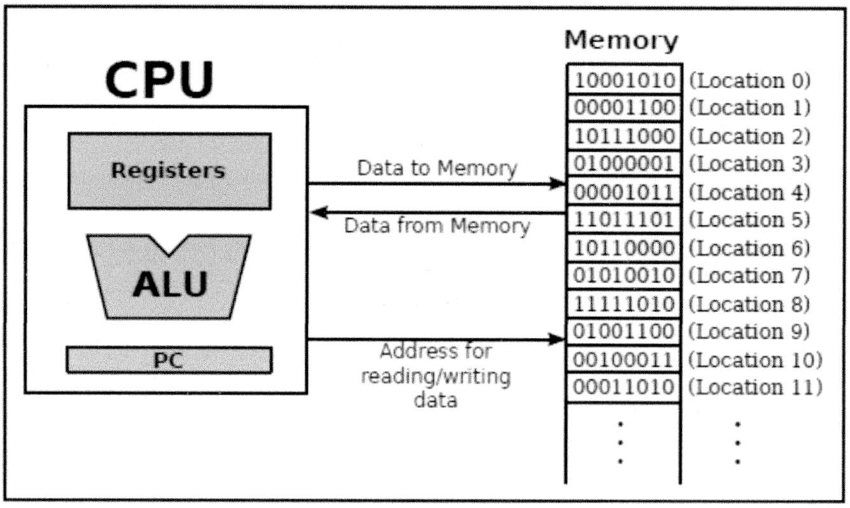

1.2 EVENTS THAT CAN'T WAIT: POLLING LOOPS AND ALARMS

The CPU spends almost all of its time fetching instructions from memory and executing them. However, the CPU and main memory are only two out of many components in a real computer system. A complete system contains other devices such as:

- A ***hard disk*** or ***solid state drive*** for storing programs and data files. (Note that main memory holds only a comparatively small amount of information, and holds it only as long as the power is turned on. A hard disk or solid state drive is used for permanent storage of larger amounts of information, but programs have to be loaded from there into main memory before they can actually be executed. A hard disk stores data on a spinning magnetic disk, while a solid state drive is a purely electronic device with no moving parts.)
- A ***keyboard*** and ***mouse*** for user input.
- A ***monitor*** and ***printer*** which can be used to display the computer's output.
- An ***audio output device*** that allows the computer to play sounds.
- A ***network interface*** that allows the computer to communicate with other computers that are connected to it on a network, either wirelessly or by wire.
- A ***scanner*** that converts images into coded binary numbers that can be stored and manipulated on the computer.

The list of devices is entirely open ended, and computer systems are built so that they can easily be expanded by adding new devices. Somehow the CPU has to communicate with and control all these devices. The CPU can only do this by executing machine language instructions (which is all it can do, period). The way this works is that for each device in a system, there is a *device driver* , which consists of software that the CPU executes when it has to deal with the device. Installing a new device on a system generally has two steps: plugging the device physically into the computer, and installing the device driver software. Without the device driver, the actual physical device would be useless, since the CPU would not be able to communicate with it.

A computer system consisting of many devices is typically organized by connecting those devices to one or more *busses*. A bus is a set of wires that carry various sorts of information between the devices connected to those wires. The wires carry data, addresses, and control signals. An address directs the data to a particular device and perhaps to a particular register or location within that device. Control signals can be used, for example, by one device to alert another that data is available for it on the data bus. A fairly simple computer system might be organized like this:

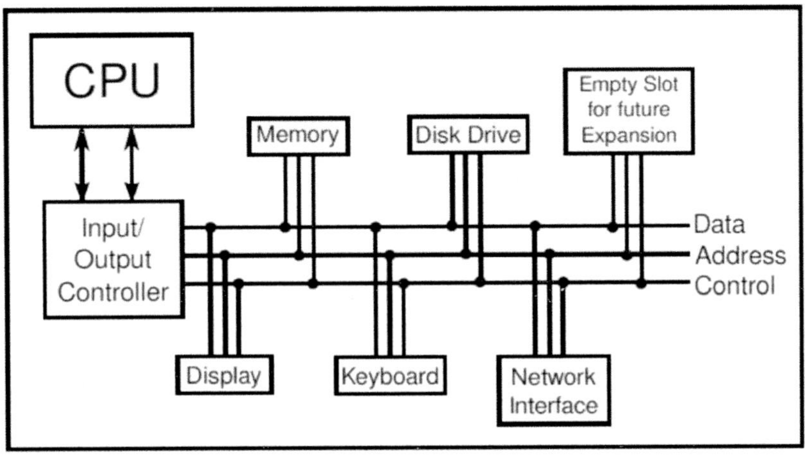

Now, devices such as keyboard, mouse, and network interface can produce input that needs to be processed by the CPU. How does the CPU know that the data is there? One simple idea, which turns out to be not very satisfactory, is for the CPU to keep checking for incoming data over and over. Whenever it finds data, it processes it. This method is called *polling* , since the CPU polls the input devices continually to see whether they have any input data to report. Unfortunately, although polling is very simple, it is also very inefficient. The CPU can waste an awful lot of time just waiting for input.

To avoid this inefficiency, *interrupts* are generally used instead of polling. An interrupt is a signal sent by another device to the CPU. The CPU responds to an interrupt signal by putting aside whatever it is doing in order to respond to the interrupt. Once it has handled the interrupt, it returns to what it was doing before the interrupt occurred. For example, when you press a key on your computer keyboard, a keyboard interrupt is sent to the CPU. The CPU responds to this signal by interrupting what it is doing, reading the key that you pressed, processing it, and then returning to the task it was performing before you pressed the key.

Again, you should understand that this is a purely mechanical process: A device signals an interrupt simply by turning on a wire. The CPU is built so that when that wire is turned on, the CPU saves enough information about what it is currently doing so that it can return to the same state later. This information consists of the contents of important internal registers such as the program counter. Then the CPU jumps to some predetermined memory location and begins executing the instructions stored there. Those instructions make up an *interrupt handler* that does the processing necessary to respond to the interrupt. (This interrupt handler is part of the device driver software for the device that signaled the interrupt.) At the end of the interrupt handler is an instruction that tells the CPU to jump back to what it was doing; it does that by restoring its previously saved state.

Interrupts allow the CPU to deal with *asynchronous events*. In the regular fetch- and-execute cycle, things happen in a predetermined order; everything that happens is "synchronized" with everything else. Interrupts make it possible for the CPU to deal efficiently with events that happen "asynchronously," that is, at unpredictable times.

As another example of how interrupts are used, consider what happens when the CPU needs to access data that is stored on a hard disk. The CPU can access data directly only if it is in main memory. Data on the disk has to be copied into memory before it can be accessed. Unfortunately, on the scale of speed at which the CPU operates, the disk drive is extremely slow. When the CPU needs data from the disk, it sends a signal to the disk drive telling it to locate the data and get it ready. (This signal is sent synchronously, under the control of a regular program.) Then, instead of just waiting the long and unpredictable amount of time that the disk drive will take to do this, the CPU goes on with some other task. When the disk drive has the data ready, it sends an interrupt signal to the CPU. The interrupt handler can then read the requested data.

Now, you might have noticed that all this only makes sense if the CPU actually has several tasks to perform. If it has nothing better to do, it might as well spend its time polling for input or waiting for disk drive operations to complete. All modern computers use *multitasking* to perform several tasks at once. Some computers can be used by several people at once. Since the CPU is so fast, it can quickly switch its attention from one user to another, devoting a fraction of a second to each user in turn. This application of multitasking is called *timesharing* . But a modern personal computer with just a single user also uses multitasking. For example, the user might be typing a paper while a clock is continuously displaying the time and a file is being downloaded over the network.

Each of the individual tasks that the CPU is working on is called a *thread* . (Or a *process*; there are technical differences between threads and processes, but they are not important here, since it is threads that are used in Java.) Many CPUs can literally execute more than one thread simultaneously—such CPUs contain multiple "cores," each of which can run a thread— but there is always a limit on the number of threads that can be executed at the same time. Since there are often more threads than can be executed simultaneously, the computer has to be able switch its attention from one thread to another, just as a timesharing computer switches its attention from one user to another. In general, a thread that is being executed will continue to run until one of several things happens:

- The thread might voluntarily *yield* control, to give other threads a chance to run.
- The thread might have to wait for some asynchronous event to occur. For example, the thread might request some data from the disk drive, or it might wait for the user to press a key. While it is waiting, the thread is said to be *blocked* , and other threads, if any, have a chance to run. When the event occurs, an interrupt will "wake up" the thread so that it can continue running.
- The thread might use up its allotted slice of time and be suspended to allow other threads to run. Most computers can "forcibly" suspend a thread in this way; computers that can do that are said to use *preemptive multitasking.* To do preemptive multitasking, a computer needs a special timer device that generates an interrupt at regular intervals, such as 100 times per second. When a timer interrupt occurs, the CPU has a chance to switch from one thread to another, whether the thread that is currently running likes it or not. All modern desktop and laptop computers, and even typical smartphones and tablets, use preemptive multitasking.

Ordinary users, and indeed ordinary programmers, have no need to deal with interrupts and interrupt handlers. They can concentrate on the different tasks that they want the computer to perform; the details of how the computer manages to get all those tasks done are not important to them. In fact, most users, and many programmers, can ignore threads and multitasking altogether. However, threads have become increasingly important as computers have become more powerful and as they have begun to make more use of multitasking and multiprocessing. In fact, the ability to work with threads is fast becoming an essential job skill for programmers. Fortunately, Java has good support for threads, which are built into the Java programming language as a fundamental programming concept. Programming with threads will be covered in Chapter 12.

Just as important in Java and in modern programming in general is the basic concept of asynchronous events. While programmers don't actually deal with interrupts directly, they do often find themselves writing event handlers, which, like interrupt handlers, are called asynchronously when specific events occur. Such "event-driven programming" has a very different feel from the more traditional straight-through, synchronous programming. We will begin with the more traditional type of programming, which is still used for programming individual tasks, but we will return to threads and events later in the text, starting in Chapter 6

By the way, the software that does all the interrupt handling, handles communication with the user and with hardware devices, and controls which thread is allowed to run is called the *operating system* . The operating system is the basic, essential software without which a computer would not be able to function. Other programs, such as word processors and Web browsers, are dependent upon the operating system. Common desktop operating systems include Linux, various versions of Windows, and MacOS. Operating systems for smartphones and tablets include Android and iOS.

1.3 THE VIRTUAL MACHINE FOR JAVA

The CPU of a computer can directly carry out the very simple rules that make up machine language. On the other hand, most programs are written in high-level languages like C++, Java, or Python. Any machine can't run a program that was written in a high-level language. It needs to be turned into machine code first. This work can be done by a tool known as a compiler. A translator takes a program written in a high-level language and turns it into a machine-language program that can be run. Once the translation is done, the machine-language program can be run as many times as needed. However, it can only be used on one type of computer at a time, since every computer has its own machine language. As it turns out, Java also depends on the operating system it is running on because it needs to work with the OS to do things like access the computer's hardware. But let's not worry about that right now. If you want the program to work on a different kind of computer, you have to use a different compiler to change it into the right machine code.

There is an alternative to compiling a high-level language program. Instead of using a compiler, which translates the program all at once, you can use an *interpreter*, which translates it instruction-by-instruction, as necessary. An interpreter is a program that acts much like a CPU, with a kind of fetch-and-execute cycle. In order to execute a program, the interpreter runs in a loop in which it repeatedly reads one instruction from the program, decides what is necessary to carry out that instruction, and then performs the appropriate machine-language commands to do so.

(A compiler is like a human translator who translates an entire book from one language to another, producing a new book in the second language. An interpreter is more like a human interpreter who translates a speech at the United Nations from one language to another at the same time that the speech is being given.)

One use of interpreters is to execute high-level language programs. For example, the programming language Lisp is usually executed by an interpreter rather than a compiler. However, interpreters have another purpose: They can let you use a machine-language program meant for one type of computer on a completely different type of computer. For example, one of the original home computers was the Commodore 64 or "C64". While you might not find an actual C64, you can find programs that run on other computers—or even in a web browser— that "emulate" one. Such an emulator can run C64 programs by acting as an interpreter for the C64 machine language.

The designers of Java chose to use a combination of compiling and interpreting. Programs written in Java are compiled into machine language, but it is a machine language for a computer that doesn't really exist. This so-called "virtual" computer is known as the *Java Virtual Machine*, or JVM. The machine language for the Java Virtual Machine is called *Java bytecode*. There is no reason why Java bytecode couldn't be used as the machine language of a real computer, rather than a virtual computer. But in fact the use of a virtual machine makes possible one of the main selling points of Java: the fact that it can actually be used on any computer. All that the computer needs is an interpreter for Java bytecode. Such an interpreter simulates the JVM in the same way that a C64 emulator simulates a Commodore 64 computer. (The term JVM is also used for the Java bytecode interpreter program that does the simulation, so we say that a computer needs a JVM in order to run Java programs. Technically, it would be more correct to say that the interpreter *implements* the JVM than to say that it *is* a JVM.)

Of course, a different Java bytecode interpreter is needed for each type of computer, but once a computer has a Java bytecode interpreter, it can run any Java bytecode program, and the same program can be run on any computer that has such an interpreter. This is one of the essential features of Java: the same compiled program can be run on many different types of computers.

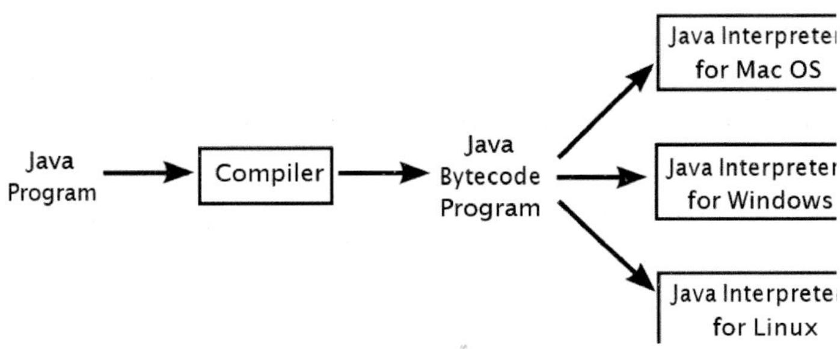

Why, you might wonder, use the intermediate Java bytecode at all? Why not just distribute the original Java program and let each person compile it into the machine language of whatever computer they want to run it on? There are several reasons. First of all, a compiler has to understand Java, a complex high-level language. The compiler is itself a complex program. A Java bytecode interpreter, on the other hand, is a relatively small, simple program. This makes it easy to write a bytecode interpreter for a new type of computer; once that is done, that computer can run any compiled Java program. It would be much harder to write a Java compiler for the same computer.

Furthermore, Java was created with the idea that some programs would be downloaded over a network. This leads to obvious security concerns: you don't want to download and run a program that will damage your computer or your files. The bytecode interpreter acts as a buffer between you and the program you download. You are really running the interpreter, which runs the downloaded program indirectly. The interpreter can protect you from potentially dangerous actions on the part of that program.

When Java was still a new language, it was criticized for being slow: Since Java bytecode was executed by an interpreter, it seemed that Java bytecode programs could never run as quickly as programs compiled into native machine language (that is, the actual machine language of the computer on which the program is running). However, this problem has been largely overcome by the use of *just-in-time compilers* for executing Java bytecode. A just-in-time compiler translates Java bytecode into native machine language. It does this while it is executing the program. Just as for a normal interpreter, the input to a just-in-time compiler is a Java bytecode program, and its task is to execute that program. But as it is executing the program, it also translates parts of it into the native machine language. The translated parts of the program can then be executed much more quickly than they could be interpreted. Since a given part of a program is often executed many times as the program runs, a just-in-time compiler can significantly speed up the overall execution time.

I should note that there is no necessary connection between Java and Java bytecode. A program written in Java could certainly be compiled into the machine language of a real computer. And programs written in other languages can be compiled into Java bytecode. However, the combination of Java and Java bytecode is platform-independent, secure, and network-compatible while allowing you to program in a modern high-level object-oriented language.

There are even some other programming languages that compile into Java bytecode. The compiled bytecode programs can then be executed by a standard JVM. New languages that have been developed specifically for programming the

JVM include Scala, Groovy, Clojure, and Processing. Jython and JRuby are versions of older languages, Python and Ruby, that target the JVM. These languages make it possible to enjoy many of the advantages of the JVM while avoiding some of the technicalities of the Java language. In fact, the use of other languages with the JVM has become important enough that several new features have been added to the JVM specifically to add better support for some of those languages. And this improvement to the JVM has in turn made possible some new features in Java.

1.4 ESSENTIAL COMPONENTS OF PROGRAMS

There are two basic aspects of programming: data and instructions. To work with data, you need to understand *variables* and *types*; to work with instructions, you need to understand *control structures* and *subroutines*. You'll spend a large part of the course becoming familiar with these concepts.

A *variable* is just a memory location (or several consecutive locations treated as a unit) that has been given a name so that it can be easily referred to and used in a program. The programmer only has to worry about the name; it is the compiler's responsibility to keep track of the memory location. As a programmer, you just need to keep in mind that the name refers to a kind of "box" in memory that can hold data, even though you don't have to know where in memory that box is located.

In Java and in many other programming languages, a variable has a *type* that indicates what sort of data it can hold. One type of variable might hold integers—whole numbers such as 3, -7, and 0—while another holds floating point numbers—numbers with decimal points such as 3.14, -2.7, or 17.0. (Yes, the computer does make a distinction between the integer 17 and the floating-point number 17.0; they actually look quite different inside the computer.) There could also be types for individual characters ('A', ';', etc.), strings ("Hello", "A string can include many characters", etc.), and less common types such as dates, colors, sounds, or any other kind of data that a program might need to store.

Programming languages always have commands for getting data into and out of variables and for doing computations with data. For example, the following "assignment statement," which might appear in a Java program, tells the computer to take the number stored in the variable named "principal", multiply that number by 0.07, and then store the result in the variable named "interest":

```
interest = principal * 0.07;
```

There are also "input commands" for getting data from the user or from files on the computer's disks, and there are "output commands" for sending data in the other direction.

These basic commands—for moving data from place to place and for performing computations—are the building blocks for all programs. These building blocks are combined into complex programs using control structures and subroutines.

A program is a sequence of instructions. In the ordinary "flow of control," the computer executes the instructions in the sequence in which they occur in the program, one after the other. However, this is obviously very limited: the computer would soon run out of instructions to execute. *Control structures* are special instructions that can change the flow of control. There are two basic types of control structure: *loops*, which allow a sequence of instructions to be repeated over and over, and *branches*, which allow the computer to decide between two or more different courses of action by testing conditions that occur as the program is running. For example, it might be that if the value of the variable "principal" is greater than 10000, then the "interest" should be computed by multiplying the principal by 0.05; if not, then the interest should be computed by multiplying the principal by 0.04. A program needs some way of expressing this type of decision. In Java, it could be expressed using the following "if statement":

```
if (principal > 10000)
    interest = principal * 0.05;
else
    interest = principal * 0.04;
```

(Don't worry about the details for now. Just remember that the computer can test a condition and decide what to do next on the basis of that test.)

Loops are used when the same task has to be performed more than once. For example, if you want to print out a mailing label for each name on a mailing list, you might say, "Get the first name and address and print the label; get the second name and address and print the label; get the third name and address and print the label. . . " But this quickly becomes ridiculous—and might not work at all if you don't know in advance how many names there are. What you would like to say is something like "While there are more names to process, get the next name and address, and print the label." A loop can be used in a program to express such repetition.

Large programs are so complex that it would be almost impossible to write them if there were not some way to break them up into manageable "chunks." Subroutines provide one way to do this. A *subroutine* consists of the instructions for performing some task, grouped together as a unit and given a name. That name can then be used as a substitute for the whole set of instructions. For example, suppose that one of the tasks that your program needs to perform is to draw a house on the screen. You can take the necessary instructions, make them into a subroutine, and give that subroutine some appropriate name—say, "drawHouse()". Then anyplace in your program where you need to draw a house, you can do so with the single command:

drawHouse();

This will have the same effect as repeating all the house-drawing instructions in each place.

The advantage here is not just that you save typing. Organizing your program into subroutines also helps you organize your thinking and your program design effort. While writing the house-drawing subroutine, you can concentrate on the problem of drawing a house without worrying for the moment about the rest of the program. And once the subroutine is written, you can forget about the details of drawing houses—that problem is solved, since you have a subroutine to do it for you. A subroutine becomes just like a built-in part of the language which you can use without thinking about the details of what goes on "inside" the subroutine.

Variables, types, loops, branches, and subroutines are the basis of what might be called "traditional programming." However, as programs become larger, additional structure is needed to help deal with their complexity. One of the most effective tools that has been found is object- oriented programming, which is discussed in the next section.

1.5 OBJECTS AND OBJECT-ORIENTED PROGRAMMING

Programs must be designed. No one can just sit down at the computer and compose a program of any complexity. The discipline called *software engineering* is concerned with the construction of correct, working, well-written programs. The software engineer tries to use accepted and proven methods for analyzing the problem to be solved and for designing a program to solve that problem.

During the 1970s and into the 80s, the primary software engineering methodology was *structured programming* . The structured programming approach to program design was based on the following advice: To solve a large problem, break the problem into several pieces and work on each piece separately; to solve each piece, treat it as a new problem which can itself be broken down into smaller problems; eventually, you will work your way down to problems that can be solved directly, without further decomposition. This approach is called *top-down programming* .

There is nothing wrong with top-down programming. It is a valuable and often-used approach to problem-solving. However, it is incomplete. For one thing, it deals almost entirely with producing the instructions necessary to solve a problem. But as time went on, people realized that the design of the data structures for a program was at least as important as the design of subroutines and control structures. Top-down programming doesn't give adequate consideration to the data that the program manipulates.

Another problem with strict top-down programming is that it makes it difficult to reuse work done for other projects. By starting with a particular problem and subdividing it into convenient pieces, top-down programming tends to produce a design that is unique to that problem. It is unlikely that you will be able to take a large chunk of programming from another program and fit it into your project, at least not without extensive modification. Producing high-quality programs is difficult and expensive, so programmers and the people who employ them are always eager to reuse past work.

So, in practice, top-down design is often combined with *bottom-up design* . In bottom-up design, the approach is to start "at the bottom," with problems that you already know how to solve (and for which you might already have a reusable software component at hand). From there, you can work upwards towards a solution to the overall problem.

The reusable components should be as "modular" as possible. A *module* is a component of a larger system that interacts with the rest of the system in a simple, well-defined, straightforward manner. The idea is that a module can be "plugged into" a system. The details of what goes on inside the module are not important to the system as a whole, as long as the module fulfills its assigned role correctly. This is called *information hiding* , and it is one of the most important principles of software engineering.

One common format for software modules is to contain some data, along with some subroutines for manipulating that data. For example, a mailing-list module might contain a list of names and addresses along with a subroutine for adding a new name, a subroutine for printing mailing labels, and so forth. In such modules, the data itself is often hidden inside the module; a program that uses the module can then manipulate the data only indirectly, by calling the subroutines provided by the module. This protects the data, since it can only be manipulated in known, well-defined ways. And it makes it easier for programs to use the module, since they don't have to worry about the details of how the data is represented. Information about the representation of the data is hidden.

Modules that could support this kind of information-hiding became common in program- ming languages in the early 1980s. Since then, a more advanced form of the same idea has more or less taken over software engineering. This latest approach is called *object-oriented programming* , often abbreviated as OOP.

The central concept of object-oriented programming is the *object*, which is a kind of module containing data and subroutines. The point-of-view in OOP is that an object is a kind of self- sufficient entity that has an internal *state* (the data it contains) and that can respond to *messages* (calls to its subroutines). A mailing list object, for example, has a state consisting of a list of names and addresses. If you send it a message telling it to add a name, it will respond by modifying its state to reflect the change. If you send it a message telling it to print itself, it will respond by printing out its list of names and addresses.

The OOP approach to software engineering is to start by identifying the objects involved in a problem and the messages that those objects should respond to. The program that results is a collection of objects, each with its own data and its own set of responsibilities. The objects interact by sending messages to each other. There is not much "top-down" in the large-scale design of such a program, and people used to more traditional programs can have a hard time getting used to OOP. However, people who use OOP would claim that object-oriented programs tend to be better models of the way the world itself works, and that they are therefore easier to write, easier to understand, and more likely to be correct.

You should think of objects as "knowing" how to respond to certain messages. Different objects might respond to the same message in different ways. For example, a "print" message would produce very different results, depending on the object it is sent to. This property of objects—that different objects can respond to the same message in different ways—is called *polymorphism*.

It is common for objects to bear a kind of "family resemblance" to one another. Objects that contain the same type of data and that respond to the same messages in the same way belong to the same *class*. (In actual programming, the class is primary; that is, a class is created and then one or more objects are created using that class as a template.) But objects can be similar without being in exactly the same class.

For example, consider a drawing program that lets the user draw lines, rectangles, ovals, polygons, and curves on the screen. In the program, each visible object on the screen could be represented by a software object in the program. There would be five classes of objects in the program, one for each type of visible object that can be drawn. All the lines would belong to one class, all the rectangles to another class, and so on. These classes are obviously related; all of them represent "drawable objects." They would, for example, all presumably be able to respond to a "draw yourself" message. Another level of grouping, based on the data needed to represent each type of object, is less obvious, but would be very useful in a program: We can group polygons and curves together as "multipoint objects," while lines, rectangles, and ovals are "two-point objects." (A line is determined by its two endpoints, a rectangle by two of its corners, and an oval by two corners of the rectangle that contains it. The rectangles that I am talking about here have sides that are vertical and horizontal, so that they can be specified by just two points; this is the common meaning of "rectangle" in drawing programs.) We could diagram these relationships as follows:

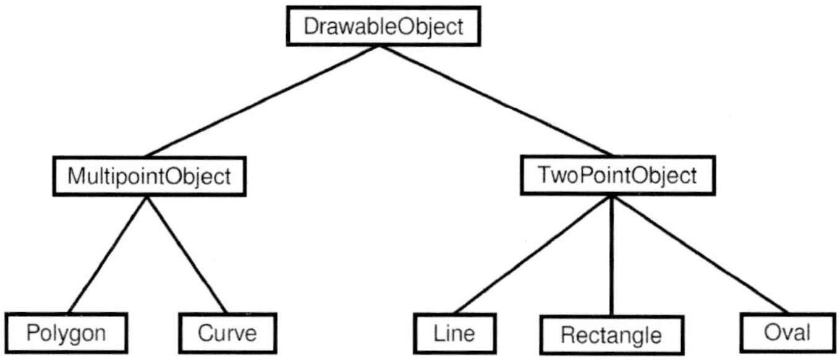

DrawableObject, MultipointObject, and TwoPointObject would be classes in the program. MultipointObject and TwoPointObject would be *subclasses* of DrawableObject. The class Line would be a subclass of TwoPointObject and (indirectly) of DrawableObject. A subclass of a class is said to *inherit* the properties of that class. The subclass can add to its inheritance and it can even "override" part of that inheritance (by defining a different response to some message). Nevertheless, lines, rectangles, and so on are drawable objects, and the class DrawableObject expresses this relationship.

Inheritance is a powerful means for organizing a program. It is also related to the problem of reusing software components. A class is the ultimate reusable component. Not only can it be reused directly if it fits exactly into a program you are trying to write, but if it just almost fits, you can still reuse it by defining a subclass and making only the small changes necessary to adapt it exactly to your needs.

So, OOP is meant to be both a superior program-development tool and a partial solution to the software reuse problem. Objects, classes, and object-oriented programming will be important themes throughout the rest of this text. You will start using objects that are built into the Java language in the next chapter, and in Chapter 5 you will begin creating your own classes and objects.

1.6 THE MODERN USER INTERFACE

When computers were first introduced, ordinary people—including most programmers— couldn't get near them. They were locked up in rooms with white-coated attendants who would take your programs and data, feed them to the computer, and return the computer's response some time later. When timesharing—where the computer switches its attention rapidly from one person to another—was invented in the 1960s, it became possible for several people to interact directly with the computer at the same time. On a timesharing system, users sit at "terminals" where they type commands to the computer, and the computer types back its re- sponse. Early personal computers also used typed commands and responses, except that there was only one person involved at a time. This type of interaction between a user and a computer is called a *command-line interface.*

Today, of course, most people interact with computers in a completely different way. They use a *Graphical User Interface*, or GUI. The computer draws interface *components* on the screen. The components include things like windows, scroll bars, menus, buttons, and icons. Usually, a *mouse* is used to manipulate such components or, on "touchscreens," your fingers. Assuming that you have not just been teleported in from the 1970s, you are no doubt already familiar with the basics of graphical user interfaces!

A lot of GUI interface components have become fairly standard. That is, they have similar appearance and behavior on many different computer platforms including MacOS, Windows, and Linux. Java programs, which are supposed to run on many different platforms without modification to the program, can use all the standard GUI components. They might vary a little in appearance from platform to platform, but their functionality should be identical on any computer on which the program runs.

Shown below is an image of a very simple Java program that demonstrates a few standard GUI interface components. When the program is run, a window similar to the picture shown here will open on the computer screen. There are four components in the window with which the user can interact: a button, a checkbox, a text field, and a pop-up menu. These components are labeled. There are a few other components in the window. The labels themselves are components (even though you can't interact with them). The right half of the window is a text area component, which can display multiple lines of text. A scrollbar component appears alongside the text area when the number of lines of text becomes larger than will fit in the text area. And in fact, the whole window can itself be considered to be a "component."

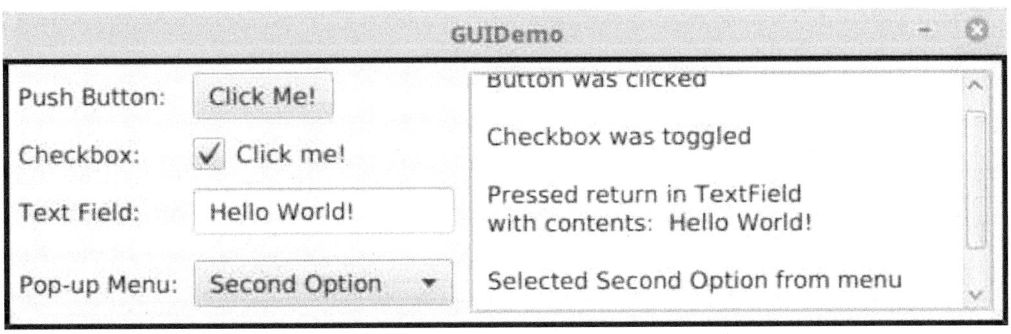

(If you would like to run this program, the source code, GUIDemo.java, is available on line. For more information on using this and other examples from this textbook see Section 2.6.)

In fact, there are three complete sets of GUI components that can be used with Java. One of these, the AWT or *Abstract Windowing Toolkit*, was part of the original version of Java. The second, which is known as *Swing* , builds on the AWT; it was introduced in Java version 1.2, and was the standard GUI toolkit for many years. The third GUI toolkit, JavaFX, briefly became a standard part of Java in Version 8 but is now distributed separately. JavaFX is meant as a more modern way to write GUI applications, but using it is complicated by the fact that it has to be downloaded and installed separately. This textbook covers JavaFX exclusively, but an alternative version of the textbook is available that covers Swing instead. Either version of the textbook can be a reasonable choice.

When a user interacts with GUI components, "events" are generated. For example, clicking a push button generates an event, and pressing a key on the keyboard generates an event. Each time an event is generated, a message is sent to the program telling it that the event has occurred, and the program responds according to its program. In fact, a typical GUI program consists largely of "event handlers" that tell the program how to respond to various types of events. In the above example, the program has been programmed to respond to each event by displaying a message in the text area. In a more realistic example, the event handlers would have more to do.

The use of the term "message" here is deliberate. Messages, as you saw in the previous section, are sent to objects. In fact, Java GUI components are implemented as objects. Java includes many predefined classes that represent various types of GUI components. Some of these classes are subclasses of others. Here is a diagram showing just a few of the JavaFX GUI classes and their relationships:

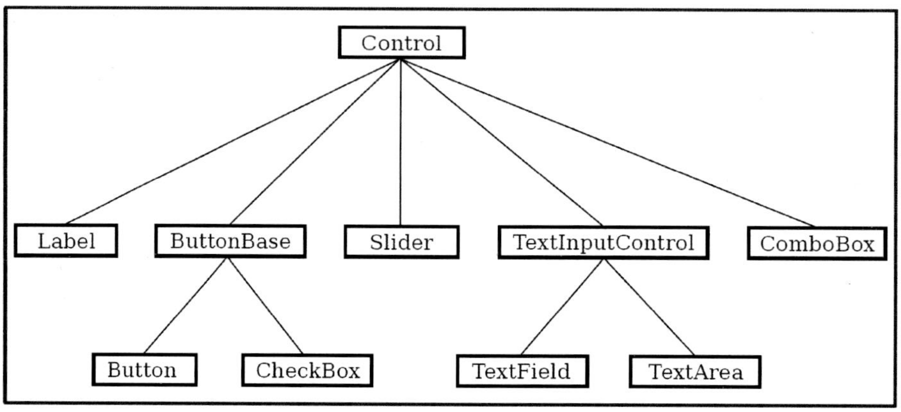

Don't worry about the details for now, but try to get some feel about how object-oriented programming and inheritance are used here. Note that all the GUI classes shown here are subclasses, directly or indirectly, of a class called *Control*, which represents general properties that are shared by many JavaFX components. In the diagram, two of the direct subclasses of *Control* themselves have subclasses. The classes *TextField* and *TextArea*, which have certain behaviors in common, are grouped together as subclasses of *TextInputControl*. Similarly *Button* and *CheckBox* are subclasses of *ButtonBase*, which represents properties common to both buttons and checkboxes. (*ComboBox*, by the way, is the class that represents pop-up menus.)

Just from this brief discussion, perhaps you can see how GUI programming can make effective use of object-oriented design. In fact, GUIs, with their "visible objects," are probably a major factor contributing to the popularity of OOP.

Programming with GUI components and events is one of the most interesting aspects of Java. However, we will spend several chapters on the basics before returning to this topic in Chapter 6.

1.7 THE INTERNET AND BEYOND

Computers can be connected together on *networks*. A computer on a network can communicate with other computers on the same network by exchanging data and files or by sending and receiving messages. Computers on a network can even work together on a large computation.

Today, millions of computers throughout the world are connected to a single huge network that we know as the *Internet* . New computers are being connected to the Internet every day, both by wireless communication and by physical connection using technologies such as DSL, cable modems, and Ethernet.

There are elaborate *protocols* for communication over the Internet. A protocol is simply a detailed specification of how communication is to proceed. For two computers to communicate at all, they must both be using the same protocols. The most basic protocols on the Internet are the *Internet Protocol* (IP), which specifies how data is to be physically transmitted from one computer to another, and the *Transmission Control Protocol* (TCP), which ensures that data sent using IP is received in its entirety and without error. These two protocols, which are referred to collectively as TCP/IP, provide a foundation for communication. Other protocols use TCP/IP to send specific types of information such as web pages, electronic mail, and data files.

All communication over the Internet is in the form of *packets*. A packet consists of some data being sent from one computer to another, along with addressing information that indicates where on the Internet that data is supposed to go. Think of a packet as an envelope with an address on the outside and a message on the inside. (The message is the data.) The packet also includes a "return address," that is, the address of the sender. A packet can hold only a limited amount of data; longer messages must be divided among several packets, which are then sent individually over the Net and reassembled at their destination.

Every computer on the Internet has an *IP address*, a number that identifies it uniquely among all the computers on the Net. (Actually, the claim about uniqueness is not quite true, but the basic idea is valid, and the full truth is complicated.) The IP address is used for addressing packets. A computer can only send data to another computer on the Internet if it knows that computer's IP address. Since people prefer to use names rather than numbers, most computers are also identified by names, called *domain names*. For example, the main computer of the Mathematics Department at Hobart and William Smith Colleges has the domain name math.hws.edu. (Domain names are just for convenience; your computer still needs to know IP addresses before it can communicate. There are computers on the Internet whose job it is to translate domain names to IP addresses. When you use a domain name, your computer sends a message to a domain name server to find out the corresponding IP address. Then, your computer uses the IP address, rather than the domain name, to communicate with the other computer.)

The Internet provides a number of services to the computers connected to it (and, of course, to the users of those computers). These services use TCP/IP to send various types of data over the Net. Among the most popular services are instant messaging, file sharing, electronic mail, and the World-Wide Web. Each service has its own protocols, which are used to control transmission of data over the network. Each service also has some sort of user interface, which allows the user to view, send, and receive data through the service.

For example, the email service uses a protocol known as *SMTP* (Simple Mail Transfer Protocol) to transfer email messages from one computer to another. Other protocols, such as POP and IMAP, are used to fetch messages from an email account so that the recipient can read them. A person who uses email, however, doesn't need to understand or even know about these protocols. Instead, they are used behind the scenes by computer programs to send and receive email messages. These programs provide the user with an easy-to-use user interface to the underlying network protocols.

The World-Wide Web is perhaps the most exciting of network services. The World-Wide Web allows you to request *pages* of information that are stored on computers all over the Internet. A Web page can contain *links* to other pages on the same computer from which it was obtained or to other computers anywhere in the world. A computer that stores such pages of information is called a *web server* . The user interface to the Web is the type of program known as a *web browser* . Common web browsers include Microsoft Edge, Firefox, Chrome, and Safari. You use a Web browser to request a page of information. The browser sends a request for that page to the computer on which the page is stored, and when a response is received from that computer, the web browser displays it to you in a neatly formatted form. A web browser is just a user interface to the Web. Behind the scenes, the web browser uses a protocol called *HTTP* (HyperText Transfer Protocol) to send each page request and to receive the response from the web server.

Now just what, you might be thinking, does all this have to do with Java? In fact, Java is intimately associated with the Internet and the World-Wide Web. When Java was first introduced, one of its big attractions was the ability to write *applets*. An applet was a small program that is transmitted over the Internet and that runs on a web page. Applets made it possible for a web page to perform complex tasks and have complex interactions with the user. Alas, applets suffered from a variety of problems, and they are no longer used. There are now other options for running programs on Web pages.

But applets were only one aspect of Java's relationship with the Internet. Java can be used to write complex, stand-alone applications that do not depend on a Web browser. Many of these programs are network-related. For example many of the largest and most complex web sites use web server software that is written in Java. Java includes excellent support for network protocols, and its platform independence makes it possible to write network programs that work on many different types of computer. You will learn about Java's network support in Chapter 11.

Its support for networking is not Java's only advantage. But many good programming languages have been invented only to be soon forgotten. Java had the good luck to ride on the coattails of the Internet's immense and increasing popularity.

As Java has evolved, its applications have extended well beyond the internet. The standard edition of Java inherently includes support for various technologies, including cryptography, data compression, audio processing, and graphics. Programmers have developed Java libraries to offer enhanced functionalities. Java can be utilized to construct intricate, high-performance systems. Hadoop, a system designed for large-scale data processing, is implemented in Java. Hadoop has been utilized by Yahoo, Facebook, and various other websites to process the substantial volumes of data produced by their users.

Moreover, Java is not confined to utilization on conventional computers. Java can be utilized to develop applications for Android handsets, but not for the iPhone. Android employs Google's own version of Java and does not utilize the standard Java graphical user interface components.

Currently, Java undoubtedly ranks among the most prevalent programming languages. It is an excellent option for nearly every programming project intended to operate on several computing devices, and it remains a viable alternative for many applications designed for a single device. It remains the most extensively taught language at colleges and universities. Its similarities to other prominent languages, including as C++, JavaScript, and Python, provide a solid foundation for acquiring proficiency in other languages as well. Learning Java serves as an excellent foundation for aspiring expert programmers. I trust you will appreciate the experience.!

2 Chapter

PROGRAMMING IN THE SMALL I: NOMENCLATURE AND ENTITIES

A computer can do only rudimentary operations at the fundamental level of machine language. A computer executes intricate tasks by concatenating numerous such operations. Such duties must be meticulously "scripted" in comprehensive and flawless detail by programs. Developing intricate programs will always pose challenges; however, the complexity can be mitigated to some degree by establishing a coherent overarching framework. The design of a program's overall structure is what I refer to as "programming in the large."

Programming in the small, also referred to as coding, pertains to the elaboration of that design's specifics. The particulars are the precise, sequential directives for doing relatively little operations. Coding involves operating "close to the machine," utilizing notions akin to those found in machine language, such as memory addresses, arithmetic operations, loops, and conditional branches. In a high-level language like Java, one engages with these concepts at a level significantly elevated above machine language. Nonetheless, it remains imperative to ensure that all elements are accurately addressed.

This chapter and the subsequent one analyze the capabilities for small-scale programming within the Java programming language. Do not be deceived by the phrase "programming in the small" into believing that this subject is simplistic or trivial. This content serves as a fundamental basis for all forms of programming. If you lack comprehension, you cannot develop programs, regardless of your proficiency in designing their large-scale architecture.

The final component of this chapter addresses programming environments. This section provides guidance about compiling and executing Java programs; it is advisable to review it prior to attempting to develop your own programs or utilizing the sample programs in this book.

2.1 THE FUNDAMENTAL JAVA APPLICATION

A program is a series of instructions that a computer can execute to accomplish a certain goal. An ostensibly straightforward concept; yet, for the computer to effectively utilize the instructions, they must be articulated in a format compatible with the machine's processing capabilities. This indicates that programs must be composed in programming languages. Programming languages are distinct from conventional human languages due to their complete unambiguity and stringent regulations about permissible constructs within a program. The regulations that dictate permissible constructs are referred to as the syntax of the language. Syntax rules specify the basic vocabulary of the language and how programs can be constructed using things like loops, branches, and subroutines. A syntactically correct program is one that can be successfully compiled or interpreted; programs that have syntax errors will be rejected (hopefully with a useful error message that will help you fix the problem).

So, to be a successful programmer, you have to develop a detailed knowledge of the syntax of the programming language that you are using. However, syntax is only part of the story. It's not enough to write a program that will run—you want a program that will run and produce the correct result! That is, the meaning of the program has to be right. The meaning of a program is referred to as its *semantics*. More correctly, the semantics of a programming language is the set of rules that determine the meaning of a program written in that language. A semantically correct program is one that does what you want it to.

Furthermore, a program can be syntactically and semantically correct but still be a pretty bad program. Using the language correctly is not the same as using it well. For example, a good program has "style." It is written in a way that will make it easy for people to read and to understand. It follows conventions that will be familiar to other programmers. And it has an overall design that will make sense to human readers. The computer is completely oblivious to such things, but to a human reader, they are paramount. These aspects of programming are sometimes referred to as *pragmatics*. (I will often use the more common term *style*.)

When I introduce a new language feature, I will explain the syntax, the semantics, and some of the pragmatics of that feature. You should memorize the syntax; that's the easy part. Then you should get a feeling for the semantics by following the examples given, making sure that you understand how they work, and, ideally, writing short programs of your own to test your understanding. And you should try to appreciate and absorb the pragmatics—this means learning how to use the language feature *well*, with style that will earn you the admiration of other programmers.

Of course, even when you've become familiar with all the individual features of the language, that doesn't make you a programmer. You still have to learn how to construct complex programs to solve particular problems. For that, you'll need both experience and taste.

We begin our exploration of Java with the problem that has become traditional for such beginnings: to write a program that displays the message "Hello World!". This might seem like a trivial problem, but getting a computer to do this is really a big first step in learning a new programming language (especially if it's your first programming language). It means that you understand the basic process of:

1. getting the program text into the computer,
2. compiling the program, and
3. running the compiled program.

The first time through, each of these steps will probably take you a few tries to get right. I won't go into the details here of how you do each of these steps; it depends on the particular computer and Java programming environment that you are using. See Section 2.6 for information about creating and running Java programs in specific programming environments. But in general, you will type the program using some sort of text editor and save the program in a file. Then, you will use some command to try to compile the file. You'll either get a message that the program contains syntax errors, or you'll get a compiled version of the program. In the case of Java, the program is compiled into Java bytecode, not into machine language. Finally, you can run the compiled program by giving some appropriate command.

For Java, you will actually use an interpreter to execute the Java bytecode. Your programming environment might automate some of the steps for you—for example, the compilation step is often done automatically—but you can be sure that the same three steps are being done in the background.

Here is a Java program to display the message "Hello World!". Don't expect to understand what's going on here just yet; some of it you won't really understand until a few chapters from now:

```
A program to display the message
    "Hello World!" on standard output.
/public class HelloWorld {
public static void main(String[] args)
    { System.out.println("Hello World!");}}
    // end of class HelloWorld
```

The command that actually displays the message is:

```
System.out.println("Hello World!");
```

This command is an example of a *subroutine call statement*. It uses a "built-in subroutine" named System.out.println to do the actual work. Recall that a subroutine consists of the instructions for performing some task, chunked together and given a name. That name can be used to "call" the subroutine whenever that task needs to be performed. A *built-in subroutine* is one that is already defined as part of the language and therefore automatically available for use in any program.

When you run this program, the message "Hello World!" (without the quotes) will be displayed on standard output. Unfortunately, I can't say exactly what that means! Java is meant to run on many different platforms, and standard output will mean different things on different platforms. However, you can expect the message to show up in some convenient or inconvenient place. (If you use a command-line interface, like that in a Java Development Kit, you type in a command to tell the computer to run the program. The computer will type the output from the program, Hello World!, on the next line. In an integrated development environment such as Eclipse, the output might appear somewhere in one of the environment's windows.)

You must be curious about all the other stuff in the above program. Part of it consists of *comments*. Comments in a program are entirely ignored by the computer; they are there for human readers only. This doesn't mean that they are unimportant. Programs are meant to be read by people as well as by computers, and without comments, a program can be very difficult to understand. Java has two types of comments. The first type begins with // and extends to the end of a line. There is a comment of this form on the last line of the above program. The computer ignores the // and everything that follows it on the same line. The second type of comment starts with /* and ends with */, and it can extend over more than one line. The first three lines of the program are an example of this second type of comment. (A comment that actually begins with /**, like this one does, has special meaning; it is a "Javadoc" comment that can be used to produce documentation for the program.

Everything else in the program is required by the rules of Java syntax. All programming in Java is done inside "classes." The first line in the above program (not counting the comment) says that this is a class named *HelloWorld*. "HelloWorld," the name of the class, also serves as the name of the program. Not every class is a program. In order to define a program, a class must include a subroutine named main, with a definition that takes the form:

```
public static void main(String[] args) {
    (statements)
}
```

When you tell the Java interpreter to run the program, the interpreter calls this main subroutine, and the statements that it contains are executed. Those statements make up the script that tells the computer exactly what to do when the program is executed. The main() routine can call other subroutines that are defined in the same class or even in other classes, but it is the main routine that determines how and in what order the other subroutines are used.

The word "public" in the first line of main means that this routine can be called from outside the program. This is essential because the main routine is called by the Java interpreter, which is something external to the program itself. The remainder of the first line of the routine is harder to explain at the moment; for now, just think of it as part of the required syntax. The definition of the subroutine—that is, the instructions that say what it does—consists of the sequence of "statements" enclosed between braces, { and }. Here, I've used ⟨*statements*⟩ as a placeholder for the actual statements that make up the program. Throughout this textbook, I will always use a similar format: anything that you see in ⟨*this style of text* ⟩ (italic in angle brackets) is a placeholder that describes something you need to type when you write an actual program.

As noted above, a subroutine can't exist by itself. It has to be part of a "class". A program is defined by a public class that takes the form:

```
⟨optional-package-declaration⟩
⟨optional-imports⟩

public class ⟨program-name⟩ {

    ⟨optional-variable-declarations-and-subroutines⟩

    public static void main(String[] args) {

            ⟨statements⟩

    }

    ⟨optional-variable-declarations-and-subroutines⟩

}
```

The first two lines have to do with using packages. A package is a group of classes. You will start learning about packages in Section 2.4, but our first few example programs will not use them.

The ⟨*program-name*⟩ in the line that begins "public class" is the name of the program, as well as the name of the class. (Remember, again, that ⟨*program-name*⟩ is a placeholder for the actual name!) If the name of the class is HelloWorld, then the class must be saved in a file called HelloWorld.java. When this file is compiled, another file named HelloWorld.class will be produced. This class file, HelloWorld.class, contains the translation of the program into Java bytecode, which can be executed by a Java interpreter. HelloWorld.java is called the *source code* for the program. To execute the program, you only need the compiled class file, not the source code.

The layout of the program on the page, such as the use of blank lines and indentation, is not part of the syntax or semantics of the language. The computer doesn't care about layout—you could run the entire program together on one line as far as it is concerned. However, layout is important to human readers, and there are certain style guidelines for layout that are followed by most programmers.

Also note that according to the above syntax specification, a program can contain other subroutines besides main(), as well as things called "variable declarations."

2.2 VARIABLES AND THE PRIMITIVE TYPES

Names are fundamental to programming. In programs, names are used to refer to many different sorts of things. In order to use those things, a programmer must understand the rules for giving names to them and the rules for using the names to work with them. That is, the programmer must understand the syntax and the semantics of names.

According to the syntax rules of Java, the most basic names are *identifiers.* Identifiers can be used to name classes, variables, and subroutines. An identifier is a sequence of one or more characters. It must begin with a letter or underscore and must consist entirely of letters, digits, and underscores. ("Underscore" refers to the character ' '.) For example, here are some legal identifiers:

N n rate x15 quite a long name HelloWorld

No spaces are allowed in identifiers; HelloWorld is a legal identifier, but "Hello World" is not. Upper case and lower case letters are considered to be different, so that HelloWorld, helloworld, HELLOWORLD, and hElloWorLD are all distinct names. Certain words are reserved for special uses in Java, and cannot be used as identifiers. These *reserved words* include: class, public, static, if, else, while, and several dozen other words. (Remember that reserved words are not identifiers, since they can't be used as names for things.)

Java is actually pretty liberal about what counts as a letter or a digit. Java uses the *Unicode* character set, which includes thousands of characters from many different languages and different alphabets, and many of these characters count as letters or digits. However, I will be sticking to what can be typed on a regular English keyboard.

The pragmatics of naming includes style guidelines about how to choose names for things. For example, it is customary for names of classes to begin with upper case letters, while names of variables and of subroutines begin with lower case letters; you can avoid a lot of confusion by following this standard convention in your own programs. Most Java programmers do not use underscores in names, although some do use them at the beginning of the names of certain kinds of variables. When a name is made up of several words, such as HelloWorld or interestRate, it is customary to capitalize each word, except possibly the first; this is sometimes referred to as *camel case,* since the upper case letters in the middle of a name are supposed to look something like the humps on a camel's back.

Finally, I'll note that in addition to simple identifiers, things in Java can have *compound names* which consist of several simple names separated by periods. (Compound names are also called *qualified names.*) You've already seen an example: System.out.println. The idea here is that things in Java can contain other things. A compound name is a kind of path to an item through one or more levels of containment. The name System.out.println indicates that something called "System" contains something called "out" which in turn contains something called "println".

2.2.1 Variables

Programs manipulate data that are stored in memory. In machine language, data can only be referred to by giving the numerical address of the location in memory where the data is stored. In a high-level language such as Java, names are used instead of numbers to refer to data. It is the job of the computer to keep track of where in memory the data is actually stored; the programmer only has to remember the name. A name used in this way—to refer to data stored in memory—is called a *variable.*

Variables are actually rather subtle. Properly speaking, a variable is not a name for the data itself but for a location in memory that can hold data. You should think of a variable as a container or box where you can store data that you will need to use later. The variable refers directly to the box and only indirectly to the data in the box. Since the data in the box can change, a variable can refer to different data values at different times during the execution of the program, but it always refers to the same box. Confusion can arise, especially for beginning programmers, because when a variable is used in a program in certain ways, it refers to the container, but when it is used in other ways, it refers to the data in the container. You'll see examples of both cases below.

In Java, the only way to get data into a variable—that is, into the box that the variable names—is with an *assignment statement.* An assignment statement takes the form:

(variable) = (expression);

where (*expression*) represents anything that refers to or computes a data value. When the computer comes to an assignment statement in the course of executing a program, it evaluates the expression and puts the resulting data value into the variable. For example, consider the simple assignment statement

rate = 0.07;

The (*variable*) in this assignment statement is rate, and the (*expression*) is the number 0.07. The computer executes this assignment statement by putting the number 0.07 in the variable rate, replacing whatever was there before. Now, consider the following more complicated assignment statement, which might come later in the same program:

*interest = rate * principal;*

Here, the value of the expression "rate * principal" is being assigned to the variable interest. In the expression, the * is a "multiplication operator" that tells the computer to multiply rate times principal. The names rate and principal are themselves variables, and it is really the values stored in those variables that are to be multiplied. We see that when a variable is used in an expression, it is the value stored in the variable that matters; in this case, the variable seems to refer to the data in the box, rather than to the box itself. When the computer executes this assignment statement, it takes the value of rate, multiplies it by the value of principal, and stores the answer in the box referred to by interest. When a variable is used on the left-hand side of an assignment statement, it refers to the box that is named by the variable.

(Note, by the way, that an assignment statement is a command that is executed by the computer at a certain time. It is not a statement of fact. For example, suppose a program includes the statement "rate = 0.07;". If the statement "interest = rate * principal;" is executed later in the program, can we say that the principal is multiplied by 0.07? No! The value of rate might have been changed in the meantime by another statement. The meaning of an assignment statement is completely different from the meaning of an equation in mathematics, even though both use the symbol "=".)

2.2.2 Types

A variable in Java is designed to hold only one particular type of data; it can legally hold that type of data and no other. The compiler will consider it to be a syntax error if you try to violate this rule by assigning a value of the wrong type to a variable. We say that Java is a *strongly typed* language because it enforces this rule.

There are eight so-called *primitive types* built into Java. The primitive types are named byte, short, int, long, float, double, char, and boolean. The first four types hold integers (whole numbers such as 17, -38477, and 0). The four integer types are distinguished by the ranges of integers they can hold. The float and double types hold real numbers (such as 3.6 and -145.99). Again, the two real types are distinguished by their range and accuracy. A variable of type char holds a single character from the Unicode character set. And a variable of type boolean holds one of the two logical values true or false.

Any data value stored in the computer's memory must be represented as a binary number, that is as a string of zeros and ones. A single zero or one is called a *bit.* A string of eight bits is called a *byte.* Memory is usually measured in terms of bytes.

Not surprisingly, the byte data type refers to a single byte of memory. A variable of type byte holds a string of eight bits, which can represent any of the integers between -128 and 127, inclusive. (There are 256 integers in that range; eight bits can represent 256—two raised to the power eight—different values.) As for the other integer types,

- short corresponds to two bytes (16 bits). Variables of type short have values in the range -32768 to 32767.
- int corresponds to four bytes (32 bits). Variables of type int have values in the range -2147483648 to 2147483647.
- long corresponds to eight bytes (64 bits). Variables of type long have values in the range -9223372036854775808 to 9223372036854775807.

You don't have to remember these numbers, but they do give you some idea of the size of integers that you can work with. Usually, for representing integer data you should just stick to the int data type, which is good enough for most purposes.

The float data type is represented in four bytes of memory, using a standard method for encoding real numbers. The maximum value for a float is about 10 raised to the power 38. A float can have about 7 significant digits. (So that 32.3989231134 and 32.3989234399 would both have to be rounded off to about 32.398923 in order to be stored in a variable of type float.) A double takes up 8 bytes, can range up to about 10 to the power 308, and has about 15 significant digits. Ordinarily, you should stick to the double type for real values.

A variable of type char occupies two bytes in memory. The value of a char variable is a single character such as A, *, x, or a space character. The value can also be a special character such a tab or a carriage return or one of the many Unicode characters that come from different languages. Values of type char are closely related to integer values, since a character is actually stored as a 16-bit integer code number. In fact, we will see that chars in Java can actually be used like integers in certain situations.

It is important to remember that a primitive type value is represented using only a certain, finite number of bits. So, an int can't be an arbitrary integer; it can only be an integer in a certain finite range of values. Similarly, float and double variables can only take on certain values. They are not true real numbers in the mathematical sense. For example, the mathematical constant π can only be approximated by a value of type float or double, since it would require an infinite number of decimal places to represent it exactly. For that matter, many simple numbers such as 1/3 can only be approximated by floats and doubles.

2.2.3 Literals

A data value is stored in the computer as a sequence of bits. In the computer's memory, it doesn't look anything like a value written on this page. You need a way to include constant values in the programs that you write. In a program, you represent constant values as *literals*. A literal is something that you can type in a program to represent a value. It is a kind of name for a constant value.

For example, to type a value of type char in a program, you must surround it with a pair of single quote marks, such as 'A', '*', or 'x'. The character and the quote marks make up a literal of type char. Without the quotes, A would be an identifier and * would be a multiplication operator. The quotes are not part of the value and are not stored in the variable; they are just a convention for naming a particular character constant in a program. If you want to store the character A in a variable ch of type char, you could do so with the assignment statement

ch = 'A';

Certain special characters have special literals that use a backslash, \, as an "escape character." In particular, a tab is represented as '\t', a carriage return as '\r', a linefeed as '\n', the single quote character as '\'', and the backslash itself as '\\'. Note that even though you type two characters between the quotes in '\t', the value represented by this literal is a single tab character.

Numeric literals are a little more complicated than you might expect. Of course, there are the obvious literals such as 317 and 17.42. But there are other possibilities for expressing numbers in a Java program. First of all, real numbers can be represented in an exponential form such as 1.3e12 or 12.3737e-108. The "e12" and "e-108" represent powers of 10, so that 1.3e12 means 1.3 times 10^{12} and 12.3737e-108 means 12.3737 times 10^{-108}. This format can be used to express very large and very small numbers. Any numeric literal that contains a decimal point or exponential is a literal of type double. To make a literal of type float, you have to append an "F" or "f" to the end of the number. For example, "1.2F" stands for 1.2 considered as a value of type float. (Occasionally, you need to know this because the rules of Java say that you can't assign a value of type double to a variable of type float, so you might be confronted with a ridiculous-seeming error message if you try to do something like "x = 1.2;" if x is a variable of type float. You have to say "x = 1.2F;". This is one reason why I advise sticking to type double for real numbers.)

Even for integer literals, there are some complications. Ordinary integers such as 177777 and -32 are literals of type byte, short, or int, depending on their size. You can make a literal of type long by adding "L" as a suffix. For example: 17L or 728476874368L. As another complication, Java allows binary, octal (base-8), and hexadecimal (base-16) literals. I don't want to cover number bases in detail, but in case you run into them in other people's programs, it's worth knowing a few things: Octal numbers use only the digits 0 through 7. In Java, a numeric literal that begins with a 0 is interpreted as an octal number; for example, the octal literal 045 represents the number 37, not the number 45. Octal numbers are rarely used, but you need to be aware of what happens when you start a number with a zero. Hexadecimal numbers use 16 digits, the usual digits 0 through 9 and the letters A, B, C, D, E, and F. Upper case and lower case letters can be used interchangeably in this context. The letters represent the numbers 10 through 15. In Java, a hexadecimal literal begins with 0x or 0X, as in 0x45 or 0xFF7A. Finally, binary literals start with 0b or 0B and contain only the digits 0 and 1; for example: 0b10110.

As a final complication, numeric literals can include the underscore character (" "), which can be used to separate groups of digits. For example, the integer constant for two billion could be written 2 000 000 000, which is a good deal easier to decipher than 2000000000. There is no rule about how many digits have to be in each group. Underscores can be especially useful in long binary numbers; for example, 0b1010 1100 1011.

I will note that hexadecimal numbers can also be used to represent arbitrary Unicode characters. A Unicode literal consists of \u followed by four hexadecimal digits. For example, the character literal '\u00E9' represents the Unicode character that is an "e" with an acute accent.

For the type boolean, there are precisely two literals: true and false. These literals are typed just as I've written them here, without quotes, but they represent constant values, not variables. Boolean values occur most often as the values of conditional expressions. For example,

rate > 0.05

is a boolean-valued expression that evaluates to true if the value of the variable rate is greater than 0.05, and to false if the value of rate is less than or equal to 0.05. As you'll see in Chapter 3, boolean-valued expressions are used extensively in control structures. Of course, boolean values can also be assigned to variables of type boolean. For example, if test is a variable of type boolean, then both of the following assignment statements are legal:

test = true;

test = rate > 0.05;

2.2.4 Strings and String Literals

Java has other types in addition to the primitive types, but all the other types represent objects rather than "primitive" data values. For the most part, we are not concerned with objects for the time being. However, there is one predefined object type that is very important: the type *String*. (*String* is a type, but not a primitive type; it is in fact the name of a class, and we will return to that aspect of strings in the next section. The fact that *String* is a class explains why the name begins with an upper case "S" rather than lower case.)

A value of type *String* is a sequence of characters. You've already seen a string literal: "Hello World!". The double quotes are part of the literal; they have to be typed in the program. However, they are not part of the actual *String* value, which consists of just the characters between the quotes. A string can contain any number of characters, even zero. A string with no characters is called the *empty string* and is represented by the literal "", a pair of double quote marks with nothing between them. Remember the difference between single quotes and double quotes! Single quotes are used for char literals and double quotes for *String* literals! There is a big difference between the *String* "A" and the char 'A'.

Within a string literal, special characters can be represented using the backslash notation.

Within this context, the double quote is itself a special character. For example, to represent the string value

I said, "Are you listening!"

with a linefeed at the end, you would have to type the string literal:

"I said, \"Are you listening!\"\n"

You can also use \t, \r, \\, and Unicode sequences such as \u00E9 to represent other special characters in string literals.

2.2.5 Variables in Programs

A variable can be used in a program only if it has first been *declared* . A *variable declaration statement* is used to declare one or more variables and to give them names. When the computer executes a variable declaration, it sets aside memory for the variable and associates the variable's name with that memory. A simple variable declaration takes the form:

(type-name) *(variable-name-or-names);*

The (*variable-name-or-names*) can be a single variable name or a list of variable names separated by commas. (We'll see later that variable declaration statements can actually be somewhat more complicated than this.) Good programming style is to declare only one variable in a declaration statement, unless the variables are closely related in some way. For example:

int numberOfStudents; String name;

double x, y; boolean isFinished;

char firstInitial, middleInitial, lastInitial;

It is also good style to include a comment with each variable declaration to explain its purpose in the program, or to give other information that might be useful to a human reader. For example:

```
double principal;     // Amount of money invested.
double interestRate; // Rate as a decimal, not percentage.
```

In this chapter, we will only use variables declared inside the main() subroutine of a program. Variables declared inside a subroutine are called *local variables* for that subroutine. They exist only inside the subroutine, while it is running, and are completely inaccessible from outside. Variable declarations can occur anywhere inside the subroutine, as long as each variable is declared before it is used in any way. Some people like to declare all the variables at the beginning of the subroutine. Others like to wait to declare a variable until it is needed. My preference: Declare important variables at the beginning of the subroutine, and use a comment to explain the purpose of each variable. Declare "utility variables" which are not important to the overall logic of the subroutine at the point in the subroutine where they are first used. Here is a simple program using some variables and assignment statements:

```
/**
This class implements a simple program that
will compute the amount of interest that is
earned on 17,000 invested at an interest
rate of 0.027 for one year.      The interest and
the value of the investment after one year are
printed to standard output.
 public class Interest {
public static void main(String[] args) {
    /* Declare the variables. */
    double principal;          // The value of the investment.
    double rate;               // The annual interest rate.
    double interest;           // Interest earned in one year.
/* Do the computations.
*/ principal = 17000;
rate = 0.027;
interest = principal * rate;    // Compute the interest.
```

```
principal = principal + interest;
    // Compute value of investment after one year, with interest.
    // (Note: The new value replaces the old value of principal.)
/* Output the results. */
System.out.print("The interest earned is ");
System.out.println(interest);
System.out.print("The value of the investment after one year is ");
System.out.println(principal);
} // end of main()
} // end of class Interest
```

This program uses several subroutine call statements to display information to the user of the program. Two different subroutines are used: System.out.print and System.out.println. The difference between these is that System.out.println adds a linefeed after the end of the information that it displays, while System.out. print does not. Thus, the value of interest, which is displayed by the subroutine call "System.out.println(interest);", follows on the same line as the string displayed by the previous System.out.print statement. Note that the value to be displayed by System.out.print or System.out.println is provided in parentheses after the subroutine name. This value is called a *parameter* to the subroutine. A parameter provides a subroutine with information it needs to perform its task. In a subroutine call statement, any parameters are listed in parentheses after the subroutine name. Not all subroutines have parameters. If there are no parameters in a subroutine call statement, the subroutine name must be followed by an empty pair of parentheses.

All the sample programs for this textbook are available in separate source code files in the on-line version of this text at https://math.hws.edu/javanotes/source. They are also included in the downloadable archive of the web site, in a folder named source. The source code for the Interest program, for example, can be found in the file Interest.java in subfolder named chapter2 inside the source folder.

2.3 STRINGS, CLASSES, OBJECTS, AND SUBROUTINES

The previous section introduced the eight primitive data types and the type *String*. There is a fundamental difference between the primitive types and *String* : Values of type *String* are objects. While we will not study objects in detail until Chapter 5, it will be useful for you to know a little about them and about a closely related topic: classes. This is not just because strings are useful but because objects and classes are essential to understanding another important programming concept, subroutines.

2.3.1 Built-in Subroutines and Functions

Recall that a subroutine is a set of program instructions that have been chunked together and given a name. A subroutine is designed to perform some task. To get that task performed in a program, you can "call" the subroutine using a subroutine call statement. In Chapter 4, you'll learn how to write your own subroutines, but you can get a lot done in a program just by calling subroutines that have already been written for you. In Java, every subroutine is contained either in a class or in an object. Some classes that are standard parts of the Java language contain predefined subroutines that you can use. A value of type *String*, which is an object, contains subroutines that you can use to manipulate that string. These subroutines are "built into" the Java language. You can call all these subroutines without understanding how they were written or how they work. Indeed, that's the whole point of subroutines: A subroutine is a "black box" which can be used without knowing what goes on inside.

Let's first consider subroutines that are part of a class. One of the purposes of a class is to group together some variables and subroutines, which are contained in that class. These variables and subroutines are called *static members* of the class. You've seen one example: In a class that defines a program, the main() routine is a static member of the class. The parts of a class definition that define static members are marked with the reserved word "static", such as the word "static" in public static void main...

When a class contains a static variable or subroutine, the name of the class is part of the full name of the variable or subroutine. For example, the standard class named *System* contains a subroutine named exit. To use that subroutine in your program, you must refer to it as System.exit. This full name consists of the name of the class that contains the subroutine, followed by a period, followed by the name of the subroutine. This subroutine requires an integer as its parameter, so you would actually use it with a subroutine call statement such as

System.exit(0);

Calling System.exit will terminate the program and shut down the Java Virtual Machine. You could use it if you had some reason to terminate the program before the end of the main routine. (The parameter tells the computer why the program was terminated. A parameter value of 0 indicates that the program ended normally. Any other value indicates that the program was terminated because an error was detected, so you could call System.exit(1) to indicate that the program is ending because of an error. The parameter is sent back to the operating system; in practice, the value is usually ignored by the operating system.)

System is just one of many standard classes that come with Java. Another useful class is called *Math*. This class gives us an example of a class that contains static variables:

It includes the variables Math.PI and Math.E whose values are the mathematical constants π and e. *Math* also contains a large number of mathematical "functions." Now, any subroutine performs some specific task, but for some subroutines, the task is to compute or retrieve some data value. Subroutines of this type are called *functions.* We say that a function *returns* a value. Generally, the returned value is meant to be used somehow in the program that calls the function.

You are familiar with the mathematical function that computes the square root of a number. The corresponding function in Java is called Math.sqrt. This function is a static member subroutine in the class named *Math.* If x is any numerical value, then Math.sqrt(x) computes and returns the square root of that value. Since Math. sqrt(x) represents a value, it doesn't make sense to put it on a line by itself in a subroutine call statement such as

```
Math.sqrt(x);          // This doesn't make sense!
```

What, after all, would the computer do with the value computed by the function in this case? You have to tell the computer to do something with the value. You might tell the computer to display it:

```
System.out.print( Math.sqrt(x) );      // Display the square root of x.
```

or you might use an assignment statement to tell the computer to store that value in a variable:

```
lengthOfSide = Math.sqrt(x);
```

The function call Math.sqrt(x) represents a value of type double, and it can be used anyplace where a numeric literal of type double could be used. The x in this formula represents the parameter to the subroutine; it could be a variable named "x", or it could be replaced by any expression that represents a numerical value. For example, Math.sqrt(2) computes the square root of 2, and Math.sqrt(a*a+b*b) would be legal as long as a and b are numeric variables.

- The *Math* class contains many static member functions. Here is a list of some of the more important of them:
- Math.abs(x), which computes the absolute value of x.
- The usual trigonometric functions, Math.sin(x), Math.cos(x), and Math. tan(x). (For all the trigonometric functions, angles are measured in radians, not degrees.)
- The inverse trigonometric functions arcsin, arccos, and arctan, which are written as: Math.asin(x), Math.acos(x), and Math.atan(x). The return value is expressed in radians, not degrees.
- The exponential function Math.exp(x) for computing the number e raised to the power x, and the natural logarithm function Math.log(x) for computing the logarithm of x in the base e.

- Math.pow(x,y) for computing x raised to the power y.
- Math.floor(x), which rounds x down to the nearest integer value that is less than or equal to x. Even though the return value is mathematically an integer, it is returned as a value of type double, rather than of type int as you might expect. For example, Math.floor(3.76) is 3.0, and Math.floor(-4.2) is -5.0. The function Math.round(x) returns the integer that is closest to x, and Math.ceil(x) rounds x up to an integer. ("Ceil" is short for "ceiling", the opposite of "floor.")
- Math.random(), which returns a randomly chosen double in the range 0.0 <= Math.random() < 1.0. (The computer actually calculates so-called "pseudorandom" numbers, which are not truly random but are effectively random enough for most pur- poses.) We will find a lot of uses for Math. random in future examples.

For these functions, the type of the parameter—the x or y inside the parentheses—can be any value of any numeric type. For most of the functions, the value returned by the function is of type double no matter what the type of the parameter. However, for Math.abs(x), the value returned will be the same type as x; if x is of type int, then so is Math.abs(x). So, for example, while Math.sqrt(9) is the double value 3.0, Math.abs(9) is the int value 9.

Note that Math.random() does not have any parameter. You still need the parentheses, even though there's nothing between them. The parentheses let the computer know that this is a subroutine rather than a variable. Another example of a subroutine that has no parameters is the function System.currentTimeMillis(), from the *System* class. When this function is executed, it retrieves the current time, expressed as the number of milliseconds that have passed since a standardized base time (the start of the year 1970, if you care). One millisecond is one- thousandth of a second. The return value of System.currentTimeMillis() is of type long (a 64-bit integer). This function can be used to measure the time that it takes the computer to perform a task. Just record the time at which the task is begun and the time at which it is finished and take the difference. For more accurate timing, you can use System.nanoTime() instead. System.nanoTime() returns the number of nanoseconds since some arbitrary starting time, where one nanosecond is one-billionth of a second. However, you should not expect the time to be truly accurate to the nanosecond.

Here is a sample program that performs a few mathematical tasks and reports the time that it takes for the program to run.

```
/**
This program performs some mathematical computations and displays the results.
It also displays the value of the constant Math.PI.        It then
```

```
reports the number of seconds that the computer spent on this task.
*/
public class TimedComputation {
public static void main(String[] args) {
    long startTime; // Starting time of program, in nanoseconds.
    long endTime;   // Time when computations are done, in nanoseconds.
    long compTime; // Run time in nanoseconds.
    double seconds; // Time difference, in seconds.
    startTime = System.nanoTime();
    double width, height, hypotenuse;       // sides of a triangle width = 42.0;
    height = 17.0;
    hypotenuse = Math.sqrt( width*width + height*height );
    System.out.print("A triangle      with sides 42 and 17 has hypotenuse ");
    System.out.println(hypotenuse);
    System.out.println("\nMathematically, sin(x)*sin(x) + "
    + "cos(x)*cos(x) - 1 should be 0."); System.out.println("Let's check this for x = 100:");
    System.out.print("       sin(100)*sin(100) + cos(100)*cos(100) - 1 is: ");
    System.out.println( Math.sin(100)*Math.sin(100)
    + Math.cos(100)*Math.cos(100) - 1 );
    System.out.println("(There can be round-off errors when"
    + " computing with real numbers!)");
    System.out.print("\nHere is a random number:     ");
    System.out.println( Math.random() );
    System.out.print("\nThe value of Math.PI is ");
    System.out.println( Math.PI );
    endTime = System.nanoTime();
    compTime = endTime - startTime;
    seconds = compTime / 1000000000.0;
    System.out.print("\nRun time in nanoseconds was: ");
    System.out.println(compTime);
    System.out.println("(This is probably not perfectly accurate!");
```

System.out.print("\nRun time in seconds was: "); System.out.println(seconds);

} // end main()

} // end class TimedComputation

2.3.2 Classes and Objects

Classes can be containers for static variables and subroutines. However classes also have another purpose. They are used to describe objects. In this role, the class is a type, in the same way that int and double are types. That is, the class name can be used to declare variables. Such variables can only hold one type of value. The values in this case are *objects*. An object is a collection of variables and subroutines. Every object has an associated class that tells what "type" of object it is. The class of an object specifies what subroutines and variables that object contains. All objects defined by the same class are similar in that they contain similar collections of variables and subroutines. For example, an object might represent a point in the plane, and it might contain variables named x and y to represent the coordinates of that point. Every point object would have an x and a y, but different points would have different values for these variables. A class, named *Point* for example, could exist to define the common structure of all point objects, and all such objects would then be values of type *Point.*

As another example, let's look again at System.out.println. *System* is a class, and out is a static variable within that class. However, the value of System.out is an object, and System.out.println is actually the full name of a subroutine that is contained in the object System.out. You don't need to understand it at this point, but the object referred to by System.out is an object of the class *PrintStream. PrintStream* is another class that is a standard part of Java. Any object of type *PrintStream* is a destination to which information can be printed; any object of type *PrintStream* has a println subroutine that can be used to send information to that destination. The object System.out is just one possible destination, and System.out.println is a subroutine that sends information to that particular destination. Other objects of type *PrintStream* might send information to other destinations such as files or across a network to other computers. This is object-oriented programming: Many different things which have something in common—they can all be used as destinations for output—can all be used in the same way—through a println subroutine. The *PrintStream* class expresses the commonalities among all these objects.

The dual role of classes—to contain static variables and subroutines and to describe objects that can also contain variables and subroutines—can be confusing, and in practice most classes are designed to perform primarily or exclusively in only one of the two possible roles. Fortunately, you will not need to worry too much about it until we start working with objects in a more serious way.

By the way, since class names and variable names are used in similar ways, it might be hard to tell which is which. Remember that all the built-in, predefined names in Java follow the rule that class names begin with an upper case letter while variable names begin with a lower case letter. While this is not a formal syntax rule, I strongly recommend that you follow it in your own programming. Subroutine names should also begin with lower case letters. There is no possibility of confusing a variable with a subroutine, since a subroutine name in a program is always followed by a left parenthesis.

As one final general note, you should be aware that subroutines in Java are often referred to as *methods*. Generally, the term "method" means a subroutine that is contained in a class or in an object. Since this is true of every subroutine in Java, every subroutine in Java is a method. The same is not true for other programming languages, and for the time being, I will prefer to use the more general term, "subroutine." However, I should note that some people prefer to use the term "method" from the beginning.

2.3.3 Operations on Strings

String is a class, and a value of type *String* is an object. That object contains data, namely the sequence of characters that make up the string. It also contains subroutines. All of these subroutines are in fact functions. For example, every string object contains a function named length that computes the number of characters in that string. Suppose that advice is a variable that refers to a *String*. For example, advice might have been declared and assigned a value as follows:

String advice;

advice = "Seize the day!";

Then advice.length() is a function call that returns the number of characters in the string "Seize the day!". In this case, the return value would be 14. In general, for any variable str of type *String*, the value of str.length() is an int equal to the number of characters in the string. Note that this function has no parameter; the particular string whose length is being computed is the value of str. The length subroutine is defined by the class *String*, and it can be used with any value of type *String*. It can even be used with *String* literals, which are, after all, just constant values of type *String*. For example, you could have a program count the characters in "Hello World" for you by saying

System.out.print("The number of characters in ");

System.out.print("the string \"Hello World\" is ");

System.out.println("Hello World".length());

initial value of the investment and the interest rate. The result is a much more useful program—for one thing, it makes sense to run it more than once! Note that this program uses formatted output to print out monetary values in their correct format.

```
import textio.TextIO;
/**
This class implements a simple program that will compute
the amount of interest that is earned on an investment over
a period of one year. The initial amount of the investment
and the interest rate are input by the user.     The value of
the investment at the end of the year is output.          The
rate must be input as a decimal, not a percentage (for
example, 0.05 rather than 5).
*/
public class Interest2 {
    public static void main(String[] args) {
            double principal;           // The value of the investment.
            double rate;       // The annual interest rate.
            double interest; // The interest earned during the year.
            System.out.print("Enter the initial investment: ");
            principal = TextIO.getlnDouble();
            System.out.print("Enter the annual interest rate (as a decimal): ");
            rate = TextIO.getlnDouble();
            interest = principal * rate;          // Compute this year's interest.
            principal = principal + interest;    // Add it to principal.
            System.out.printf("The amount of interest is %1.2f%n", interest);
            System.out.printf("The value after one year is %1.2f%n", principal);
    } // end of main()
} // end of class Interest2
```

(You might be wondering why there is only one output routine, System.out.println, which can output data values of any type, while there is a separate input routine for each data type. For the output function, the computer can tell what type of value is being output by looking at the parameter. However, the input routines don't have parameters, so the different input routines can only be distinguished by having different names.)

2.4.3 Introduction to File I/O

System.out sends its output to the output destination known as "standard output." But standard output is just one possible output destination. For example, data can be written to a *file* that is stored on the user's hard drive. The advantage to this, of course, is that the data is saved in the file even after the program ends, and the user can print the file, email it to someone else, edit it with another program, and so on. Similarly, System.in has only one possible source for input data.

TextIO has the ability to write data to files and to read data from files. *TextIO* includes output functions TextIO.put, TextIO.putln, and TextIO.putf. Ordinarily, these functions work exactly like System.out.print, System.out.println, and System. out.printf and are interchangeable with them. However, they can also be used to output text to files and to other destinations.

When you write output using TextIO.put, TextIO.putln, or TextIO.putf, the output is sent to the *current output destination.* By default, the current output destination is standard output. However, *TextIO* has subroutines that can be used to change the current output destination. To write to a file named "result.txt", for example, you would use the statement:

TextIO.writeFile("result.txt");

After this statement is executed, any output from *TextIO* output statements will be sent to the file named "result.txt" instead of to standard output. The file will be created if it does not already exist. Note that if a file with the same name already exists, its previous contents will be erased without any warning!

When you call TextIO.writeFile, *TextIO* remembers the file and automatically sends any output from TextIO.put or other output functions to that file. If you want to go back to writing to standard output, you can call

TextIO.writeStandardOutput();

Here is a simple program that asks the user some questions and outputs the user's responses to a file named "profile.txt." As an example, it uses *TextIO* for output to standard output as well as to the file, but System.out could also have been used for the output to standard output.

import textio.TextIO;

public class CreateProfile {

public static void main(String[] args) { String name; // The user's name.

String email; // The user's email address. double salary; // the user's yearly salary.

```
        String favColor; // The user's favorite color.
        TextIO.putln("Good Afternoon!    This program will create");
        TextIO.putln("your profile file, if you will just answer");
        TextIO.putln("a few simple questions.");
        TextIO.putln();
        /* Gather responses from the user. */
        TextIO.put("What is your name?  ");
        name = TextIO.getln();
        TextIO.put("What is your email address?  ");
        email = TextIO.getln();
        TextIO.put("What is your yearly income?  ");
        salary = TextIO.getlnDouble();
        TextIO.put("What is your favorite color? ");
        favColor = TextIO.getln();
        /* Write the user's information to the file named profile.txt. */
        TextIO.writeFile("profile.txt");            // subsequent output goes to file
        TextIO.putln("Name:        " + name);
        TextIO.putln("Email:       " + email);
        TextIO.putln("Favorite Color:      " + favColor);
        TextIO.putf( "Yearly Income:      %,1.2f%n", salary);
        /* Print a final message to standard output. */
        TextIO.writeStandardOutput();
        TextIO.putln("Thank you.        Your profile has been written to profile
        txt.");
    }
}
```

In many cases, you want to let the user select the file that will be used for output. You could ask the user to type in the file name, but that is error-prone, and users are more familiar with selecting a file from a file dialog box. The statement

```
TextIO.writeUserSelectedFile();
```

will open a typical graphical-user-interface file selection dialog where the user can specify the output file. This also has the advantage of alerting the user if they are about to replace an existing file. It is possible for the user to cancel the dialog box without selecting a file. TextIO.writeUserSelectedFile is a function that returns a boolean value. The return value is true if the user selected a file, and is false if the user canceled the dialog box. Your program can check the return value if it needs to know whether it is actually going to write to a file or not.

TextIO can also read from files, as an alternative to reading from standard input. You can specify an input source for *TextIO's* various "get" functions. The default input source is standard input. You can use the statement TextIO.readFile("data.txt") to read from a file named "data.txt" instead, or you can let the user select the input file with a GUI-style dialog box by saying TextIO.readUserSelectedFile(). After you have done this, any input will come from the file instead of being typed by the user. You can go back to reading the user's input with TextIO.readStandardInput().

When your program is reading from standard input, the user gets a chance to correct any errors in the input. This is not possible when the program is reading from a file. If illegal data is found when a program tries to read from a file, an error occurs that will crash the program. (Later, we will see that it is possible to "catch" such errors and recover from them.) Errors can also occur, though more rarely, when writing to files.

A complete understanding of input/output in Java requires a knowledge of object oriented programming. We will return to the topic later in Chapter 11. The file I/O capabilities in the *TextIO* class are rather primitive by comparison. Nevertheless, they are sufficient for many applications, and they will allow you to get some experience with files sooner rather than later.

2.4.4 Other TextIO Features

The *TextIO* input functions that we have seen so far can only read one value from a line of input. Sometimes, however, you do want to read more than one value from the same line of input. For example, you might want the user to be able to type something like "42 17" to input the two numbers 42 and 17 on the same line. *TextIO* provides the following alternative input functions to allow you to do this:

```
j = TextIO.getInt();    // Reads a value of type int.
y = TextIO.getDouble();         // Reads a value of type double.
a = TextIO.getBoolean(); // Reads a value of type boolean
c = TextIO.getChar(); // Reads a value of type char.
w = TextIO.getWord();           // Reads one "word" as a value of type String.
```

The names of these functions start with "get" instead of "getln". "Getln" is short for "get line" and should remind you that the functions whose names begin with "getln" will consume an entire line of data. A function without the "ln" will read an input value in the same way, but will then save the rest of the input line in a chunk of internal memory called the *input buffer* . The next time the computer wants to read an input value, it will look in the input buffer before prompting the user for input. This allows the computer to read several values from one line of the user's input. Strictly speaking, the computer actually reads only from the input buffer. The first time the program tries to read input from the user, the computer will wait while the user types in an entire line of input. *TextIO* stores that line in the input buffer until the data on the line has been read or discarded (by one of the "getln" functions). The user only gets to type when the buffer is empty.

Previously, I said that TextIO.getln() reads a full line of input. Given the way that *TextIO* uses the input buffer, that is not quite true. In fact, if TextIO.getln() is called when the buffer is not empty, then it will simply return whatever characters remain in the buffer without getting a new line of input from the user. If you ever want to empty the input buffer and simply discard the input, you can call TextIO. getln() as a subroutine, without assigning the returned value to a variable:

TextIO.getln();

Note, by the way, that although most *TextIO* input functions will skip past blank spaces and carriage returns while looking for input, they will not skip past other characters. For example, if you try to read two ints and the user types "42,17", the computer will read the first number correctly, but when it tries to read the second number, it will see the comma. It will regard this as an error and will force the user to retype the number. If you want to input several numbers from one line, you should make sure that the user knows to separate them with spaces, not commas. Alternatively, if you want to require a comma between the numbers, use getChar() to read the comma before reading the second number.

There is another character input function, TextIO.getAnyChar(), which does not skip past blanks or carriage returns. It simply reads and returns the next character typed by the user, even if it's a blank or carriage return. If the user typed a carriage return, then the char returned by getAnyChar() is the special linefeed character '\n'. There is also a function, TextIO.peek(), that lets you look ahead at the next character in the input without actually reading it. After you "peek" at the next character, it will still be there when you read the next item from input. This allows you to look ahead and see what's coming up in the input, so that you can take different actions depending on what's there.

The TextIO class provides a number of other functions. To learn more about them, you can look at the comments in the source code file, TextIO.java.

Clearly, the semantics of input is much more complicated than the semantics of output! Fortunately, for the majority of applications, it's pretty straightforward in practice. You only need to follow the details if you want to do something fancy. In particular, I strongly advise you to use the "getln" versions of the input routines, rather than the "get" versions, unless you really want to read several items from the same line of input, precisely because the semantics of the "getln" versions is much simpler.

2.4.5 Using Scanner for Input

TextIO makes it easy to get input from the user. However, since it is not a standard class, you have to remember to make TextIO.java available to any program that uses it. Another option for input is the *Scanner* class. One advantage of using *Scanner* is that it's a standard part of Java and so is always there when you want it.

It's not that hard to use a Scanner for user input, and it has some nice features, but using it requires some syntax that will not be introduced until Chapter 4 and Chapter 5. I'll tell you how to do it here, without explaining why it works. You won't understand all the syntax at this point.

First, since *Scanner* is defined in the package *java.util*, you should add the following import directive to your program at the beginning of the source code file, before the "public class. . . ":

import java.util.Scanner;

Then include the following statement at the beginning of your main() routine:

Scanner stdin = new Scanner(System.in);

This creates a variable named stdin of type *Scanner*. (You can use a different name for the variable if you want; "stdin" stands for "standard input.") You can then use stdin in your program to access a variety of subroutines for reading user input. For example, the function stdin.nextInt() reads one value of type int from the user and returns it. It is almost the same as TextIO.getInt() except for two things: If the value entered by the user is not a legal int, then stdin.nextInt() will crash rather than prompt the user to re-enter the value. And the integer entered by the user must be followed by a blank space or by an end-of-line, whereas TextIO.getInt() will stop reading at any character that is not a digit.

There are corresponding methods for reading other types of data, including stdin. nextDouble(), stdin.nextLong(), and stdin.nextBoolean(). (stdin.nextBoolean() will only accept "true" or "false" as input.) These subroutines can read more than one value from a line, so they are more similar to the "get" versions of *TextIO* subroutines rather than the "getln" versions. The method stdin.nextLine() is equivalent to TextIO.getln(), and stdin.next(), like TextIO.getWord(), returns a string of non-blank characters.

As a simple example, here is a version of the sample program Interest2.java that uses *Scanner* instead of *TextIO* for user input:

```
import java.util.Scanner;
public class Interest2WithScanner {
    public static void main(String[] args) {
            Scanner stdin = new Scanner( System.in ); // Create the Scanner.
            double principal;           // The value of the investment.
            double rate;        // The annual interest rate.
            double interest; // The interest earned during the year.
            System.out.print("Enter the initial investment: ");
            principal = stdin.nextDouble();
            System.out.print("Enter the annual interest rate (as a decimal): ");
            rate = stdin.nextDouble();
            interest = principal * rate;          // Compute this year's interest.
            principal = principal + interest;     // Add it to principal.
            System.out.printf("The amount of interest is %1.2f%n", interest);
            System.out.printf("The value after one year is %1.2f%n", principal);
    } // end of main()
} // end of class Interest2WithScanner
```

Note the inclusion of the two lines given above to import Scanner and create stdin. Also note the substitution of stdin.nextDouble() for TextIO.getlnDouble(). (In fact, stdin.nextDouble() is really equivalent to TextIO.getDouble() rather than to the "getln" version, but this will not affect the behavior of the program as long as the user types just one number on each line of input.)

I will continue to use *TextIO* for input for the time being, but I will give a few more examples of using *Scanner* in the on-line solutions to the end-of-chapter exercises. There will be more detailed coverage of *Scanner* later in the book.

2.5 SPECIFICATIONS OF EXPRESSIONS

This section takes a closer look at expressions. Recall that an expression is a piece of program code that represents or computes a value. An expression can be a literal, a variable, a function call, or several of these things combined with operators such as + and >. The value of an expression can be assigned to a variable, used as a parameter in a subroutine call, or combined with other values into a more complicated expression. (The value can even, in some cases, be ignored, if that's what you want to do; this is more common than you might think.) Expressions are an essential part of programming. So far, this book has dealt only informally with expressions. This section tells you the more-or-less complete story (leaving out some of the less commonly used operators).

The basic building blocks of expressions are literals (such as 674, 3.14, true, 'X', and "Hello"), variables, and function calls. Recall that a function is a subroutine that returns a value. You've already seen some examples of functions, such as the input routines from the *TextIO* class and the mathematical functions from the *Math* class.

The *Math* class also contains a couple of mathematical constants that are useful in mathematical expressions: Math.PI represents π (the ratio of the circumference of a circle to its diameter), and Math.E represents *e* (the base of the natural logarithms). These "constants" are actually member variables in *Math* of type double. They are only approximations for the mathematical constants, which would require an infinite number of digits to specify exactly. The standard class *Integer* contains a couple of constants related to the int data type: Integer.MAX VALUE is the largest possible int, 2147483647, and Integer.MIN VALUE is the smallest int, -2147483648. Similarly, the class *Double* contains some constants related to type double. Double. MAX VALUE is the largest value of type double, and Double.MIN VALUE is the smallest positive value. It also has constants to represent infinite values, Double. POSITIVE INFINITY and Double.NEGATIVE INFINITY, and the special value Double. NaN to represent an undefined value. For example, the value of Math.sqrt(-1) is Double.NaN.

Literals, variables, and function calls are simple expressions. More complex expressions can be built up by using *operators* to combine simpler expressions. Operators include + for adding two numbers, > for comparing two values, and so on. When several operators appear in an expression, there is a question of *precedence*, which determines how the operators are grouped for evaluation. For example, in the expression "A + B * C", B*C is computed first and then the result is added to A. We say that multiplication (*) has *higher precedence* than addition (+). If the default precedence is not what you want, you can use parentheses to explicitly specify the grouping you want. For example, you could use "(A + B) * C" if you want to add A to B first and then multiply the result by C.

The rest of this section gives details of operators in Java. The number of operators in Java is quite large. I will not cover them all here, but most of the important ones are here.

2.5.1 Arithmetic Operators

Arithmetic operators include addition, subtraction, multiplication, and division. They are indicated by +, -, *, and /. These operations can be used on values of any numeric type: byte, short, int, long, float, or double. They can also be used with values of type char, which are treated as integers in this context; a char is converted into its Unicode code number when it is used with an arithmetic operator. When the computer actually calculates one of these operations, the two values that it combines must be of the same type. If your program tells the computer to combine two values of different types, the computer will convert one of the values from one type to another. For example, to compute 37.4 + 10, the computer will convert the integer 10 to a real number 10.0 and will then compute 37.4 + 10.0. This is called a *type conversion* . Ordinarily, you don't have to worry about type conversion in expressions, because the computer does it automatically.

When two numerical values are combined (after doing type conversion on one of them, if necessary), the answer will be of the same type. If you multiply two ints, you get an int; if you multiply two doubles, you get a double. This is what you would expect, but you have to be very careful when you use the division operator /. When you divide two integers, the answer will always be an integer; if the quotient has a fractional part, it is discarded. For example, the value of 7/2 is 3, not 3.5. If N is an integer variable, then N/100 is an integer, and 1/N is equal to zero for any N greater than one! This fact is a common source of programming errors. You can force the computer to compute a real number as the answer by making one of the operands real: For example, when the computer evaluates 1.0/N, it first converts N to a real number in order to match the type of 1.0, so you get a real number as the answer.

Java also has an operator for computing the remainder when one number is divided by another. This operator is indicated by %. If A and B are integers, then A % B represents the remainder when A is divided by B. (However, for negative operands, % is not quite the same as the usual mathematical "modulus" operator, since if A is negative, then the value of A % B will be negative.) For example, 7 % 2 is 1, while 34577 % 100 is 77, and 50 % 8 is 2. A common use of % is to test whether a given integer is even or odd: N is even if and only if N % 2 is zero. (If N is odd, then N % 2 is plus or minus 1, depending on whether N is positive or negative.) More generally, you can check whether an integer N is evenly divisible by an integer M by checking whether N % M is zero.

The % operator also works with real numbers. In general, A % B is what is left over after you remove as many copies of B as possible from A. For example, 7.52 % 0.5 is 0.02.

Finally, you might need the *unary minus* operator, which takes the negative of a number. For example, -X has the same value as (-1)*X. For completeness, Java also has a unary plus operator, as in +X, even though it doesn't really do anything.

By the way, recall that the + operator can also be used to concatenate a value of any type onto a *String*. When you use + to combine a string with a value of some other type, it is another example of type conversion, since any type can be automatically converted into type *String*.

2.5.2 Increment and Decrement

You'll find that adding 1 to a variable is an extremely common operation in programming. Subtracting 1 from a variable is also pretty common. You might perform the operation of adding 1 to a variable with assignment statements such as:

```
counter = counter + 1;
goalsScored = goalsScored + 1;
```

The effect of the assignment statement x = x + 1 is to take the old value of the variable x, compute the result of adding 1 to that value, and store the answer as the new value of x. The same operation can be accomplished by writing x++ (or, if you prefer, ++x). This actually changes the value of x, so that it has the same effect as writing "x = x + 1". The two statements above could be written

```
counter++;
goalsScored++;
```

Similarly, you could write x-- (or --x) to subtract 1 from x. That is, x-- performs the same computation as x = x - 1. Adding 1 to a variable is called *incrementing* that variable, and subtracting 1 is called *decrementing* . The operators ++ and -- are called the increment operator and the decrement operator, respectively. These operators can be used on variables belonging to any of the numerical types and also on variables of type char. (If ch is 'A' then ch++ changes the value of ch to 'B'.)

Usually, the operators ++ or -- are used in statements like "x++;" or "x--;". These statements are commands to change the value of x. However, it is also legal to use x++, ++x, x--, or --x as expressions, or as parts of larger expressions. That is, you can write things like:

```
y = x++;
y = ++x;
TextIO.putln(--x);
z = (++x) * (y--);
```

The statement "y = x++;" has the effects of adding 1 to the value of x and, in addition, assigning some value to y. The value assigned to y is defined to be the old value of x, before the 1 is added. Thus, if the value of x is 6, the statement "y = x++;" will change the value of x to 7, but it will change the value of y to 6, because the value assigned to y is the old value of x. On the other hand, the value of ++x is defined to be the new value of x, after the 1 is added. So if x is 6, then the statement "y = ++x;" changes the values of both x and y to 7. The decrement operator, --, works in a similar way.

Note in particular that the statement x = x++; does not change the value of x! This is because the value that is being assigned to x is the old value of x, the one that it had before the statement was executed. The net result is that x is incremented but then immediately changed back to its previous value! You also need to remember that x++ is not the same as x + 1. The expression x++ changes the value of x; the expression x + 1 does not.

This can be confusing, and I have seen many bugs in student programs resulting from the confusion. My advice is: Don't be confused. Use ++ and -- only as stand-alone statements, not as expressions. I will follow this advice in almost all examples in these notes.

2.5.3 Relational Operators

Java has boolean variables and boolean-valued expressions that can be used to express conditions that can be either true or false. One way to form a boolean-valued expression is to compare two values using a *relational operator* . Relational operators are used to test whether two values are equal, whether one value is greater than another, and so forth. The relational operators in Java are: ==, !=, <, >, <=, and >=. The meanings of these operators are:

A == B	*Is A "equal to" B?*		
A != B	*Is A "not equal to" B? A < B*	*Is A "less than" B?*	
A > B	*Is A "greater than" B?*		
A <= B	*Is A "less than or equal to" B?*		
A >= B	*Is A "greater than or equal to" B?*		

These operators can be used to compare values of any of the numeric types. They can also be used to compare values of type char. For characters, < and > are defined according the numeric Unicode values of the characters. (This might not always be what you want. It is not the same as alphabetical order because all the upper case letters come before all the lower case letters.) When using boolean expressions, you should remember that as far as the computer is concerned, there is nothing special about boolean values. In the next chapter, you will see how to use them in loop and branch statements. But you can also assign boolean-valued expressions to boolean variables, just as you can assign numeric values to numeric variables and functions can return boolean values.

By the way, the operators == and != can be used to compare boolean values too. This is occasionally useful. For example, can you figure out what this does:

```
boolean sameSign;
sameSign = ((x > 0) == (y > 0));
```

One thing that you cannot do with the relational operators <, >, <=, and >= is to use them to compare values of type String. You can legally use == and != to compare Strings, but because of peculiarities in the way objects behave, they might not give the results you want. (The == operator checks whether two objects are stored in the same memory location, rather than whether they contain the same value. Occasionally, for some objects, you do want to make such a check—but rarely for strings. I'll get back to this in a later chapter.) Instead, you should compare strings using subroutines such as equals and compareTo, which were described in Subsection 2.3.3.

Another place where == and != don't always work as you would expect is with Double.NaN, the constant that represents an undefined value of type double. The value of x == Double.NaN is defined to be false for any x, and x != Double.NaN is defined to be true in all cases. Those values hold even when x is Double.NaN! To test whether a real value x is the undefined value Double.NaN, use the boolean-valued function Double.isNaN(x).

2.5.4 Boolean Operators

In English, complicated conditions can be formed using the words "and", "or", and "not." For example, "If there is a test and you did not study for it. . . ". "And", "or", and "not" are *boolean operators*, and they exist in Java as well as in English.

In Java, the boolean operator "and" is represented by &&. The && operator is used to combine two boolean values. The result is also a boolean value. The result is true if both of the combined values are true, and the result is false if either of the combined values is false. For example, "(x == 0) && (y == 0)" is true if and only if both x is equal to 0 and y is equal to 0.

The boolean operator "or" is represented by ||. (That's supposed to be two of the vertical line characters, |.) The expression "A || B" is true if either A is true or B is true, or if both are true. "A || B" is false only if both A and B are false.

The operators && and || are said to be *short-circuited* versions of the boolean operators. This means that the second operand of && or || is not necessarily evaluated. Consider the test

(x != 0) && (y/x > 1)

Suppose that the value of x is in fact zero. In that case, the division y/x is undefined mathematically. However, the computer will never perform the division, since when the computer evaluates (x != 0), it finds that the result is false, and so it knows that ((x != 0) && anything) has to be false. Therefore, it doesn't bother to evaluate the second operand. The evaluation has been short-circuited and the division by zero is avoided. (This may seem like a technicality, and it is. But at times, it will make your programming life a little easier.)

The boolean operator "not" is a unary operator. In Java, it is indicated by ! and is written in front of its single operand. For example, if test is a boolean variable, then

test = ! test;

will reverse the value of test, changing it from true to false, or from false to true.

2.5.5 Conditional Operator

Any good programming language has some nifty little features that aren't really necessary but that let you feel cool when you use them. Java has the conditional operator. It's a ternary operator—that is, it has three operands—and it comes in two pieces, ? and :, that have to be used together. It takes the form

(boolean-expression) ? (expression1) : (expression2)

The computer tests the value of (*boolean-expression*). If the value is true, it evaluates (*expression1*); otherwise, it evaluates (*expression2*). The two expressions must be of the same type. For example:

*next = (N % 2 == 0) ? (N/2) : (3*N+1);*

will assign the value N/2 to next if N is even (that is, if N % 2 == 0 is true), and it will assign the value (3*N+1) to next if N is odd. (The parentheses in this example are not required, but they do make the expression easier to read.)

2.5.6 Assignment Operators and Type Conversion

You are already familiar with the assignment statement, which uses the symbol "=" to assign the value of an expression to a variable. In fact, = is really an operator in the sense that an assignment can itself be used as an expression or as part of a more complex expression. The value of an assignment such as A=B is the same as the value that is assigned to A. So, if you want to assign the value of B to A and test at the same time whether that value is zero, you could say:

if ((A=B) == 0)...

Usually, I would say, don't do things like that!

In general, the type of the expression on the right-hand side of an assignment statement must be the same as the type of the variable on the left-hand side. However, in some cases, the computer will automatically convert the value computed by the expression to match the type of the variable. Consider the list of numeric types: byte, short, int, long, float, double. A value of a type that occurs earlier in this list can be converted automatically to a value that occurs later. For example:

int A

double X;

```
short B;
A = 17;
X = A;        // OK; A is converted to a double
B = A;        // illegal; no automatic conversion
              //        from int to short
```

The idea is that conversion should only be done automatically when it can be done without changing the semantics of the value. Any int can be converted to a double with the same numeric value. However, there are int values that lie outside the legal range of shorts. There is simply no way to represent the int 100000 as a short, for example, since the largest value of type short is 32767.

In some cases, you might want to force a conversion that wouldn't be done automatically. For this, you can use what is called a *type cast*. A type cast is indicated by putting a type name, in parentheses, in front of the value you want to convert. For example,

```
int A;
short B;
A = 17;
B = (short)A;// OK; A is explicitly type cast
              //        to a value of type short
```

You can do type casts from any numeric type to any other numeric type. However, you should note that you might change the numeric value of a number by type-casting it. For example, (short)100000 is -31072. (The -31072 is obtained by taking the 4-byte int 100000 and throwing away two of those bytes to obtain a short—you've lost the real information that was in those two bytes.)

When you type-cast a real number to an integer, the fractional part is discarded. For example, (int)7.9453 is 7. As another example of type casts, consider the problem of getting a random integer between 1 and 6. The function Math.random() gives a real number between 0.0 and 0.9999. . . , and so 6*Math.random() is between 0.0 and 5.999. . . . The type- cast operator, (int), can be used to convert this to an integer: (int)(6*Math.random()). Thus, (int)(6*Math.random()) is one of the integers 0, 1, 2, 3, 4, and 5. To get a number between 1 and 6, we can add 1: "(int)(6*Math. random()) + 1". (The parentheses around 6*Math.random() are necessary because of precedence rules; without the parentheses, the type cast operator would apply only to the 6.)

The type char is almost an integer type. You can assign char values to int variables, and you can assign integer constants in the range 0 to 65535 to char variables. You can also use explicit type-casts between char and the numeric types. For example, (char)97 is 'a', (int)'+' is 43, and (char)('A' + 2) is 'C'.

Type conversion between *String* and other types cannot be done with type-casts. One way to convert a value of any type into a string is to concatenate it with an empty string. For example, "" + 42 is the string "42". But a better way is to use the function String.valueOf(x), a static member function in the *String* class. String.valueOf(x) returns the value of x, converted into a string. For example, String.valueOf(42) is the string "42", and if ch is a char variable, then String.valueOf(ch) is a string of length one containing the single character that is the value of ch.

It is also possible to convert certain strings into values of other types. For example, the string "10" should be convertible into the int value 10, and the string "17.42e-2" into the double value 0.1742. In Java, these conversions are handled by built-in functions.

The standard class *Integer* contains a static member function for converting from *String* to int. In particular, if str is any expression of type *String*, then Integer.parseInt(str) is a function call that attempts to convert the value of str into a value of type int. For example, the value of Integer.parseInt("10") is the int value 10. If the parameter to Integer.parseInt does not represent a legal int value, then an error occurs.

Similarly, the standard class *Double* includes a function Double.parseDouble. If str is a *String*, then the function call Double.parseDouble(str) tries to convert str into a value of type double. An error occurs if str does not represent a legal double value.

Getting back to assignment statements, Java has several variations on the assignment operator, which exist to save typing. For example, "A += B" is defined to be the same as "A = A + B". Many of Java's operators give rise to similar assignment operators. For example:

```
x -= y;     // same as: x = x - y;
x *= y;     // same as: x = x * y;
x /= y;     // same as: x = x / y;
x %= y;     // same as: x = x % y;
```

The combined assignment operator += even works with strings. Recall that when the + operator is used with a string as one of the operands, it represents concatenation. Since str += x is equivalent to str = str + x, when += is used with a string on the left-hand side, it appends the value on the right-hand side onto the string. For example, if str has the value "tire", then the statement str += 'd'; changes the value of str to "tired".

2.5.7 Precedence Rules

If you use several operators in one expression, and if you don't use parentheses to explicitly indicate the order of evaluation, then you have to worry about the precedence rules that determine the order of evaluation. (Advice: don't confuse yourself or the reader of your program; use parentheses liberally.)

Here is a listing of the operators discussed in this section, listed in order from highest precedence (evaluated first) to lowest precedence (evaluated last):

- *Unary operators:* ++, --, !, unary -, unary +, type-cast
- *Multiplication and division:* *, /, %
- *Addition and subtraction:* +, -
- *Relational operators:* <, >, <=, >=
- *Equality and inequality:* ==, !=
- *Boolean and:* &&
- *Boolean or:* ||
- *Conditional operator:* ?:
- *Assignment operators:* =, +=, -=, *=, /=, %=

Operators on the same line have the same precedence. When operators of the same precedence are strung together in the absence of parentheses, unary operators and assignment operators are evaluated right-to-left, while the remaining operators are evaluated left-to-right. For example, A*B/C means (A*B)/C, while A=B=C means A=(B=C). (Can you see how the expression A=B=C might be useful, given that the value of B=C as an expression is the same as the value that is assigned to B?)

2.6 PROGRAMMING ENVIRONMENTS

Although the Java language is highly standardized, the procedures for creating, compiling, and editing Java programs vary widely from one programming environment to another. There are two basic approaches: a command line environment , where the user types commands and the computer responds, and an integrated development environment (IDE), where the user uses the keyboard and mouse to interact with a graphical user interface. While there is essentially just one command line environment for Java programming, there are several common IDEs, including Eclipse, IntelliJ IDEA, and BlueJ. I cannot give complete or definitive information on Java programming environments in this section, but I will try to give enough information to let you compile and run the examples from this textbook using the command line, Eclipse, or BlueJ. (Readers are strongly encouraged to read, compile, and run the examples. Source code for sample programs and solutions to end-of-chapter exercises can be downloaded from the book's web page, https://math.hws.edu/javanotes.)

One thing to keep in mind is that you do not have to pay any money to do Java programming (aside from buying a computer, of course). Everything that you need can be downloaded for free on the Internet.

This textbook is meant for use with Java 17 or later, although the large majority of it it is valid for versions as old as Java 8. In this section, I will try to give you enough information to make it possible to install Java and use it with this textbook. Since Java 8, new versions of Java are released much more frequently than in the past, about twice a year, but only some of the releases are "long-term support" (LTS) releases that will continue to receive bug fixes and security updates over an extended period of time. Java 8, Java 11, and Java 17 are long- term support releases. I recommend that you use Java 17, or Java 11 if you already have that installed, and avoid non-long-term-support releases unless you have specific need for some feature that they offer.

2.6.1 Getting a JDK

The basic development system for Java programming is usually referred to as a *JDK* (Java Development Kit). Note that Java comes in two versions: a Development Kit version (the JDK) and a Runtime Environment version (the JRE). A Runtime Environment can be used to run Java programs, but it does not allow you to compile your own Java programs. A Development Kit includes the Runtime Environment but also lets you compile programs. (It has become harder find a separate JRE download, but you will still see the term used — sometimes to refer, in fact, to a JDK.) A JDK will include the command line environment that you need to work with Java on the command line. If you decide to use an IDE, you might still need to download a JDK first; note, however, that both the Eclipse IDE and BlueJ now include a JDK, so you do not need to download a separate JDK to use them.

Java was developed by Sun Microsystems, Inc., which was acquired by the Oracle corporation. It is possible to download a JDK directly from Oracle's web site, but starting with Java 11, the Oracle JDK is meant mostly for commercial use. For personal and educational use, it is probably preferable to use OpenJDK, which has the same functionality as the version available from Oracle and is distributed under a fully free, open-source license. Although OpenJDK can be downloaded from https://jdk.java.net/, which is also owned by Oracle, I recommend downloading from Adoptium at this address:

https://adoptium.net/

This site is run by the Eclipse Foundation, and it distributes a version of the OpenJDk under the name "Eclipse Temurin." You will want to download Temurin 17 or later. The JDK comes in different versions, depending on the operating system and type of CPU for your computer, but the Adoptium web page should detect your operating system and CPU, so that you just need to click the "Latest release" download button to get the appropriate version. (If you need to select the version yourself, note that the CPU type is referred to as "Architecture." You are most likely to be using the "x64" architecture, which works for Intel and AMD CPUs, but the newer M1 Macs use "aarch64," which refers to ARM CPUs.)

The Adoptium site provides installers for MacOS and Windows that make it easier to set up Java on those platforms. (The installer for MacOS is a .pkg file, and the installer for Windows is a .msi file.) If you use the Linux operating system, you can probably install an OpenJDK using the usual software manager for your distribution; if not, you can download a version from Adoptium, but it will just be a compressed archive rather than an installer.

If you download a JDK installer for Windows or MacOS from Adoptium, you can just double-click the installer file to start the installation, if it does not start automatically. If you use the default installation, the installer will set up your computer so that you can use the javac and java commands on the command line.

The GUI programs in this book use a programming library known as *JavaFX* , which must be downloaded separately from the OpenJDK. You will need to download JavaFX even if you use Eclipse for all of your Java work. (BlueJ comes with JavaFX.) Information about downloading and using JavaFX is given at the end of this section.

(An OpenJDK can also be downloaded as a compressed archive, which you can decompress and place anywhere on your computer. However, to use the javac and java commands, you will either need to put the bin directory from the OpenJDK directory on your PATH environment variable, or use full path names for the javac and java commands. The Adoptium installers for Windows and for MacOS will take care of this detail for you.)

2.6.2 Command Line Environment

Many modern computer users find the command line environment to be pretty alien and unintuitive. It is certainly very different from the graphical user interfaces that most people are used to. However, it takes only a little practice to learn the basics of the command line environment and to become productive using it. It is useful to know how to use the command line, and it is particularly important for computer science students, but you can skip this subsection if you plan to do all of your work with Java in an IDE.

To use a command line programming environment, you will have to open a window where you can type commands. In Windows, you can open such a command window by running a program named *cmd* . In MacOS, you want to run the *Terminal* program, which can be found in the Utilities folder inside the Applications folder. In Linux, there are several possibilities, including a very old program called *xterm* ; but try looking for "Terminal" in your Applications menu.

No matter what type of computer you are using, when you open a command window, it will display a prompt of some sort. Type in a command at the prompt and press return. The computer will carry out the command, displaying any output in the command window, and will then redisplay the prompt so that you can type another command. One of the central concepts in the command line environment is the *current directory* or *working directory* , which contains files that can be used by the commands that you type. (The words "directory" and "folder" mean the same thing.) Often, the name of the current directory is part of the command prompt. You can get a list of the files in the current directory by typing in the command *dir* (on Windows) or *ls* (on Linux and MacOS). When the window first opens, the current directory is your *home directory* , where your personal files are stored. You can change the current directory using the *cd* command with the name of the directory that you want to use. For example, if the current directory is your home directory, then you can change into your Desktop directory by typing the command cd Desktop (and then pressing return).

You might want to create a directory (that is, a folder) to hold your Java work. For example, you might create a directory named javawork in your home directory. You can do this using your computer's GUI; another way is to use the command line: Open a command window. If you want to put your work directory in a different folder from your home directory, *cd* into the directory where you want to put it. Then enter the command mkdir javawork to make the directory. When you want to work on programming, open a command window and use the *cd* command to change into your Java work directory. Of course, you can have more than one working directory for your Java work; you can organize your files any way you like.

The most basic commands for using Java on the command line are *javac* and *java.* The javac command is used to compile Java source code, and java is used to run Java programs. These commands, and other commands for working with Java, can be found in a directory named *bin* inside the directory that holds the JDK. If you set things up correctly on your computer, it should recognize these commands when you type them on the command line. Try typing the commands java -version and javac -version. The output from these commands should tell you which version of Java is being used. If you get a message such as "Command not found," then Java is not correctly configured.

Java should already be configured correctly on Linux, if you have installed Java from the Linux software repositories. The same is true on MacOS and Windows, if you have used an installer from Adoptium.

To test the javac command, place a copy of HelloWorld.java into your working directory. (If you downloaded the Web site of this book, you can find it in the directory named chapter2 inside the directory named source; you can use your computer's GUI to copy-and-paste this file into your working directory, or you could cd into the chapter2 folder and work there. Alternatively, you can navigate to HelloWorld.java on the book's Web site and use the "Save As" command in your Web browser to save a copy of the file into your working directory.) Type the command (while working in the directory that contains the file HelloWorld.java):

javac HelloWorld.java

This will compile HelloWorld.java and will create a bytecode file named HelloWorld.class in the same directory. Note that if the command succeeds, you will not get any response from the computer; it will just redisplay the command prompt to tell you it's ready for another command. You will then be able to run the program using the java command:

java HelloWorld

The computer should respond by outputting the message "Hello World!". Note that although the compiled program is stored in a file named HelloWorld.class, the java command uses the name of the class, *HelloWorld*, not the name of the file. To run the program, you only need

.class file, not the .java file.

Many of the sample programs for this book use TextIO to read input from the user. Since TextIO is not a standard part of Java, you must make it available to any program that uses it. This means that your working directory should contain a folder named textio, and inside that folder should be the file TextIO.java. You can copy TextIO.java from this book's source directory, or your can download it from the web site, but you should be sure to place it inside a folder named textio in the same directory as the program that uses TextIO.

Once you have TextIO.java you can run a sample program such as Interest2.java to test user input. First, compile the program with the command

javac Interest2.java

If successful, this will create the compiled file named Interest2.class. But you will also notice that it creates the file TextIO.class inside the textio folder, if that file does not already exist. More generally, the javac command will compile not just the file that you specify but also any additional Java files that are needed. Once you have Interest2.class, you can run it using the command

java Interest2

You will be asked to enter some information, and you will respond by typing your answers into the command window, pressing return at the end of each line. When the program ends, you will see the command prompt, and you can enter another command. (Note, by the way, that "java TextIO" would not make sense, since TextIO does not have a main() routine, and so it is not possible to execute it as a program.)

You can follow a similar procedure to run all of the examples in this book that do not use JavaFX. For running JavaFX programs.

To create your own programs, you will need a *text editor*. A text editor is a computer program that allows you to create and save documents that contain plain text. It is important that the documents be saved as plain text, that is without any special encoding or formatting information. Word processor documents are not appropriate, unless you can get your word processor to save as plain text. A good text editor can make programming a lot more pleasant. Linux comes with several text editors. On Windows, you can use notepad in a pinch, but you will probably want something better. For MacOS, you might download the BBEdit application, which can be used for free. One possibility that will work on any platform is to use *jedit*, a programmer's text editor that is itself written in Java and that can be downloaded for free from www.jedit.org. Another popular cross-platform programming editor is Atom, available from atom.io.

To work on your programs, you can open a command line window and cd into the working directory where you will store your source code files. Start up your text editor program, such as by double-clicking its icon or selecting it from a Start menu. Type your code into the editor window, or open an existing source code file that you want to modify. Save the file into your working directory. Remember that the name of a Java source code file must end in ".java", and the rest of the file name must match the name of the class that is defined in the file. Once the file is saved in your working directory, go to the command window and use the javac command to compile it, as discussed above. If there are syntax errors in the code, they will be listed in the command window. Each error message contains the line number in the file where the computer found the error. Go back to the editor and try to fix one or more errors, save your changes, and then try the javac command again. (It's usually a good idea to just work on the first few errors; sometimes fixing those will make other errors go away.) Remember that when the javac command finally succeeds, you will get no message at all, or possibly just some "warnings"; warnings do not stop a program from running. Then you can use the java command to run your program, as described above. Once you've compiled the program, you can run it as many times as you like without recompiling it.

That's really all there is to it: Keep both editor and command-line window open. Edit, save, and compile until you have eliminated all the syntax errors. (Always remember to save the file before compiling it—the compiler only sees the saved file, not the version in the editor window.) When you run the program, you might find that it has semantic errors that cause it to run incorrectly. In that case, you have to go back to the edit/save/compile loop to try to find and fix the problem.

2.6.3 Eclipse IDE (Integrated Development Environment)

In an Integrated Development Environment, everything you need to create, compile, and run programs is integrated into a single package, with a graphical user interface that will be familiar to most computer users. There are a number of different IDEs for Java program development, ranging from fairly simple wrappers around the JDK to highly complex applications with a multitude of features. For a beginning programmer, there is a danger in using an IDE, since the difficulty of learning to use the IDE, on top of the difficulty of learning to program, can be daunting. However, for my own programming, I generally use the *Eclipse* IDE, and I introduce my students to it after they have had some experience with the command line. I will discuss Eclipse in some detail and a much simpler alternative, BlueJ, more briefly. IDEs have features that are very useful even for a beginning programmer, although a beginner will want to ignore many of their advanced features.

Unless you happen to be using Oracle's JDK for Java 8, 9, or 10, using Eclipse for JavaFX programs will require some extra configuration. Subsection 2.6.8 discusses using JavaFX in Eclipse. This subsection tells you how to use it for programs that use only standard Java classes.

You can download an Eclipse IDE from eclipse.org. When I install Eclipse, I get the "Eclipse IDE for Java Developers" package (not the "installer") from this web page:

https://www.eclipse.org/downloads/packages/

For Windows and Linux, the package download is a compressed archive file. You can simply extract the contents of the archive and place the resulting directory wherever you want it on your computer. You will find the Eclipse application in that directory, and you can start Eclipse by double-clicking the application icon. For MacOS, the download is a .dmg file that contains the Eclipse application. You can open the .dmg file and drag the application to any location that you prefer (probably the Applications folder). Note that the MacOS and Linux packages are available in two versions, for x86 64 and AArch64. This refers to the type of CPU that the computer uses. Newer "M1" Macs can use the AArch64 version; the x86 64 version is for older Macs that use Intel CPUs. For Linux, you are most likely to need the x86 64 version, which will work for Intel and AMD CPUs.

Eclipse is a free program. It is itself written in Java. Recent versions of Eclipse include an OpenJDK (although Eclipse calls it a JRE), so you can use it without downloading a separate JDK. The March 2022 version includes a Java 17 SDK.

The first time you start Eclipse, you will be asked to specify a *workspace*, which is the directory where your work will be stored. You can accept the default name, or provide one of your own. You can use multiple workspaces and select the one that you want to use at startup. When a new workspace is first opened, the Eclipse window will be filled by a large "Welcome" screen that includes links to extensive documentation and tutorials. You should close this screen, by clicking the "X" next to the word "Welcome"; you can get back to it later by choosing "Welcome" from the "Help" menu.

The Eclipse GUI consists of one large window that is divided into several sections. Each section contains one or more *views*. For example, a view can be a text editor, it can be a place where a program can do I/O, or it can contain a list of your projects. If there are several views in one section of the window, then there will be tabs at the top of the section to select the view that is displayed in that section. This will happen, for example, if you have several editor views open at the same time.

Each view displays a different type of information. The whole set of views in the window is called a *perspective*. Eclipse uses different perspectives, that is, different sets of views of different types of information, for different tasks. For compiling and running programs, the only perspective that you will need is the "Java Perspective," which is the default. As you become more experienced, you might want to use the "Debug Perspective," which has features designed to help you find semantic errors in programs. There are small buttons in the Eclipse toolbar that can be used to switch between perspectives.

The Java Perspective includes a large area in the center of the window that contains text editor views. This is where you will create and edit your programs. To the left of this is the Package Explorer view, which will contain a list of your Java projects and source code files. To the right are one or more other views that you might or might not find useful; I usually close them by clicking the small "X" next to the name of each one. Several other views that will certainly be useful appear under different tabs in a section of the window below the editing area. If you accidently close one of the important views, such as the Package Explorer, you can get it back by selecting it from the "Show View" submenu of the "Window" menu. You can also reset the whole window to its default contents by selecting "Reset Perspective" from the "Window" menu.

To do any work in Eclipse, you need a *project* . To start a Java project, go to the "New" submenu in the "File" menu, and select the "Java Project" command. In the window that pops up, you will need to fill in a "Project Name," which can be anything you like. There are two other sections of the window that you might need to pay attention to:

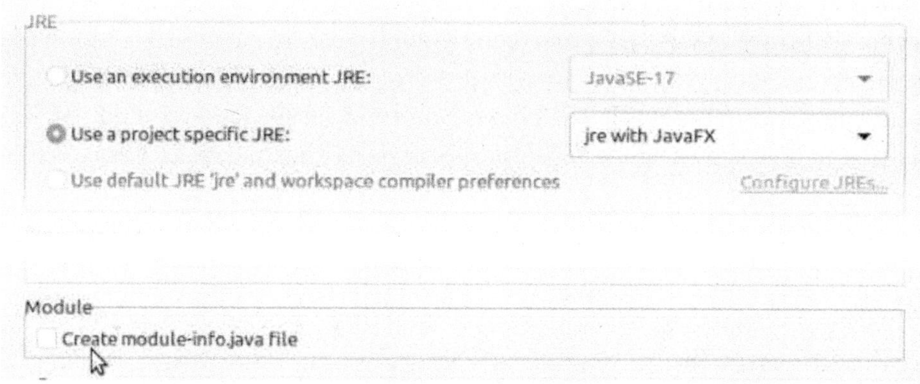

If the project will use JavaFX, you must already have configured the workspace for JavaFX, as described at the end of this section. You should make sure that the JRE configuration that you have created for JavaFX is selected in the "JRE" section of the dialog box, as shown here. For a project that does not require JavaFX, you can set the JRE to be an "execution environment," which should be set to JavaSE 17 or later. And for any program from this textbook, you need to uncheck the option labeled "Create module-info.java file" in the "Module" section. This textbook does not use modular programs! Note that the workspace will remember these two settings for the next time that you create a new project and that it is harmless to use a JRE with JavaFX support even for a project that does not use JavaFX.

After entering a project name, and changing the options if necessary, click the "Finish" button. The project should appear in the "Package Explorer" view on the left side of the Eclipse window. Click on the small triangle or plus sign next to the project name to see the contents of the project. Assuming that you use the default settings, there should be a directory named "src," which is where your Java source code files will go. The project also contains the "JRE System Library". This is the collection of standard built-in classes that come with Java; if you have configured the project for JavaFX, it will also include the JavaFX classes.

To run any of the sample Java programs from this textbook, you need to copy the source code file into your Eclipse Java project. Assuming that you have downloaded the source code file onto your computer, you can copy-and-paste it into the Eclipse window. (Right-click the file icon (or control-click on MacOS); select "Copy" from the pop-up menu; then right-click the project's src folder in the Eclipse window, and select "Paste". Be sure to paste it into the src folder, not into the project itself; files outside the src folder are not treated as Java source code files.) Alternatively, you can try dragging the file icon from a file browser window onto the src folder in the Eclipse window.

To use the *TextIO*-based examples from this textbook, you must add the source code file TextIO.java to your project. This file has to be in a "package" named textio.

If you already have TextIO.java in a folder named "textio," as described above, then you can simply copy- and-paste the textio folder into the "src" folder of your project. Alternatively, you can create the textio package using the "New/Package" command from the "File" menu. This will make a folder named "textio" in your project, inside the src folder, and you can then copy-and-paste TextIO.java into that folder. In any case, package *textio* should appear under "src" in your project, with TextIO.java inside it. (You can drag files from one location to another in the Package Explorer view, if you accidently put a file in the wrong location.)

Once a Java program is in the project, you can open it in an editor by double-clicking the file name in the "Package Explorer" view. To run the program, right-click in the editor window, or on the file name in the Package Explorer view (or control-click in MacOS). In the menu that pops up, go to the "Run As" submenu, and select "Java Application". The program will be executed. If the program writes to standard output, the output will appear in the "Console" view, in the section of the Eclipse window below the editor section. If the program uses *TextIO* or *Scanner* for input, you will have to type the required input into the "Console" view—click the "Console" view before you start typing so that the characters that you type will be sent to the correct part of the window. (For an easier way to run a program, find and click the small "Run" button in Eclipse's tool bar. This will run either the program in the editor window, the program selected in the Package Explorer view, or the program that was run most recently, depending on context.) Note that when you run a program in Eclipse, it is compiled automatically. There is no separate compilation step.

You can have more than one program in the same Eclipse project, or you can create additional projects to organize your work better. Remember to place a copy of TextIO.java, inside a folder named textio, in any project that requires it.

To create a new Java program in Eclipse, you must create a new Java class. To do that, right-click the Java project name in the "Project Explorer" view. Go to the "New" submenu of the popup menu, and select "Class". (Alternatively, there is a small icon in the toolbar at the top of the Eclipse window that you can click to create a new Java class.) In the window that opens, type in the name of the class that you want to create. The class name must be a legal Java identifier. Note that you want the name of the class, not the name of the source code file, so don't add ".java" at the end of the name. The window also includes an input box labeled "Package" where you can specify the name of a package to contain the class. Most examples in this book use the "default package," but you can create your own programs in any package. To use the default package, the "Package" input box should be empty. Finally, click the "Finish" button to create the class. The class should appear inside the "src" folder, in a folder corresponding to its package. The new file should automatically open in the editing area so that you can start typing your program.

Eclipse has several features that aid you as you type your code. It will underline any syntax error with a jagged red line, and in some cases will place an error marker in the left border of the edit window. If you hover the mouse cursor over the error marker or over the error itself, a description of the error will appear. Note that you do not have to get rid of every error immediately as you type; many errors will go away as you type in more of the program!

If an error marker displays a small "light bulb," Eclipse is offering to try to fix the error for you. Click the light bulb—or simply hover your mouse over the actual error—to get a list of possible fixes, then click the fix that you want to apply. For example, if you use an undeclared variable in your program, Eclipse will offer to declare it for you. You can actually use this error-correcting feature to get Eclipse to write certain types of code for you! Unfortunately, you'll find that you won't understand a lot of the proposed fixes until you learn more about the Java language, and it is not a good idea to apply a fix that you don't understand—often that will just make things worse in the end.

Eclipse will also look for spelling errors in comments and will underline them with jagged red lines. Hover your mouse over the error to get a list of possible correct spellings.

Another essential Eclipse feature is *content assist*. Content assist can be invoked by typing Control-Space. It will offer possible completions of whatever you are typing at the moment. For example, if you type part of an identifier and hit Control-Space, you will get a list of identifiers that start with the characters that you have typed; use the up and down arrow keys to select one of the items in the list, and press Return or Enter. (You can also click an item with the mouse to select it, or hit Escape to dismiss the list.) If there is only one possible completion when you hit Control-Space, it will be inserted automatically. By default, Content Assist will also pop up automatically, when you type a period or certain other characters. For example, if you type "TextIO.", you will get a list of all the subroutines in the *TextIO* class. Personally, I find this auto-activation annoying. You can disable it in the Eclipse Preferences. (Look under Java / Editor / Content Assist, and turn off the "Enable auto activation" option.) You can still call up Code Assist manually with Control-Space.

Once you have an error-free program, you can run it as described above. If you find a problem when you run it, it's very easy to go back to the editor, make changes, and run it again.

(As a side note, it is possible to use the JDK that is included with Eclipse on the command line. That JDK is a directory inside the Eclipse installation, with a long, complex name. The best way to find the name might be to open The "Installed JREs" section of the Eclipse preferences, as described above, select the built-in JRE in the list of "Installed JREs", and click "Edit." The name of the JDK directory will be in the "JRE home" section of the dialog, and you can copy-and-paste it from there. You need to add /bin— or \bin on Windows—to that directory name to get the name of the directory that contains the JDK command line programs such as javac. You can add the full name of that bin directory to your PATH environment variable, or you can use full path names for the javac and java commands.)

2.6.4 BlueJ

As a simpler alternative to Eclipse, I will mention BlueJ, a small IDE that is designed specifically for people who are learning to program. It is much less complex than Eclipse, but it does have some features that make it useful for education. BlueJ can be downloaded from bluej.org. There are installers available for Windows, for MacOS, and for Debian-based Linux (such as Ubuntu Linux and Linux Mint). The installers include an OpenJDK as well as JavaFX (which is required to run BlueJ), so you will not need to do any additional downloading or configuration. As of March, 2022, BlueJ supports Java 11 but not later versions.

In BlueJ, you can begin a project with the "New Project" command in the "Project" menu. A BlueJ project is simply a folder. When you create a project, you will have to select a folder name that does not already exist. The folder will be created and a window will be opened to show the contents of the folder. Files are shown as icons in the BlueJ window. You can drag .java files from the file system onto that window to add files to the project; they will be copied into the project folder as well as shown in the window. You can also copy files directly into the project folder, but BlueJ won't see them until the next time you open the project. When you restart BlueJ, it should show the project that you were working on most recently, but you can open any project with a command from the "Project" menu.

There is a button in the project window for creating a new class. An icon for the class is added to the window, and a .java source code file is created in the project folder. The file is not automatically opened for editing. To edit a file, double-click its icon in the project window. An editor will be opened in a separate window. (A newly created class will contain some default code that you probably don't want; you can erase it and add a main() routine instead.) The BlueJ editor does not show errors as you type. Errors will be reported when you compile the program. Also, it does not offer automatic fixes for errors. It has a less capable version of Eclipse's Content Assist, which seems only to work for getting a list of available subroutines in a class or object; call up the list by hitting Control-Space after typing the period following the name of a class or object.

An editor window contains a button for compiling the program in the window. There is also a compile button in the project window, which compiles all the classes in the project.

To run a program, it must already be compiled. Right-click the icon of a compiled program. In the menu that pops up, you will see "void main(String[] args)" or, for a JavaFX program, "Run JavaFX Application"). Select that option from the menu to run the program.

One of the neatest features of BlueJ is that you can actually use it to run any subroutine, not just main(). If a class contains other subroutines, you will see them in the list that you get by right-clicking its icon. A pop-up dialog allows you to enter any parameters required by the routine, and if the routine is a function, you will get another dialog box after the routine has been executed to tell you its return value. This allows easy testing of individual subroutines. Furthermore, you can also use BlueJ to create new objects from a class. An icon for the object will be added at the bottom of the project window, and you can right-click that icon to get a list of subroutines in the object.

2.6.5 The Problem of Packages

Every class in Java is contained in something called a *package*. Classes that are not explicitly put into a package are in the "default" package. All of Java's standard classes are in named packages. This includes even classes like *String* and *System*, which are in a package named *java.lang*. Classes in *java.lang* are automatically imported into any Java file, but classes in other packages must be imported using an import directive. My *TextIO* class is in a package named *textio*, and it must be imported into a program that wants to use it.

Although most of my examples are in the default package, the use of the default package is in fact discouraged, according to official Java style guidelines. Nevertheless, I have chosen to use it, since it seems easier for beginning programmers to avoid packages as much as possible, at least at first. If Eclipse tries to put a class into a package, you can delete the package name from the class-creation dialog to get it to use the default package instead. But if you do create a class in a package, the source code starts with a line that specifies which package the class is in. For example, if the class is in a package named test.pkg, then the first line of the source code will be

package test.pkg;

For example, the source code for *TextIO* begins with "package textio;". I put *TextIO* in a package because a class that is in a non-default package cannot use a class from the default package. That is, if *TextIO* were in the default package, then it could only be used by programs that are also in the default package. (In fact, in earlier versions of this textbook, *TextIO* was in the default package.

When packages are used in a command-line environment, some complications arise. For example, if a program is in a package named *test.pkg*, then the source code file must be in a subdirectory named "pkg" inside a directory named "test" that is in turn inside your main Java working directory. Nevertheless, when you compile or execute the program, you should be working in the main directory, not in the subdirectory. When you compile the source code file, you have to include the name of the directory in the command: For example, for a program in package *test.pkg* use "javac test/pkg/ClassName.java" on Linux or MacOS, or "javac test\pkg\ClassName.java" on Windows. The command for executing the program is then "java test.pkg.ClassName", with a period separating the package name from the class name.

2.6.6 About jshell

I will mention one more command-line tool for working with Java: *jshell*. The jshell command is a standard part of the JDK (after Java 8). If you can use the javac and java commands on the command line, then you can also use jshell. The purpose of jshell is to let you type in and execute Java code without the bother of creating a .java file and writing a main program. To start jshell, just enter the command on a line by itself. You will get a jshell prompt where you can enter either a Java statement or a Java expression. If you enter a statement, it will be executed. If you enter an expression, its value will be printed. You do not have to place a semicolon at the end of a line. Here is a short example of a jshell session.

```
jshell
|  Welcome to JShell -- Version 17.0.2
|  For an introduction type: /help intro
jshell> System.out.println("Hello World")
Hello World
jshell> int x = 42 x ==> 42
jshell> x * x
 3 ==> 1764
jshell> /exit
|  Goodbye
```

Using jshell can be a great way to learn Java and to experiment with its features. I won't give any more detailed information about it in this book, but you can learn more at https://docs.oracle.com/en/java/javase/17/jshell/introduction-jshell.html or you can use the /help command inside jshell to learn more about it.

2.6.7 JavaFX on the Command Line

Version 7 of this textbook used Swing for GUI programming. When I began work on Version 8, JavaFX had been added to the standard JDK, and it seemed to be the furture of Java GUIs. So, in Version 8, I made the switch to JavaFX. Not long after that, however, JavaFX was removed from the JDK, and it is now developed and distributed separately. This has made it somewhat more difficult to use. So for Version 9, I decided to make the book available in two editions, one covering Swing and one covering JavaFX. The only significant differences are in the chapters that cover GUI programming, Chapter 6 and Chapter 13. This edition covers JavaFX. If you also want to learn Swing, you can read those two chapters in the Swing edition.

To use JavaFX on the command line or in Eclipse, you have to download it onto your computer. You can find download links on this page:

https://gluonhq.com/products/javafx/

You need to download a JavaFX "SDK"—not "jmods" or "Monocle SDK"—that is appropriate for your operating system (Linux, MacOS, or Windows) and for the JDK that you are using. You should get the version number that matches the version of the JDK; that probably means JavaFX version 17.0.2. (Only the major version number, 17, has to match.) Furthermore, you need to select the "Architecture," which refers to the CPU type. The architecture should match the architecture used by your JDK. If you are using an "x64" JDK from Adoptium or if you are using an "x86 64" Eclipse package, then you need JavaFX for the x64 architecture. If you are using an "aarch64" JDK from Adoptium or an "AArch64" package from Eclipse, then you need the aarch64 architecture.

When you download the JavaFX SDK, it will be in the form of a compressed archive file. You will need to extract the contents of the archive. Usually, simply double-clicking the icon of the archive file will either extract the contents or open a program that you can use to extract the contents. You will get a directory with a name something like *javafx-sdk-17.0.2*. You can put the directory anywhere on your computer, but you will need to know where it is located.

JavaFX is a collection of Java classes that can be used for making GUI programs. In this book, it is first used in Section 3.9 and is covered extensively. It is also used in example programs in several other chapters. This subsection explains how to use JavaFX on the command line. It assumes that you have already downloaded the JavaFX SDK, as described above. JavaFX is distributed as a set of "modules." (See Subsection 4.6.4) The modules are stored in .jar files in the *lib* subdirectory of the JavaFX SDK. When using the javac and java commands on a program that uses JavaFX, you need to tell the command where to find the JavaFX modules.

The modules are specified for the javac and java commands using two command options: -- module-path and --add-modules. The first option specifies the directory that contains the JavaFX .jar files, and the second says which modules you actually want to use. For the purposes of this textbook, you can set the value of --add-modules to ALL-MODULE-PATH, which makes all of JavaFX available to your program. The value of --module-path is a path to the *lib* directory that contains the JavaFX .jar files. For example, let's say that the JavaFX SDK directory is named *openjfx-sdk-17.0.2* and that it is in my home directory, */home/eck*. Then the full path to the *lib* directory is /home/eck/openjfx-sdk-17.0.2/lib, and the javac command for compiling JavaFX programs would be:

javac --module-path=/home/eck/openjfx-sdk-17.0.2/lib --add-modules=ALL-MODULE-PATH

This would be followed on the same line by the .java files that you want to compile. Exactly the same options would be used with the java command to run JavaFX programs. The option -- module-path can also be abbreviated to -p, with no equals sign. So this can also be written

javac -p /home/eck/openjfx-sdk-17.0.2/lib --add-modules=ALL-MODULE-PATH

If you don't know the full path to the JavaFX SDK, open a command window and use the *cd* command to move to the SDK's *lib* directory. On Mac or Linux, enter the command *pwd* to print out the full path of the working directory. On windows, use the command *cd*, with no directory specified, to print out the path. Use the output from that command as the value for the --module-path. On windows, a typical java command for use with javafx might look something like this:

java -p C:\Users\eck\openjfx-sdk-17.0.2\lib --add-modules=ALL-MODULE-PATH

If the path name includes a space, or certain other special characters, it must be enclosed in quotation marks. For example,

java -p "C:\JavaFX Support\openjfx-sdk-17.0.2\lib" --add-modules=ALL-MODULE-PATH

Of course, this is very verbose, and it would be nice not to have to retype it all the time. On MacOS or Linux, it is easy to define *aliases*, which are shortcuts for long commands. On my computer, I use an alias to define a *jfxc* command for compiling JavaFX programs. The alias is defined as follows:

alias jfxc='javac -p /home/eck/javafx-sdk-17.0.2/lib --add-modules=ALL-MODULE-PATH'

Similarly, I defined an alias for running JavaFX programs:

alias jfx='java -p /home/eck/javafx-sdk-17.0.2/lib --add-modules=ALL-MODULE-PATH'

This lets me compile and run JavaFX programs using commands such as

jfxc MyJavaFXProgram.java

jfx MyJavaFXProgram

To make the alias definitions permanent on my Linux computer, I added them to a file named *.bashrc*. On MacOS, I would put them in a file named *.zshrc* (for MacOS 10.15 and later) or in a file named *.bash profile* (for earlier versions of MacOS). That file must be placed in your home directory. The file might or might not already exist; if it doesn't exist, you can create it. The file is executed whenever you open a Terminal window. (In particular, changes do not become effective until you open a new Terminal.) Note that the file name begins with a period, which makes it a "hidden file." That means that it won't show up in a usual directory listing or file browser, but you should be able to set your file browser to show hidden files.

Unfortunately, Windows currently does not have an equivalent of a .bashrc or .zshrc for its *cmd* command window. One option is to make a batch script file to run the command. For compilation, you could create a file named *jfxc.bat* containing just one line similar to

*javac -p C:\Users\eck\javafx-sdk-17.0.2\lib --add-modules=ALL-MODULE-PATH %**

but, of course, using the appropriate JavaFX location for your own computer. The "%*" at the end represents the inputs to the javac command. The file can be in the current directory or somewhere on the system path, such as the JDK *bin* directory. Then you can use jfxc as a command for compiling JavaFX programs. You can handle the java command with a similar .bat file.

2.6.8 Using JavaFX in Eclipse

To compile and run JavaFX programs in Eclipse, you need to configure your Eclipse workspace to support it. My goal here is not to present the most "correct" or general way to configure Eclipse for JavaFX; I just want to make it possible to easily work with basic JavaFX programs like the ones that come with this textbook. I will discuss a one-time configuration of an Eclipse workspace that seems to work reliably for all the versions of Eclipse in which I have tried it.

The first step is to download a JavaFX SDK from the JavaFX download site, as discussed in the previous subsection.

To begin, open the Eclipse preferences, using the "Preferences" command (which is in the "Windows" menu on Linux and Windows and in the "Eclipse" menu on MacOS). Expand the Java section in the list on the left, by clicking the small triangle or plus sign next to the word "Java." Click on "Installed JREs." You will see a list of the Java environments that Eclipse knows about. The list should include at least the JRE that is included in Eclipse, and it might also include other JREs that have been installed. You can click on a JRE to select it and click the "Duplicate" button to make a copy. You can then add JavaFX support to the copy. (You could also just "Edit" the original JRE, or "Add" a completely new configuration. I recommend using "Duplicate", but if you add a new configuration, you would have the freedom to use a different JDK that you have downloaded, along with a matching JavaFX.)

When you "Duplicate" an existing JRE, you should see a dialog box similar to the following. The "JRE home" and "JRE name" will already be filled in, and there will be just one entry under "JRE system libraries".

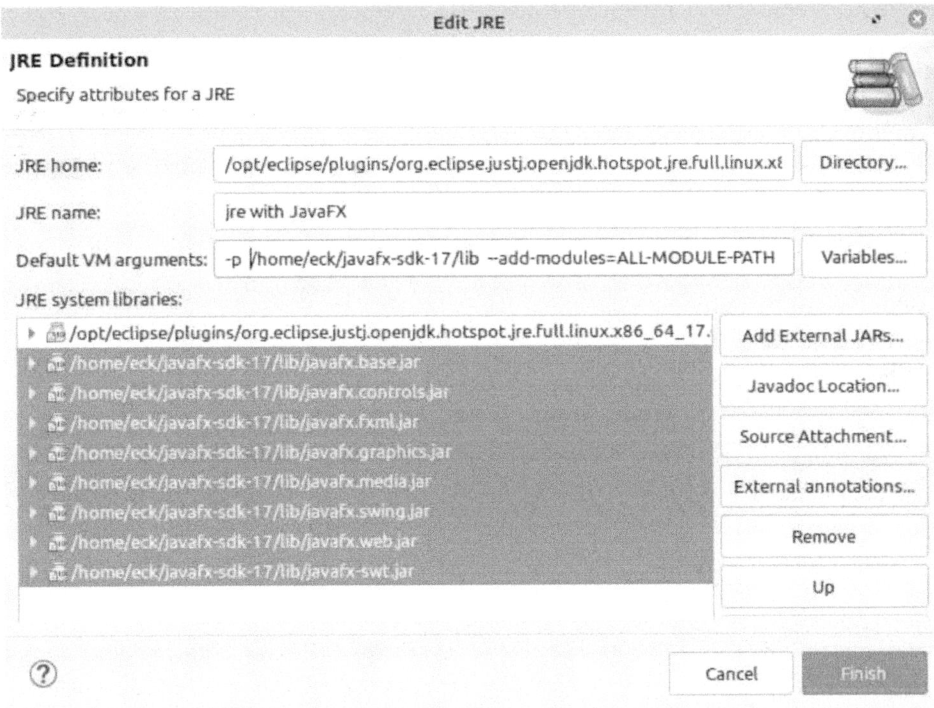

You should change the "JRE name" to something that indicates that it supports JavaFX. This is just so that you will recognize the name when you create a new project in Eclipse. But the main thing is to add the JavaFX configuration.

Remember that to use JavaFX, you need to make it available to your program both at compile time and at run time. The first step in the configuration is to make it available at compile time. To do that, you want to add the JavaFX .jar files to the JRE system libraries: Click the "Add External JARs" button, and navigate to the *lib* directory in the JavaFX SDK that you downloaded. You should see the JavaFX .jar files. Select them all, and click "OK". They should appear in the "JRE system libraries" list.

The second step is to configure the JavaFX source file. This step is optional, but it will allow Eclipse to find the documentation for JavaFX, which can be very useful when you are writing programs. For this step, make sure that all of the JavaFX jar files are selected in the list of .jar files, as shown in the above illustration. Click the "Source Attachment" button. In the "Source Attachment Configuration" dialog box, select "External Location", and click "External File".

Select the file *src.zip* from the JavaFX SDK directory, and click "OK". That's all there is to it. Finally, you must make JavaFX available to your programs at run time. To do that, you need to fill in the "Default VM arguments" input box by typing in the JavaFX command line options for the *java* command. The input box contains options that will be added to the *java* command every time you run a program in Eclipse using this JRE. The -p (or --module-path) and -- add-modules options that are needed were discussed in the previous subsection. Examples appropriate for my own computer are shown in the above illustration. The value of the -p option is the location of the JavaFX *lib* directory. It should be exactly the same as the beginning of the paths for the JavaFX .jar files as shown in the "JRE system libraries" list. (But enclose the value in quotation marks if it includes spaces or other special characters.) The value for

--add-modules can be ALL-MODULE-PATH, as shown in the illustration.

When everything is set up, click "Finish" and then click "Apply and Close" in the main "Preferences" dialog box. When you create a new Java project in the workspace, make sure that the JRE that you set up to use JavaFX is selected in the project creation dialog box. Look in the "JRE" section of the dialog box, select "Use project-specific JRE," and select the JRE with JavaFX from the popup menu. You should then be able to use JavaFX in that project. If not, check your JRE configuration. You can "Edit" it in the same Java preferences where you set it up in the first place. If you can't compile JavaFX programs, make sure that you are using a JavaFX SDK with the same major version number as the built-in JDK in Eclipse (JavaFX 17 for the March 2022 version of Eclipse, for example). If you can compile JavaFX programs but not run them, check the "Default VM arguments" and check that you have the JavaFX SDK for the correct operating system and architecture

Chapter 3 HOW TO PROGRAM THE SMALL II: TAKE CHARGE

The fundamental components of programs—variables, expressions, assignment statements, and subroutine call statements—were addressed in the preceding chapter. This chapter examines the assembly of these foundational elements to create intricate programs exhibiting more engaging behaviors. This chapter focuses on the complexity that can arise within a single function, as we continue to explore "programming in the small." At this level, complexity is introduced by control structures. Control structures, namely loops and branches, facilitate the repetition of a sequence of statements or the selection among multiple potential courses of action. Java encompasses several control structures of each category, and we shall examine each in detail. Program complexity is evident not just in control structures but also in data structures. A data structure is a systematically arranged collection of data, grouped together to function as a single entity. Section 3.8 of this chapter presents an introduction to a prevalent data structure: arrays.

This chapter will initiate the examination of program design. How can one develop a software to address a given problem? We will examine a partial response to this inquiry in Section 3.2. Section 3.9 provides a concise introductory overview of GUI programming..

3.1 BLOCKS, LOOPS, AND BRANCHES

The ability of a computer to perform complex tasks is built on just a few ways of combining simple commands into control structures. In Java, there are just six such structures that are used to determine the normal flow of control in a program—and, in fact, just three of them would be enough to write programs to perform any task. The six control structures are: the *block* , the *while loop*, the *do..while loop*, the *for loop*, the *if statement*, and the *switch statement*. Each of these structures is considered to be a single "statement," but it is a structured statement that can contain one or more other statements inside itself.

3.1.1 Blocks

The *block* is the simplest type of structured statement. Its purpose is simply to group a sequence of statements into a single statement. The format of a block is:

```
{
    (statements )
}
```

That is, it consists of a sequence of statements enclosed between a pair of braces, "{" and "}". In fact, it is possible for a block to contain no statements at all; such a block is called an *empty block* , and can actually be useful at times. An empty block consists of nothing but an empty pair of braces. Block statements usually occur inside other statements, where their purpose is to group together several statements into a unit. However, a block can be legally used wherever a statement can occur. There is one place where a block is required: As you might have already noticed in the case of the main subroutine of a program, the definition of a subroutine is a block, since it is a sequence of statements enclosed inside a pair of braces.

I should probably note again at this point that Java is what is called a free-format language. There are no syntax rules about how the language has to be arranged on a page. So, for example, you could write an entire block on one line if you want. But as a matter of good programming style, you should lay out your program on the page in a way that will make its structure as clear as possible. In general, this means putting one statement per line and using indentation to indicate statements that are contained inside control structures. This is the format that I will use in my examples.

Here are two examples of blocks:

```
{
    System.out.print("The answer is ");
    System.out.println(ans);
}

{   // This block exchanges the values of x and y
    int temp;         // A temporary variable for use in this block.
    temp = x;         // Save a copy of the value of x in temp.
    x = y;   // Copy the value of y into x.
    y = temp;         // Copy the value of temp into y.
}
```

In the second example, a variable, temp, is declared inside the block. This is perfectly legal, and it is good style to declare a variable inside a block if that variable is used nowhere else but inside the block. A variable declared inside a block is completely inaccessible and invisible from outside that block. When the computer executes the variable declaration statement, it allocates memory to hold the value of the variable (at least conceptually). When the block ends, that memory is discarded (that is, made available for reuse). The variable is said to be *local* to the block. There is a general concept called the "scope" of an identifier. The *scope* of an identifier is the part of the program in which that identifier is valid. The scope of a variable defined inside a block is limited to that block, and more specifically to the part of the block that comes after the declaration of the variable.

3.1.2 The Basic While Loop

The block statement by itself really doesn't affect the flow of control in a program. The five remaining control structures do. They can be divided into two classes: loop statements and branching statements. You really just need one control structure from each category in order to have a completely general-purpose programming language. More than that is just convenience.

In this section, I'll introduce the while loop and the if statement. I'll give the full details of these statements and of the other three control structures in later sections.

A *while loop* is used to repeat a given statement over and over. Of course, it's not likely that you would want to keep repeating it forever. That would be an *infinite loop*, which is generally a bad thing. (There is an old story about computer pioneer Grace Murray Hopper, who read instructions on a bottle of shampoo telling her to "lather, rinse, repeat." As the story goes, she claims that she tried to follow the directions, but she ran out of shampoo. (In case you don't get it, she was making a joke about the way that computers mindlessly follow instructions.)) By the way, if you are working on the command line and need to stop a program that has gotten into an infinite loop, you should be able to do so with Control-C, that is, hold down the Control key and press the C key.

To be more specific, a while loop will repeat a statement over and over, but only so long as a specified condition remains true. A while loop has the form:

while ((boolean-expression))

(statement)

Since the statement can be, and usually is, a block, most while loops have the form:

while ((boolean-expression)) {

(statements)

}

Some programmers think that the braces should always be included as a matter of style, even when there is only one statement between them, but I don't always follow that advice myself. The semantics of the while statement go like this: When the computer comes to a while statement, it evaluates the (*boolean-expression*), which yields either true or false as its value.

If the value is false, the computer skips over the rest of the while loop and proceeds to the next command in the program. If the value of the expression is true, the computer executes the (*statement*) or block of (*statements*) inside the loop. Then it returns to the beginning of the while loop and repeats the process. That is, it re-evaluates the (*boolean-expression*), ends the loop if the value is false, and continues it if the value is true. This will continue over and over until the value of the expression is false when the computer evaluates it; if that never happens, then there will be an infinite loop.

Here is an example of a while loop that simply prints out the numbers 1, 2, 3, 4, 5:

```
int number; // The number to be printed.
number = 1; // Start with 1.
while ( number < 6 ) {          // Keep going as long as number is < 6.
    System.out.println(number);
    number = number + 1;    // Go on to the next number.
}
System.out.println("Done!");
```

The variable number is initialized with the value 1. So when the computer evaluates the expression "number < 6" for the first time, it is asking whether 1 is less than 6, which is true. The computer therefore proceeds to execute the two statements inside the loop. The first statement prints out "1". The second statement adds 1 to number and stores the result back into the variable number; the value of number has been changed to 2. The computer has reached the end of the loop, so it returns to the beginning and asks again whether number is less than 6. Once again this is true, so the computer executes the loop again, this time printing out 2 as the value of number and then changing the value of number to 3. It continues in this way until eventually number becomes equal to 6. At that point, the expression "number < 6" evaluates to false. So, the computer jumps past the end of the loop to the next statement and prints out the message "Done!". Note that when the loop ends, the value of number is 6, but the last value that was printed was 5.

By the way, you should remember that you'll never see a while loop standing by itself in a real program. It will always be inside a subroutine which is itself defined inside some class. As an example of a while loop used inside a complete program, here is a little program that computes the interest on an investment over several years. This is an improvement over examples from the previous chapter that just reported the results for one year:

```
import textio.TextIO;
/**
This class implements a simple program that will compute the amount of
interest that is earned on an investment over a period of 5 years.        The
initial amount of the investment and the interest rate are input by the
user.        The value of the investment at the end of each year is output.
*/
public class Interest3 {
    public static void main(String[] args) {
            double principal;           // The value of the investment.
            double rate;       // The annual interest rate.
            /* Get the initial investment and interest rate from the user. */
            System.out.print("Enter the initial investment: ");
            principal = TextIO.getlnDouble();
            System.out.println();
            System.out.println("Enter the annual interest rate.");
            System.out.print("Enter a decimal, not a percentage: ");
            rate = TextIO.getlnDouble();
            System.out.println();
            /* Simulate the investment for 5 years. */
            int years;          // Counts the number of years that have passed.
            years = 0;
            while (years < 5) {
                    double interest; // Interest for this year.
                    interest = principal * rate;
                    principal = principal + interest;    // Add it to principal.
                    years = years + 1;            // Count the current year.
                    System.out.print("The value of the investment after ");
                    System.out.print(years);
                    System.out.print(" years is ");
                    System.out.printf("%1.2f", principal);
```

```
            System.out.println();
        } // end of while loop
    } // end of main()
} // end of class Interest3
```

You should study this program, and make sure that you understand what the computer does step-by-step as it executes the while loop.

3.1.3 The Basic If Statement

An *if statement* tells the computer to take one of two alternative courses of action, depending on whether the value of a given boolean-valued expression is true or false. It is an example of a "branching" or "decision" statement. An if statement has the form:

```
if ( (boolean-expression ) )
    (statement1 )
else
    (statement2 )
```

When the computer executes an if statement, it evaluates the boolean expression. If the value is true, the computer executes the first statement and skips the statement that follows the "else". If the value of the expression is false, then the computer skips the first statement and executes the second one. Note that in any case, one and only one of the two statements inside the if statement is executed. The two statements represent alternative courses of action; the computer decides between these courses of action based on the value of the boolean expression.

In many cases, you want the computer to choose between doing something and not doing it. You can do this with an if statement that omits the else part:

```
if ( (boolean-expression ) )
    (statement )
```

To execute this statement, the computer evaluates the expression. If the value is true, the computer executes the (*statement*) that is contained inside the if statement; if the value is false, the computer skips over that (*statement*). In either case, the computer then continues with whatever follows the if statement in the program.

Sometimes, novice programmers confuse while statements with simple if statements (with no else part), although their meanings are quite different. The (*statement*) in an if is executed at most once, while the (*statement*) in a while can be executed any number of times. It can be helpful to look at diagrams of the flow of control for while and simple if statements:

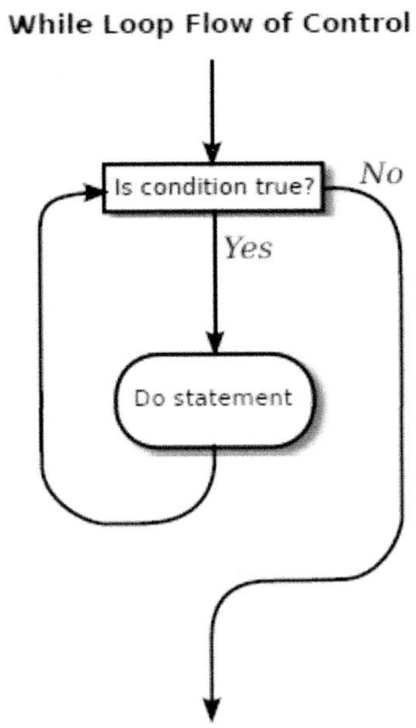

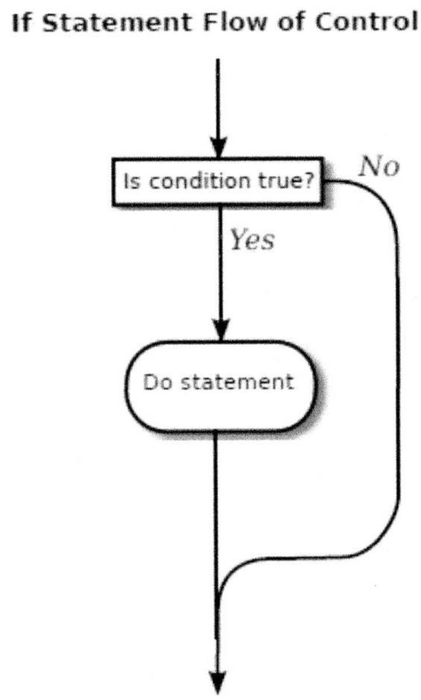

In these diagrams, the arrows represent the flow of time as the statement is executed. Control enters the diagram at the top and leaves at the bottom. Similarly, a flow control diagram for an if..else statement makes it clear that exactly one of the two nested statements is executed:

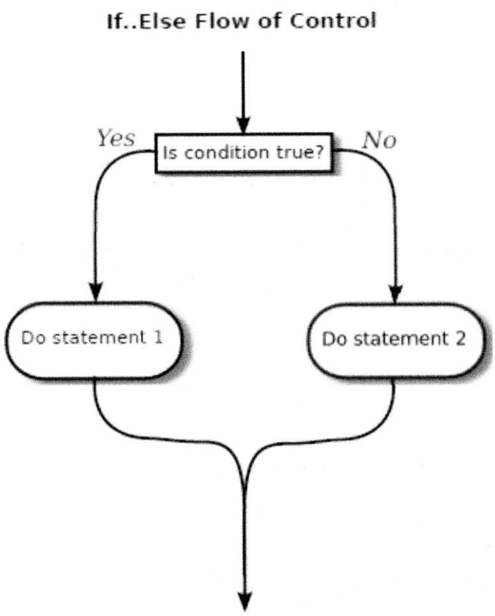

Of course, either or both of the (*statements*) in an if statement can be a block, and again many programmers prefer to add the braces even when they contain just a single statement. So an if statement often looks like:

```
if ( (boolean-expression ) ) {
    (statements )
}
else {
    (statements )
if ( (boolean-expression ) ) {
    (statements )
}
```

As an example, here is an if statement that exchanges the value of two variables, x and y, but only if x is greater than y to begin with. After this if statement has been executed, we can be sure that the value of x is definitely less than or equal to the value of y:

```
if ( x > y ) {
    int temp;        // A temporary variable for use in this block.
    temp = x;        // Save a copy of the value of x in temp.
    x = y;   // Copy the value of y into x.
    y = temp;        // Copy the value of temp into y.
}
```

Finally, here is an example of an if statement that includes an else part. See if you can figure out what it does, and why it would be used:

```
if ( years > 1 ) {       // handle case for 2 or more years
    System.out.print("The value of the investment after ");
    System.out.print(years);
    System.out.print(" years is ");
}
else {          // handle case for 1 year
    System.out.print("The value of the investment after 1 year is ");
}   // end of if statement
System.out.printf("%1.2f", principal);// this is done in any case
```

I'll have more to say about control structures later in this chapter. But you already know the essentials. If you never learned anything more about control structures, you would already know enough to perform any possible computing task. Simple looping and branching are all you really need!

3.1.4 Control Abstractiont

Control structures such as if statements and while loops allow you to control processes that go on inside the CPU of a computer. But as to what actually goes on in the CPU, there is no such thing as an if statements or a while loops. A CPU can only execute simple machine language instructions. Loops and branches must be implemented in machine language using jump instructions, which change the value stored in the program counter register, and conditional jump instructions, which might or might not change the program counter, depending on the result of a simple test.

Implementing Java control structures in machine language can get rather complicated. Fortunately, you don't need to know how to do it. You can use Java control structures without knowing how they are implemented in machine language. In fact, you don't need to know anything about machine language or how CPUs work. This is an example of *abstraction* .

Abstraction is a central concept in computer science. Abstraction allows you to work with something without understanding how it works in detail. It allows you to work on a "higher level." If statements and while loops are examples of *control abstractions.* They allow you to work with a high-level programming language like Java, rather than with very low-level machine language.

You will encounter other kinds of abstraction later in this book. In fact, you've already encountered one: A variable is a basic example of *data abstraction* . A variable lets you use a name to work with a data value of a certain type. The computer has to keep track of the numerical address of that data in memory, how many bytes of memory the data occupies, and how to interpret the bits that are stored in that memory to represent the value. The variable is an abstraction that lets you avoid all that detail.

3.1.5 Definite Assignment

I will finish this introduction to control structures with a somewhat technical issue that you might not fully understand the first time you encounter it. Consider the following two code segments, which seem to be entirely equivalent:

int y;	int y;
if (x < 0) {	if (x < 0)
{ y = 1;	y = 1;
}	}
else {	if (x >= 0) {
y = 2;	y = 2;

```
}                             }
System.out.println(y);        System.out.println(y);
```

In the version on the left, y is assigned the value 1 if x < 0 and it is assigned the value 2 otherwise, that is, if x >= 0. Exactly the same is true of the version on the right. However, there is a subtle difference. In fact, the Java compiler will report an error for the System.out.println statement in the code on the right, while the code on the left is perfectly fine!

The problem is that in the code on the right, the computer can't tell that the variable y has definitely been assigned a value. When an if statement has no else part, the statement inside the if might or might not be executed, depending on the value of the condition. The compiler can't tell whether it will be executed or not, since the condition will only be evaluated when the program is running. For the code on the right above, as far as the compiler is concerned, it is possible that neither statement, y = 1 or y = 2, will be evaluated, so it is possible that the output statement is trying to print an undefined value. The compiler considers this to be an error. The value of a variable can only be used if the compiler can verify that the variable will have been assigned a value at that point when the program is running. This is called *definite assignment*. (It doesn't matter that you can tell that y will always be assigned a value in this example. The question is whether the compiler can tell.)

Note that in the code on the left above, y is definitely assigned a value, since in an if..else statement, one of the two alternatives will be executed no matter what the value of the condition in the if. It is important that you understand that there is a difference between an if..else statement and a pair of plain if statements. Here is another pair of code segments that might seem to do the same thing, but don't. What's the value of x after each code segment is executed?

```
int x;              int x;
x = -1;             x = -1;
if (x < 0)          if (x < 0)
x = 1;              x = 1;
else if (x >= 0)
x = 2;              x = 2;
```

After the code on the left is executed, x is 1; after the code on the right, x is 2. If you don't believe this, work though the code step-by-step, doing exactly what the computer does when it executes each step. The key point is that for the code on the right, both assignment statements, x = 1 and x = 2, are executed. Make sure that you understand why.

3.2 ALGORITHM DEVELOPMENT

Programming is difficult (like many activities that are useful and worthwhile—and like most of those activities, it can also be rewarding and a lot of fun). When you write a program, you have to tell the computer every small detail of what to do. And you have to get everything exactly right, since the computer will blindly follow your program exactly as written. How, then, do people write any but the most simple programs? It's not a big mystery, actually. It's a matter of learning to think in the right way.

A program is an expression of an idea. A programmer starts with a general idea of a task for the computer to perform. Presumably, the programmer has some idea of how to perform the task by hand, at least in general outline. The problem is to flesh out that outline into a complete, unambiguous, step-by-step procedure for carrying out the task. Such a procedure is called an "algorithm." (Technically, an *algorithm* is an unambiguous, step-by-step procedure that always terminates after a finite number of steps. We don't want to count procedures that might go on forever.) An algorithm is not the same as a program. A program is written in some particular programming language. An algorithm is more like the idea behind the program, but it's the idea of the steps the program will take to perform its task, not just the idea of what the task needs to accomplish in the end. When describing an algorithm, the steps don't necessarily have to be specified in complete detail, as long as the steps are unambiguous and it's clear that carrying out the steps will accomplish the assigned task. An algorithm can be expressed in any language, including English. Of course, an algorithm can only be expressed as an actual program if all the details have been filled in.

So, where do algorithms come from? Usually, they have to be developed, often with a lot of thought and hard work. Skill at algorithm development is something that comes with practice, but there are techniques and guidelines that can help. I'll talk here about some techniques and guidelines that are relevant to "programming in the small," and I will return to the subject several times in later chapters.

3.2.1 Pseudocode and Stepwise Refinement

When programming in the small, you have a few basics to work with: variables, assignment statements, and input/output routines. You might also have some subroutines, objects, or other building blocks that have already been written by you or someone else. (Input/output routines fall into this class.) You can build sequences of these basic instructions, and you can also combine them into more complex control structures such as while loops and if statements. Suppose you have a task in mind that you want the computer to perform. One way to proceed is to write a description of the task, and take that description as an outline of the algorithm you want to develop. Then you can refine and elaborate that description, gradually adding steps and detail, until you have a complete algorithm that can be translated directly into programming language. This method is called *stepwise refinement*, and it is a type of top-down design. As you proceed through the stages of stepwise refinement, you can write out descriptions of your algorithm in *pseudocode*—informal instructions that imitate the structure of programming languages without the complete detail and perfect syntax of actual program code.

As an example, let's see how one might develop the program from the previous section, which computes the value of an investment over five years. The task that you want the program to perform is: "Compute and display the value of an investment for each of the next five years, where the initial investment and interest rate are to be specified by the user." You might then write—or more likely just think—that this can be expanded as:

Get the user's input

Compute the value of the investment after 1 year

Display the value

Compute the value after 2 years

Display the value

Compute the value after 3 years

Display the value

Compute the value after 4 years

Display the value

Compute the value after 5 years

Display the value

This is correct, but rather repetitive. And seeing that repetition, you might notice an opportunity to use a loop. A loop would take less typing. More important, it would be more general: Essentially the same loop will work no matter how many years you want to process. So, you might rewrite the above sequence of steps as:

Get the user's input

while there are more years to process: Compute the value after the next year Display the value

Following this algorithm would certainly solve the problem, but for a computer we'll have to be more explicit about how to "Get the user's input," how to "Compute the value after the next year," and what it means to say "there are more years to process." We can expand the step, "Get the user's input" into

Ask the user for the initial investment

Read the user's response

Ask the user for the interest rate

Read the user's response

To fill in the details of the step "Compute the value after the next year," you have to know how to do the computation yourself. (Maybe you need to ask your boss or professor for clarification?) Let's say you know that the value is computed by adding some interest to the previous value. Then we can refine the while loop to:

while there are more years to process:

> *Compute the interest*
>
> *Add the interest to the value*
>
> *Display the value*

As for testing whether there are more years to process, the only way that we can do that is by counting the years ourselves. This displays a very common pattern, and you should expect to use something similar in a lot of programs: We have to start with zero years, add one each time we process a year, and stop when we reach the desired number of years. This is sometimes called a *counting loop*. So the while loop becomes:

years = 0

while years < 5:

> *years = years + 1*
>
> *Compute the interest*
>
> *Add the interest to the value*
>
> *Display the value*

We still have to know how to compute the interest. Let's say that the interest is to be computed by multiplying the interest rate by the current value of the investment. Putting this together with the part of the algorithm that gets the user's inputs, we have the complete algorithm:

Ask the user for the initial investment

Read the user's response

Ask the user for the interest rate

Read the user's response

years = 0

while years < 5:

> *years = years + 1*

*Compute interest = value * interest rate*

Add the interest to the value

Display the value

Finally, we are at the point where we can translate pretty directly into proper programming- language syntax. We still have to choose names for the variables, decide exactly what we want to say to the user, and so forth. Having done this, we could express our algorithm in Java as:

```
double principal, rate, interest;          // declare the variables
int years;
System.out.print("Type initial investment: ");
principal = TextIO.getlnDouble();
System.out.print("Type interest rate: ");
rate = TextIO.getlnDouble(); years = 0;
while (years < 5) {
     years = years + 1;
     interest = principal * rate;
     principal = principal + interest;
     System.out.println(principal);
}
```

This still needs to be wrapped inside a complete program, it still needs to be commented, and it really needs to print out more information in a nicer format for the user. But it's essentially the same program as the one in the previous section. (Note that the pseudocode algorithm used indentation to show which statements are inside the loop. In Java, indentation is completely ignored by the computer, so you need a pair of braces to tell the computer which statements are in the loop. If you leave out the braces, the only statement inside the loop would be "years = years + 1;". The other statements would only be executed once, after the loop ends. The nasty thing is that the computer won't notice this error for you, like it would if you left out the parentheses around "(years < 5)". The parentheses are required by the syntax of the while statement. The braces are only required semantically. The computer can recognize syntax errors but not semantic errors.)

One thing you should have noticed here is that my original specification of the problem— "Compute and display the value of an investment for each of the next five years"—was far from being complete. Before you start writing a program, you should make sure you have a complete specification of exactly what the program is supposed to do. In particular, you need to know what information the program is going to input and output and what computation it is going to perform. Here is what a reasonably complete specification of the problem might look like in this example:

"Write a program that will compute and display the value of an investment for each of the next five years. Each year, interest is added to the value. The interest is computed by multiplying the current value by a fixed interest rate. Assume that the initial value and the rate of interest are to be input by the user when the program is run."

3.2.2 The 3N+1 Problem

Let's do another example, working this time with a program that you haven't already seen. The assignment here is an abstract mathematical problem that is one of my favorite programming exercises. This time, we'll start with a more complete specification of the task to be performed:

> *"Given a positive integer, N, define the '3N+1' sequence starting from N as follows: If N is an even number, then divide N by two; but if N is odd, then multiply N by 3 and add 1. Continue to generate numbers in this way until N becomes equal to 1. For example, starting from N = 3, which is odd, we multiply by 3 and add 1, giving N = 3*3+1 = 10. Then, since N is even, we divide by 2, giving N = 10/2 = 5. We continue in this way, stopping when we reach 1. The complete sequence is: 3, 10, 5, 16, 8, 4, 2,*
>
> *1.*
>
> *"Write a program that will read a positive integer from the user and will print out the 3N+1 sequence starting from that integer. The program should also count and print out the number of terms in the sequence."*

A general outline of the algorithm for the program we want is:

Get a positive integer N from the user.

Compute, print, and count each number in the sequence.

Output the number of terms.

The bulk of the program is in the second step. We'll need a loop, since we want to keep computing numbers until we get 1. To put this in terms appropriate for a while loop, we need to know when to continue the loop rather than when to stop it: We want to continue as long as the number is not 1. So, we can expand our pseudocode algorithm to:

Get a positive integer N from the user;

while N is not 1:

    Compute N = next term;

Output N;

Count this term;

Output the number of terms;

In order to compute the next term, the computer must take different actions depending on whether N is even or odd. We need an if statement to decide between the two cases:

Get a positive integer N from the user;

while N is not 1:

if N is even:

Compute N = N/2;

else

*Compute N = 3 * N + 1;*

Output N;

Count this term;

Output the number of terms;

We are almost there. The one problem that remains is counting. Counting means that you start with zero, and every time you have something to count, you add one. We need a variable to do the counting. The variable must be set to zero once, before the loop starts, and it must be incremented within the loop. (Again, this is a common pattern that you should expect to see over and over.) With the counter added, we get:

Get a positive integer N from the user;

Let counter = 0;

while N is not 1:

if N is even:

Compute N = N/2;

else

*Compute N = 3 * N + 1;*

Output N;

Add 1 to counter;

Output the counter;

We still have to worry about the very first step. How can we get a positive integer from the user? If we just read in a number, it's possible that the user might type in a negative number or zero. If you follow what happens when the value of N is negative or zero, you'll see that the program will go on forever, since the value of N will never become equal to 1. This is bad. In this case, the problem is probably no big deal, but in general you should try to write programs that are foolproof. One way to fix this is to keep reading in numbers until the user types in a positive number:

```
Ask user to input a positive number;
Let N be the user's response;
while N is not positive:
    Print an error message;
    Read another value for N;
Let counter = 0;
while N is not 1:
    if N is even:
            Compute N = N/2;
    else
            Compute N = 3 * N + 1;
    Output N;
    Add 1 to counter;
Output the counter;
```

The first while loop will end only when N is a positive number, as required. (A common beginning programmer's error is to use an if statement instead of a while statement here: "If N is not positive, ask the user to input another value." The problem arises if the second number input by the user is also non-positive. The if statement is only executed once, so the second input number is never tested, and the program proceeds into an infinite loop. With the while loop, after the second number is input, the computer jumps back to the beginning of the loop and tests whether the second number is positive. If not, it asks the user for a third number, and it will continue asking for numbers until the user enters an acceptable input. After the while loop ends, we can be absolutely sure that N is a positive number.)

Here is a Java program implementing this algorithm. It uses the operators <= to mean "is less than or equal to" and != to mean "is not equal to." To test whether N is even, it uses "N % 2 == 0".

```
import textio.TextIO;
/**
```

```
This program prints out a 3N+1 sequence starting from a positive
integer specified by the user. It also counts the number of
terms in the sequence, and prints out that number.
*/
public class ThreeN1 {
    public static void main(String[] args) {
            int N;    // for computing terms in the sequence
            int counter; // for counting the terms
            System.out.print("Starting point for sequence: ");
            N = TextIO.getlnInt();
            while (N <= 0) {
                    System.out.print(
                            "The starting point must be positive. Please try again: " );
                    N = TextIO.getlnInt();
            }
            // At this point, we know that N > 0
            counter = 0;
            while (N != 1) {
                    if (N % 2 == 0)
                            N = N / 2;
                    else
                            N = 3 * N + 1;
                    System.out.println(N);
                    counter = counter + 1;
            }
            System.out.println();
            System.out.print("There were ");
            System.out.print(counter);
            System.out.println(" terms in the sequence.");
    }       // end of main()
}   // end of class ThreeN1
```

Two final notes on this program: First, you might have noticed that the first term of the sequence—the value of N input by the user—is not printed or counted by this program. Is this an error? It's hard to say. Was the specification of the program careful enough to decide? This is the type of thing that might send you back to the boss/professor for clarification. The problem (if it is one!) can be fixed easily enough. Just replace the line "counter = 0" before the while loop with the two lines:

```
System.out.println(N);          // print out initial term
counter = 1; // and count it
```

Second, there is the question of why this problem might be interesting. Well, it's interesting to mathematicians and computer scientists because of a simple question about the problem that they haven't been able to answer: Will the process of computing the 3N+1 sequence finish after a finite number of steps for all possible starting values of N? Although individual sequences are easy to compute, no one has been able to answer the general question. To put this another way, no one knows whether the process of computing 3N+1 sequences can properly be called an algorithm, since an algorithm is required to terminate after a finite number of steps.

3.2.3 Coding, Testing, Debugging

It would be nice if, having developed an algorithm for your program, you could relax, press a button, and get a perfectly working program. Unfortunately, the process of turning an algorithm into Java source code doesn't always go smoothly. And when you do get to the stage of a working program, it's often only working in the sense that it does something. Unfortunately not what you want it to do.

After program design comes coding: translating the design into a program written in Java or some other language. Usually, no matter how careful you are, a few syntax errors will creep in from somewhere, and the Java compiler will reject your program with some kind of error message. Unfortunately, while a compiler will always detect syntax errors, it's not very good about telling you exactly what's wrong. Sometimes, it's not even good about telling you where the real error is. A spelling error or missing "{" on line 45 might cause the compiler to choke on line 105. You can avoid lots of errors by making sure that you really understand the syntax rules of the language and by following some basic programming guidelines. For example, I never type a "{" without typing the matching "}". Then I go back and fill in the statements between the braces. A missing or extra brace can be one of the hardest errors to find in a large program. Always, always indent your program nicely. If you change the program, change the indentation to match. It's worth the trouble. Use a consistent naming scheme, so you don't have to struggle to remember whether you called that variable interestrate or interestRate. In general, when the compiler gives multiple error messages, don't try to fix the second error message from the compiler until you've fixed the first one. Once the compiler hits an error in your program, it can get confused, and the rest of the error messages might just be guesses. Maybe the best advice is: Take the time to understand the error before you try to fix it. Programming is not an experimental science.

When your program compiles without error, you are still not done. You have to test the program to make sure it works correctly. Remember that the goal is not to get the right output for the two sample inputs that the professor gave in class. The goal is a program that will work correctly for all reasonable inputs. Ideally, when faced with an unreasonable input, it should respond by gently chiding the user rather than by crashing. Test your program on a wide variety of inputs. Try to find a set of inputs that will test the full range of functionality that you've coded into your program. As you begin writing larger programs, write them in stages and test each stage along the way. You might even have to write some extra code to do the testing—for example to call a subroutine that you've just written. You don't want to be faced, if you can avoid it, with 500 newly written lines of code that have an error in there somewhere.

The point of testing is to find *bugs*—semantic errors that show up as incorrect behavior rather than as compilation errors. And the sad fact is that you will probably find them. Again, you can minimize bugs by careful design and careful coding, but no one has found a way to avoid them altogether. Once you've detected a bug, it's time for *debugging* . You have to track down the cause of the bug in the program's source code and eliminate it. Debugging is a skill that, like other aspects of programming, requires practice to master. So don't be afraid of bugs. Learn from them. One essential debugging skill is the ability to read source code—the ability to put aside preconceptions about what you *think* it does and to follow it the way the computer does—mechanically, step-by-step—to see what it really does. This is hard. I can still remember the time I spent hours looking for a bug only to find that a line of code that I had looked at ten times had a "1" where it should have had an "i", or the time when I wrote a subroutine named WindowClosing which would have done exactly what I wanted except that the computer was looking for windowClosing (with a lower case "w"). Sometimes it can help to have someone who doesn't share your preconceptions look at your code.

Often, it's a problem just to find the part of the program that contains the error. Most programming environments come with a *debugger* , which is a program that can help you find bugs. Typically, your program can be run under the control of the debugger. The debugger allows you to set "breakpoints" in your program. A breakpoint is a point in the program where the debugger will pause the program so you can look at the values of the program's variables. The idea is to track down exactly when things start to go wrong during the program's execution. The debugger will also let you execute your program one line at a time, so that you can watch what happens in detail once you know the general area in the program where the bug is lurking. I will confess that I only occasionally use debuggers myself. A more traditional approach to debugging is to insert *debugging statements* into your program. These are output statements that print out information about the state of the program. Typically, a debugging statement would say something like

System.out.println("At start of while loop, N = " + N);

You need to be able to tell from the output where in your program the output is coming from, and you want to know the value of important variables. Sometimes, you will find that the computer isn't even getting to a part of the program that you think it should be executing. Remember that the goal is to find the first point in the program where the state is not what you expect it to be. That's where the bug is.

And finally, remember the golden rule of debugging: If you are absolutely sure that everything in your program is right, and if it still doesn't work, then one of the things that you are absolutely sure of is wrong.

3.3 THE WHILE AND DO..WHILE STATEMENTS

Statements in Java can be either simple statements or compound statements. Simple statements, such as assignment statements and subroutine call statements, are the basic building blocks of a program. Compound statements, such as while loops and if statements, are used to organize simple statements into complex structures, which are called control structures because they control the order in which the statements are executed. The next five sections explore the details of control structures that are available in Java, starting with the while statement and the do..while statement in this section. At the same time, we'll look at examples of programming with each control structure and apply the techniques for designing algorithms that were introduced in the previous section.

3.3.1 The while Statement

A while loop has the form

while ((boolean-expression))

(statement)

The (*statement*) can, of course, be a block statement consisting of several statements grouped together between a pair of braces. This statement is called the *body of the loop*. The body of the loop is repeated as long as the (*boolean-expression*) is true. This boolean expression is called the *continuation condition* , or more simply the *test*, of the loop. There are a few points that might need some clarification. What happens if the condition is false in the first place, before the body of the loop is executed even once? In that case, the body of the loop is never executed at all. The body of a while loop can be executed any number of times, including zero. What happens if the condition is true, but it becomes false somewhere in the middle of the loop body? Does the loop end as soon as this happens? It doesn't, because the computer continues executing the body of the loop until it gets to the end. Only then does it jump back to the beginning of the loop and test the condition, and only then can the loop end.

Let's look at a typical problem that can be solved using a while loop: finding the average of a set of positive integers entered by the user. The average is the sum of the integers, divided by the number of integers. The program will ask the user to enter one integer at a time. It will keep count of the number of integers entered, and it will keep a running total of all the numbers it has read so far. Here is a pseudocode algorithm for the program:

Let sum = 0 // The sum of the integers entered by the user.

Let count = 0 // The number of integers entered by the user.

while there are more integers to process:

Read an integer

Add it to the sum

Count it

Divide sum by count to get the average

Print out the average

But how can we test whether there are more integers to process? A typical solution is to tell the user to type in zero after all the data have been entered. This will work because we are assuming that all the data are positive numbers, so zero is not a legal data value. The zero is not itself part of the data to be averaged. It's just there to mark the end of the real data. A data value used in this way is sometimes called a *sentinel value*. So now the test in the while loop becomes "while the input integer is not zero". But there is another problem! The first time the test is evaluated, before the body of the loop has ever been executed, no integer has yet been read. There is no "input integer" yet, so testing whether the input integer is zero doesn't make sense. So, we have to do something before the while loop to make sure that the test makes sense. Setting things up so that the test in a while loop makes sense the first time it is executed is called *priming the loop*. In this case, we can simply read the first integer before the beginning of the loop. Here is a revised algorithm:

Let sum = 0

Let count = 0

Read an integer

while the integer is not zero:

Add the integer to the sum

Count it

Read an integer

Divide sum by count to get the average

Print out the average

Notice that I've rearranged the body of the loop. Since an integer is read before the loop, the loop has to begin by processing that integer. At the end of the loop, the computer reads a new integer. The computer then jumps back to the beginning of the loop and tests the integer that it has just read. Note that when the computer finally reads the sentinel value, the loop ends before the sentinel value is processed. It is not added to the sum, and it is not counted. This is the way it's supposed to work. The sentinel is not part of the data. The original algorithm, even if it could have been made to work without priming, was incorrect since it would have summed and counted all the integers, including the sentinel. (Since the sentinel is zero, the sum would still be correct, but the count would be off by one. Such so-called *off-by-one errors* are very common. Counting turns out to be harder than it looks!)

We can easily turn the algorithm into a complete program. Note that the program cannot use the statement "average = sum/count;" to compute the average. Since sum and count are both variables of type int, the value of sum/count is an integer. The average should be a real number. We've seen this problem before: we have to convert one of the int values to a double to force the computer to compute the quotient as a real number. This can be done by type-casting one of the variables to type double. The type cast "(double)sum" converts the value of sum to a real number, so in the program the average is computed as "average = ((double)sum) / count;". Another solution in this case would have been to declare sum to be a variable of type double in the first place.

One other issue is addressed by the program: If the user enters zero as the first input value, there are no data to process. We can test for this case by checking whether count is still equal to zero after the while loop. This might seem like a minor point, but a careful programmer should cover all the bases.

Here is the full source code for the program (with comments added, of course!):

```
import textio.TextIO;

/**

This program reads a sequence of positive integers input

by the user, and it will print out the average of those
```

```
integers.     The user is prompted to enter one integer at a
time.         The user must enter a 0 to mark the end of the
data.         (The zero is not counted as part of the data to
be averaged.)          The program does not check whether the
user's input is positive, so it will actually add up
both positive and negative input values.
*/
public class ComputeAverage {
    public static void main(String[] args) {
            int inputNumber;          // One of the integers input by the user.
            int sum;// The sum of the positive integers.
            int count;          // The number of positive integers.
            double average; // The average of the positive integers.
            /* Initialize the summation and counting variables. */
            sum = 0;
            count = 0;
            /* Read and process the user's input. */
            System.out.print("Enter your first positive integer: ");
            inputNumber = TextIO.getlnInt();
            while (inputNumber != 0) {
                    sum += inputNumber;     // Add inputNumber to running sum.
                    count++;// Count the input by adding 1 to count.
                    System.out.print("Enter your next positive integer, or 0 to end: ");
                    inputNumber = TextIO.getlnInt();
            }
            /* Display the result.*
             if (count == 0) {
                    System.out.println("You didn't enter any data!");
            }
            else {
                    average = ((double)sum) / count;
```

```
            System.out.println();
            System.out.println("You entered " + count + " positive integers.");
            System.out.printf("Their average is %1.3f.\n", average);
        }
    } // end main()
} // end class ComputeAverage
```

3.3.2 The do..while Statement

Sometimes it is more convenient to test the continuation condition at the end of a loop, instead of at the beginning, as is done in the while loop. The do..while statement is very similar to the while statement, except that the word "while," along with the condition that it tests, has been moved to the end. The word "do" is added to mark the beginning of the loop. A do..while statement has the form

```
do
    (statement )
while ( (boolean-expression ) );
```

or, since, as usual, the (statement) can be a block,

```
do {
    (statements )
} while ( (boolean-expression ) );
```

Note the semicolon, ';', at the very end. This semicolon is part of the statement, just as the semicolon at the end of an assignment statement or declaration is part of the statement. Omitting it is a syntax error. (More generally, every statement in Java ends either with a semicolon or a right brace, '}'.)

To execute a do loop, the computer first executes the body of the loop—that is, the statement or statements inside the loop—and then it evaluates the boolean expression. If the value of the expression is true, the computer returns to the beginning of the do loop and repeats the process; if the value is false, it ends the loop and continues with the next part of the program. Since the condition is not tested until the end of the loop, the body of a do loop is always executed at least once.

For example, consider the following pseudocode for a game-playing program. The do loop makes sense here instead of a while loop because with the do loop, you know there will be at least one game. Also, the test that is used at the end of the loop wouldn't even make sense at the beginning:

```
do {
    Play a Game
    Ask user if he wants to play another game
    Read the user's response
} while ( the user's response is yes );
```

Let's convert this into proper Java code. Since I don't want to talk about game playing at the moment, let's say that we have a class named Checkers, and that the Checkers class contains a static member subroutine named playGame() that plays one game of checkers against the user. Then, the pseudocode "Play a game" can be expressed as the subroutine call statement "Checkers.playGame();". We need a variable to store the user's response. The *TextIO* class makes it convenient to use a boolean variable to store the answer to a yes/no question. The input function TextIO.getlnBoolean() allows the user to enter the value as "yes" or "no" (among other acceptable responses). "Yes" is considered to be true, and "no" is considered to be false. So, the algorithm can be coded as

```
boolean wantsToContinue;    // True if user wants to play again.
do {
    Checkers.playGame();
    System.out.print("Do you want to play again? ");
    wantsToContinue = TextIO.getlnBoolean();
} while (wantsToContinue == true);
```

When the value of the boolean variable is set to false, it is a signal that the loop should end. When a boolean variable is used in this way—as a signal that is set in one part of the program and tested in another part—it is sometimes called a *flag* or *flag variable* (in the sense of a signal flag).

By the way, a more-than-usually-pedantic programmer would sneer at the test "while (wantsToContinue == true)". This test is exactly equivalent to "while (wantsToContinue)". Testing whether "wantsToContinue == true" is true amounts to the same thing as testing whether "wantsToContinue" is true. A little less offensive is an expression of the form "flag == false", where flag is a boolean variable. The value of "flag == false" is exactly the same as the value of "!flag", where ! is the boolean negation operator. So you can write "while (!flag)" instead of "while (flag == false)", and you can write "if (!flag)" instead of "if (flag == false)".

Although a do..while statement is sometimes more convenient than a while statement, having two kinds of loops does not make the language more powerful. Any problem that can be solved using do..while loops can also be solved using only while statements, and vice versa.

In fact, if (*doSomething*) represents any block of program code, then

```
do {
    (doSomething )
} while ( (boolean-expression ) );
```

has exactly the same effect as

```
(doSomething )
while ( (boolean-expression ) ) {
    (doSomething )
}
```

Similarly,

```
while ( (boolean-expression ) ) {
    (doSomething )
}
```

can be replaced by

```
if ( (boolean-expression ) ) { do {
    (doSomething )
} while ( (boolean-expression ) );
}
```

without changing the meaning of the program in any way.

3.3.3 break and continue

The syntax of the while and do..while loops allows you to test the continuation condition at either the beginning of a loop or at the end. Sometimes, it is more natural to have the test in the middle of the loop, or to have several tests at different places in the same loop. Java provides a general method for breaking out of the middle of any loop. It's called the break statement, which takes the form

```
break;
```

When the computer executes a break statement in a loop, it will immediately jump out of the loop. It then continues on to whatever follows the loop in the program. Consider for example:

```
while (true) {          // looks like it will run forever!
    System.out.print("Enter a positive number: ");
```

```
        N = TextIO.getlnInt();
        if (N > 0)          // the input value is OK, so jump out of loop
                break;
        System.out.println("Your answer must be > 0.");
    }
    // continue here after break
```

If the number entered by the user is greater than zero, the break statement will be executed and the computer will jump out of the loop. Otherwise, the computer will print out "Your answer must be > 0." and will jump back to the start of the loop to read another input value. The first line of this loop, "while (true)" might look a bit strange, but it's perfectly legitimate. The condition in a while loop can be any boolean-valued expression. The computer evaluates this expression and checks whether the value is true or false. The boolean literal "true" is just a boolean expression that always evaluates to true. So "while (true)" can be used to write an infinite loop, or one that will be terminated by a break statement.

A break statement terminates the loop that immediately encloses the break statement. It is possible to have *nested* loops, where one loop statement is contained inside another. If you use a break statement inside a nested loop, it will only break out of that loop, not out of the loop that contains the nested loop. There is something called a *labeled break* statement that allows you to specify which loop you want to break. This is not very common, so I will go over it quickly. Labels work like this: You can put a *label* in front of any loop. A label consists of a simple identifier followed by a colon. For example, a while with a label might look like "mainloop: while...". Inside this loop you can use the labeled break statement "break mainloop;" to break out of the labeled loop. For example, here is a code segment that checks whether two strings, s1 and s2, have a character in common. If a common character is found, the value of the flag variable nothingInCommon is set to false, and a labeled break is used to end the processing at that point:

```
    boolean nothingInCommon;
    nothingInCommon = true;     // Assume s1 and s2 have no chars in common.
    int i,j;        // Variables for iterating through the chars in s1 and s2.
    i = 0;
    bigloop: while (i < s1.length()) {
        j = 0;
        while (j < s2.length()) {
                if (s1.charAt(i) == s2.charAt(j)) { // s1 and s2 have a common char...
```

```
                nothingInCommon = false; // so nothingInCommon is actually false.
                break bigloop; // break out of BOTH loops
            }
            j++;        // Go on to the next char in s2.
        }
        i++;        //Go on to the next char in s1.
    }
```

The continue statement is related to break, but less commonly used. A continue statement tells the computer to skip the rest of the current iteration of the loop. However, instead of jumping out of the loop altogether, it jumps back to the beginning of the loop and continues with the next iteration (including evaluating the loop's continuation condition to see whether any further iterations are required). As with break, when a continue is in a nested loop, it will continue the loop that directly contains it; a "labeled continue" can be used to continue the containing loop instead.

Break and continue can be used in while loops and do..while loops. They can also be used in for loops, we'll see that break can also be used to break out of a switch statement. A break can occur inside an if statement, but only if the if statement is nested inside a loop or inside a switch statement. In that case, it does not mean to break out of the if. Instead, it breaks out of the loop or switch statement that contains the if statement. The same consideration applies to continue statements inside ifs.

3.4 THE FOR STATEMENT

We turn in this section to another type of loop, the for statement. Any for loop is equivalent to some while loop, so the language doesn't get any additional power by having for statements. But for a certain type of problem, a for loop can be easier to construct and easier to read than the corresponding while loop. It's quite possible that in real programs, for loops actually outnumber while loops (and I know of at least one person who only uses for loops).

3.4.1 For Loops

The for statement makes a common type of while loop easier to write. Many while loops have the general form:

```
(initialization )
while ( (continuation-condition ) ) {
    (statements )
```

```
        (update )
    }
```

For example, consider this example, copied from an example in Section 3.2:

```
    years = 0;    // initialize the variable years
    while ( years < 5 ) {  // condition for continuing loop
        interest = principal * rate;          //
        principal += interest;      // do three statements
        System.out.println(principal);    //
        years++;// update the value of the variable, years
    }
```

This loop can be written as the following equivalent for statement:

```
    for ( years = 0;         years < 5;          years++ ) {
        interest = principal * rate;
        principal += interest;
        System.out.println(principal);
    }
```

The initialization, continuation condition, and updating have all been combined in the first line of the for loop. This keeps everything involved in the "control" of the loop in one place, which helps make the loop easier to read and understand. The for loop is executed in exactly the same way as the original code: The initialization part is executed once, before the loop begins. The continuation condition is executed before each execution of the loop (including the first execution), and the loop ends when this condition is false. The update part is executed at the end of each execution of the loop, just before jumping back to check the condition.

The formal syntax of the for statement is as follows:

```
    for ( (initialization ); (continuation-condition ); (update ) )
        (statement )
```

or, using a block statement:

```
    for ( (initialization ); (continuation-condition ); (update ) ) {
        (statements )
    }
```

The (*continuation-condition*) must be a boolean-valued expression. The (*initialization*) is usually a declaration or an assignment statement, but it can be any expression that would be allowed as a statement in a program. The (*update*) can be any simple statement, but is usually an increment, a decrement, or an assignment statement. Any of the three parts can be empty, but the two semicolons are required in any case. If the continuation condition is empty, it is treated as if it were "true," so the loop will be repeated forever or until it ends for some other reason, such as a break statement. (Some people like to begin an infinite loop with "for (;;)" instead of "while (true)".) Here's a flow control diagram for a for statement:

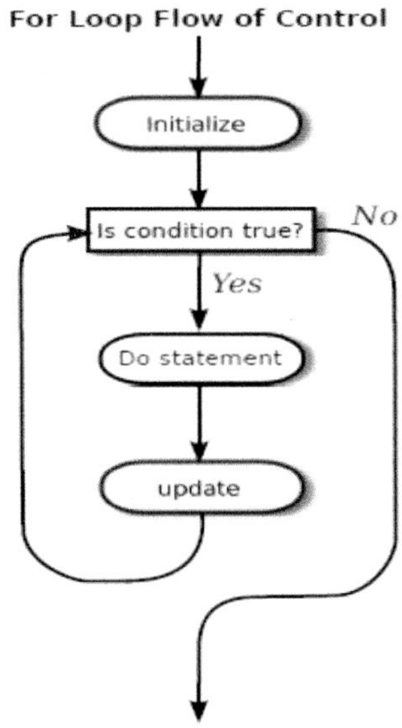

Usually, the initialization part of a for statement assigns a value to some variable, and the update changes the value of that variable with an assignment statement or with an increment or decrement operation. The value of the variable is tested in the continuation condition, and the loop ends when this condition evaluates to false. A variable used in this way is called a *loop control variable*. In the example given above, the loop control variable was years.

Certainly, the most common type of for loop is the *counting loop*, where a loop control variable takes on all integer values between some minimum and some maximum value. A counting loop has the form

```
for ( (variable ) = (min );      (variable ) <= (max ); (variable )++ ) {
     (statements )
}
```

where (*min*) and (*max*) are integer-valued expressions (usually constants). The (*variable*) takes on the values (*min*), (*min*)+1, (*min*)+2, . . . , (*max*). The value of the loop control variable is often used in the body of the loop. The for loop at the beginning of this section is a counting loop in which the loop control variable, years, takes on the values 1, 2, 3, 4, 5. Here is an even simpler example, in which the numbers 1, 2, . . . , 10 are displayed on standard output:

```
for ( N = 1 ;  N <= 10 ;N++ )
        System.out.println( N );
```

For various reasons, Java programmers like to start counting at 0 instead of 1, and they tend to use a "<" in the condition, rather than a "<=". The following variation of the above loop prints out the ten numbers 0, 1, 2, . . . , 9:

```
for ( N = 0 ;  N < 10 ;  N++ )
        System.out.println( N );
```

Using < instead of <= in the test, or vice versa, is a common source of off-by-one errors in programs. You should always stop and think, Do I want the final value to be processed or not? It's easy to count down from 10 to 1 instead of counting up. Just start with 10, decrement the loop control variable instead of incrementing it, and continue as long as the variable is greater than or equal to one.

```
for ( N = 10 ; N >= 1 ;  N-- )
        System.out.println( N );
```

Now, in fact, the official syntax of a for statement actually allows both the initialization part and the update part to consist of several expressions, separated by commas. So we can even count up from 1 to 10 and count down from 10 to 1 at the same time!

```
for ( i=1, j=10;          i <= 10;  i++, j-- ) {
        System.out.printf("%5d", i); // Output i in a 5-character wide column.
        System.out.printf("%5d", j); // Output j in a 5-character column.
        System.out.println();      //        and end the line.
}
```

As a final introductory example, let's say that we want to use a for loop that prints out just the even numbers between 2 and 20, that is: 2, 4, 6, 8, 10, 12, 14, 16, 18, 20. There are several ways to do this. Just to show how even a very simple problem can be solved in many ways, here are four different solutions (three of which would get full credit):

```
// There are 10 numbers to print.
// Use a for loop to count 1, 2,
// ..., 10.     The numbers we want
// to print are 2*1, 2*2, ... 2*10.
```

```
for (N = 1; N <= 10; N++) {
      System.out.println( 2*N );
}
// Use a for loop that counts
// 2, 4, ..., 20 directly by
// adding 2 to N each time through
// the loop.
for (N = 2; N <= 20; N = N + 2) {
      System.out.println( N );
}

// Count off all the numbers
// 2, 3, 4, ..., 19, 20, but
// only print out the numbers
// that are even.
for (N = 2; N <= 20; N++) {
      if ( N % 2 == 0 ) // is N even?
            System.out.println( N );
}

// Irritate the professor with
// a solution that follows the
// letter of this silly assignment
// while making fun of it.
for (N = 1; N <= 1; N++) {
      System.out.println("2 4 6 8 10 12 14 16 18 20");
}
```

Perhaps it is worth stressing one more time that a for statement, like any statement except for a variable declaration, never occurs on its own in a real program. A statement must be inside the main routine of a program or inside some other subroutine. And that subroutine must be defined inside a class. I should also remind you that every variable must be declared before it can be used, and that includes the loop control variable in a for statement. In all the examples that you have seen so far in this section, the loop control variables should be declared to be of type int. It is not required that a loop control variable be an integer. Here, for example, is a for loop in which the variable, ch, is of type char, using the fact that the ++ operator can be applied to characters as well as to numbers:

```
// Print out the alphabet on one line of output.
char ch;     // The loop control variable;
             //              one of the letters to be printed.
for ( ch = 'A';ch <= 'Z';    ch++ )
    System.out.print(ch);
System.out.println();
```

3.4.2 Example: Counting Divisors

Let's look at a less trivial problem that can be solved with a for loop. If N and D are positive integers, we say that D is a *divisor* of N if the remainder when D is divided into N is zero. (Equivalently, we could say that N is an even multiple of D.) In terms of Java programming, D is a divisor of N if N % D is zero.

Let's write a program that inputs a positive integer, N, from the user and computes how many different divisors N has. The numbers that could possibly be divisors of N are 1, 2, . . . , N. To compute the number of divisors of N, we can just test each possible divisor of N and count the ones that actually do divide N evenly. (This is a correct solution, but there are much more efficient ways to perform this task.) In pseudocode, the algorithm takes the form

```
Get a positive integer, N, from the user
Let divisorCount = 0
for each number, testDivisor, in the range from 1 to N:
    if testDivisor is a divisor of N:
            Count it by adding 1 to divisorCount
Output the count
```

This algorithm displays a common programming pattern that is used when some, but not all, of a sequence of items are to be processed. The general pattern is

```
for each item in the sequence:
    if the item passes the test:
            process it
```

The for loop in our divisor-counting algorithm can be translated into Java code as

```
for (testDivisor = 1; testDivisor <= N; testDivisor++) {
```

```
    if ( N % testDivisor == 0 )
        divisorCount++;
}
```

On a modern computer, this loop can be executed very quickly. It is not impossible to run it even for the largest legal int value, 2147483647. (If you wanted to run it for even larger values, you could use variables of type long rather than int.) However, it does take a significant amount of time for very large numbers. So when I implemented this algorithm, I decided to output a dot every time the computer has tested ten million possible divisors. In the improved version of the program, there are two types of counting going on. We have to count the number of divisors and we also have to count the number of possible divisors that have been tested. So the program needs two counters. When the second counter reaches 10000000, the program outputs a '.' and resets the counter to zero so that we can start counting the next group of ten million. Reverting to pseudocode, the algorithm now looks like

```
Get a positive integer, N, from the user
Let divisorCount = 0          // Number of divisors found.
Let numberTested = 0          // Number of possible divisors tested
                              //     since the last period was output.
for each number, testDivisor, in the range from 1 to N:
    if testDivisor is a divisor of N:
        Count it by adding 1 to divisorCount
    Add 1 to numberTested
    if numberTested is 10000000:
        print out a '.'
        Reset numberTested to 0
Output the count
```

Finally, we can translate the algorithm into a complete Java program:

```
import textio.TextIO;
/**
This program reads a positive integer from the user.
It counts how many divisors that number has, and
then it prints the result.
*/
```

```
public class CountDivisors {
    public static void main(String[] args) {
            int N;   // A positive integer entered by the user.
                     // Divisors of this number will be counted.
    int testDivisor; // A number between 1 and N that is a
                     // possible divisor of N.
    int divisorCount;// Number of divisors of N that have been found.
    int numberTested;       // Used to count how many possible divisors
                            // of N have been tested. When the number
                            // reaches 10000000, a period is output and
                            // the value of numberTested is reset to zero.
    /* Get a positive integer from the user. */
    while (true) {
            System.out.print("Enter a positive integer: ");
            N = TextIO.getlnInt();
            if (N > 0)
                    break;
            System.out.println("That number is not positive.  Please try again.");
    }
    /* Count the divisors, printing a "." after every 10000000 tests. */
    divisorCount = 0;
    numberTested = 0;
    for (testDivisor = 1; testDivisor <= N; testDivisor++)
            if ( N % testDivisor == 0 )
                    divisorCount++;
            numberTested++;
            if (numberTested == 10000000) {
                    System.out.print('.');
                    numberTested = 0;
            }
    }
```

```
/* Display the result. */
System.out.println();
System.out.println("The number of divisors of " + N
                         + " is " + divisorCount);
    } // end main()
} // end class CountDivisors
```

3.4.3 Nested for Loops

Control structures in Java are statements that contain other, simpler statements. In particular, control structures can contain control structures. You've already seen several examples of if statements inside loops, and one example of a while loop inside another while, but any combination of one control structure inside another is possible. We say that one structure is *nested* inside another. You can even have multiple levels of nesting, such as a while loop inside an if statement inside another while loop. The syntax of Java does not set a limit on the number of levels of nesting. As a practical matter, though, it's difficult to understand a program that has more than a few levels of nesting, and it is a style rule that excessive nesting should be avoided.

Nested for loops arise naturally in many algorithms, and it is important to understand how they work. Let's look at a couple of examples. First, consider the problem of printing out a multiplication table like this one:

```
 1   2   3   4   5   6   7   8   9  10  11  12
 2   4   6   8  10  12  14  16  18  20  22  24
 3   6   9  12  15  18  21  24  27  30  33  36
 4   8  12  16  20  24  28  32  36  40  44  48
 5  10  15  20  25  30  35  40  45  50  55  60
 6  12  18  24  30  36  42  48  54  60  66  72
 7  14  21  28  35  42  49  56  63  70  77  84
 8  16  24  32  40  48  56  64  72  80  88  96
 9  18  27  36  45  54  63  72  81  90  99 108
10  20  30  40  50  60  70  80  90 100 110 120
11  22  33  44  55  66  77  88  99 110 121 132
12  24  36  48  60  72  84  96 108 120 132 144
```

The data in the table are arranged into 12 rows and 12 columns. The process of printing them out can be expressed in a pseudocode algorithm as

for each rowNumber = 1, 2, 3, ..., 12:

Print the first twelve multiples of rowNumber on one line

Output a carriage return

The first step in the for loop can itself be expressed as a for loop. We can expand "Print the first twelve multiples of rowNumber on one line" as:

```
for N = 1, 2, 3, ..., 12:
    Print N * rowNumber
```

so a refined algorithm for printing the table has one for loop nested inside another:

```
for each rowNumber = 1, 2, 3, ..., 12:
    for N = 1, 2, 3, ..., 12:
            Print N * rowNumber
    Output a carriage return
```

We want to print the output in neat columns, with each output number taking up four spaces. This can be done using formatted output with format specifier %4d. Assuming that rowNumber and N have been declared to be variables of type int, the algorithm can be expressed in Java as

```
for ( rowNumber = 1; rowNumber <= 12;  rowNumber++ ) {
    for ( N = 1;        N <= 12; N++ ) {
                        // print in 4-character columns
            System.out.printf( "%4d", N * rowNumber );        // No carriage return !
    }
    System.out.println();     // Add a carriage return at end of the line.
}
```

This section has been weighed down with lots of examples of numerical processing. For our next example, let's do some text processing. Consider the problem of finding which of the 26 letters of the alphabet occur in a given string. For example, the letters that occur in "Hello World" are D, E, H, L, O, R, and W. More specifically, we will write a program that will list all the letters contained in a string and will also count the number of different letters. The string will be input by the user. Let's start with a pseudocode algorithm for the program.

```
Ask the user to input a string
Read the response into a variable, str
Let count = 0 (for counting the number of different letters)
for each letter of the alphabet:
    if the letter occurs in str:
            Print the letter
            Add 1 to count
```

Output the count

Since we want to process the entire line of text that is entered by the user, we'll use TextIO.getln() to read it. The line of the algorithm that reads "for each letter of the alphabet" can be expressed as "for (letter='A'; letter<='Z'; letter++)". But the if statement inside the for loop needs still more thought before we can write the program. How do we check whether the given letter, letter, occurs in str? One idea is to look at each character in the string in turn, and check whether that character is equal to letter. We can get the i-th character of str with the function call str. charAt(i), where i ranges from 0 to str.length() - 1.

One more difficulty: A letter such as 'A' can occur in str in either upper or lower case, 'A' or 'a'. We have to check for both of these. But we can avoid this difficulty by converting str

to upper case before processing it. Then, we only have to check for the upper case letter. We can now flesh out the algorithm fully:

```
Ask the user to input a string
Read the response into a variable, str Convert str to upper case
Let count = 0
for letter = 'A', 'B', ..., 'Z':
    for i = 0, 1, ..., str.length()-1:
            if letter == str.charAt(i):
                    Print letter
                    Add 1 to count
                    break    // jump out of the loop, to avoid counting letter twice
Output the count
```

Note the use of break in the nested for loop. It is required to avoid printing or counting a given letter more than once (in the case where it occurs more than once in the string). The break statement breaks out of the inner for loop, but not the outer for loop. Upon executing the break, the computer continues the outer loop with the next value of letter. You should try to figure out exactly what count would be at the end of this program, if the break statement were omitted. Here is the complete program:

```
import textio.TextIO;
/**
This program reads a line of text entered by the user.
It prints a list of the letters that occur in the text,
```

```
and it reports how many different letters were found.
*/
public class ListLetters {
    public static void main(String[] args) {
            String str;        // Line of text entered by the user.
            int count;         // Number of different letters found in str.
            char letter; // A letter of the alphabet.
            System.out.println("Please type in a line of text.");
            str = TextIO.getln();
            str = str.toUpperCase();
            count = 0;
            System.out.println("Your input contains the following letters:");
            System.out.println();
            System.out.print("        ");
            for ( letter = 'A'; letter <= 'Z'; letter++ ) {
                    int i;     // Position of a character in str.
                    for ( i = 0; i < str.length(); i++ ) {
                            if ( letter == str.charAt(i) ) {
                                    System.out.print(letter);
                                    System.out.print(' ')
                                    count++;
                                    break;
                            }
                    }
            }
            System.out.println();
            System.out.println();
            System.out.println("There were " + count + " different letters.");
    } // end main()
} // end class ListLetters
```

In fact, there is actually an easier way to determine whether a given letter occurs in a string, str. The built-in function str.indexOf(letter) will return -1 if letter does not occur in the string. It returns a number greater than or equal to zero if it does occur. So, we could check whether letter occurs in str simply by checking "if (str. indexOf(letter) >= 0)". If we used this technique in the above program, we wouldn't need a nested for loop. This gives you a preview of how subroutines can be used to deal with complexity.

3.5 THE IF STATEMENT

The first of the two branching statements in Java is the if statement. It takes the form

if ((boolean-expression))

(statement-1)

else

(statement-2)

As usual, the statements inside an if statement can be blocks. The if statement represents a two-way branch. The else part of an if statement—consisting of the word "else" and the statement that follows it—can be omitted.

3.5.1 The Dangling else Problem

Now, an if statement is, in particular, a statement. This means that either (*statement-1*) or (*statement-2*) in the above if statement can itself be an if statement. A problem arises, however, if (*statement-1*) is an if statement that has no else part. This special case is effectively forbidden by the syntax of Java. Suppose, for example, that you type

```
if ( x > 0 )
    if (y > 0)
            System.out.println("First case");
else
    System.out.println("Second case");
```

Now, remember that the way you've indented this doesn't mean anything at all to the computer. You might think that the else part is the second half of your "if (x > 0)" statement, but the rule that the computer follows attaches the else to "if (y > 0)", which is closer. That is, the computer reads your statement as if it were formatted:

```
if ( x > 0 )
    if (y > 0)
    System.out.println("First case");
```

```
else
    System.out.println("Second case");
```

You can force the computer to use the other interpretation by enclosing the nested if in a block:

```
if ( x > 0 ) {
    if (y > 0)
            System.out.println("First case");
}
else
    System.out.println("Second case");
```

These two if statements have different meanings: In the case when x <= 0, the first statement doesn't print anything, but the second statement prints "Second case".

3.5.2 Multiway Branching

Much more interesting than this technicality is the case where (*statement-2*), the else part of the if statement, is itself an if statement. The statement would look like this (perhaps without the final else part):

```
if ((boolean-expression-1 ))
    (statement-1 )
else
    if ((boolean-expression-2 ))
            (statement-2 )
    else
            (statement-3 )
```

However, since the computer doesn't care how a program is laid out on the page, this is almost always written in the format:

```
if ((boolean-expression-1 ))
    (statement-1 )
else
if ((boolean-expression-2 ))
    (statement-2 )
else
    (statement-3 )
```

You should think of this as a single statement representing a three-way branch. When the computer executes this, one and only one of the three statements—(*statement-1*), (*statement- 2*), or (*statement-3*)—will be executed. The computer starts by evaluating (*boolean-expression- 1*). If it is true, the computer executes (*statement-1*) and then jumps all the way to the end of the outer if statement, skipping the other two (*statements*). If (*boolean-expression-1*) is false, the computer skips (*statement-1*) and executes the second, nested if statement. To do this, it tests the value of (*boolean-expression-2*) and uses it to decide between (*statement-2*) and (*statement-3*).

Here is an example that will print out one of three different messages, depending on the value of a variable named temperature:

```
if (temperature < 50)
    System.out.println("It's cold.");
else if (temperature < 80)
    System.out.println("It's nice.");
else
    System.out.println("It's hot.");
```

If temperature is, say, 42, the first test is true. The computer prints out the message "It's cold", and skips the rest—without even evaluating the second condition. For a temperature of 75, the first test is false, so the computer goes on to the second test. This test is true, so the computer prints "It's nice" and skips the rest. If the temperature is 173, both of the tests evaluate to false, so the computer says "It's hot" (unless its circuits have been fried by the heat, that is).

You can go on stringing together "else-if's" to make multiway branches with any number of cases:

```
if ((test-1 ))
    (statement-1 )
else if ((test-2 ))
    (statement-2 )
else if ((test-3 ))
    (statement-3 )
.
. // (more cases)
.
else if ((test-N ))
    (statement-N )
```

else

(statement-(N+1))

The computer evaluates the tests, which are boolean expressions, one after the other until it comes to one that is true. It executes the associated statement and skips the rest. If none of the boolean expressions evaluate to true, then the statement in the else part is executed. This statement is called a multiway branch because one and only one of the statements will be executed. The final else part can be omitted. In that case, if all the boolean expressions are false, none of the statements are executed. Of course, each of the statements can be a block, consisting of a number of statements enclosed between { and }. Admittedly, there is lot of syntax here; as you study and practice, you'll become comfortable with it. It might be useful to look at a flow control diagram for the general "if..else if" statement shown above:

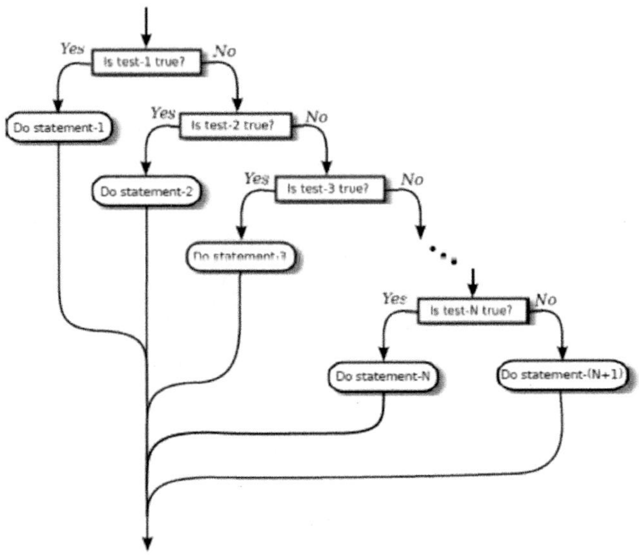

3.5.3 If Statement Examples

As an example of using if statements, let's suppose that x, y, and z are variables of type int, and that each variable has already been assigned a value. Consider the problem of printing out the values of the three variables in increasing order. For example, if the values are 42, 17, and 20, then the output should be in the order 17, 20, 42.

One way to approach this is to ask, where does x belong in the list? It comes first if it's less than both y and z. It comes last if it's greater than both y and z. Otherwise, it comes in the middle. We can express this with a 3-way if statement, but we still have to worry about the order in which y and z should be printed. In pseudocode,

```
if (x < y && x < z) {
    output x, followed by y and z in their correct order
}
else if (x > y && x > z) {
    output y and z in their correct order, followed by x
}
else {
    output x in between y and z in their correct order
}
```

Determining the relative order of y and z requires another if statement, so this becomes

```
if (x < y && x < z) { // x comes first
    if (y < z)
            System.out.println( x + " " + y + " " + z );
    else
            System.out.println( x + " " + z + " " + y );
}
else if (x > y && x > z) { // x comes last
    if (y < z)
            System.out.println( y + " " + z + " " + x );
    else
            System.out.println( z + " " + y + " " + x );
}
else { // x in the middle
    if (y < z)
            System.out.println( y + " " + x + " " + z);
    else
    System.out.println( z + " " + x + " " + y);
}
```

You might check that this code will work correctly even if some of the values are the same. If the values of two variables are the same, it doesn't matter which order you print them in.

Note, by the way, that even though you can say in English "if x is less than y and z," you can't say in Java "if (x < y && z)". The && operator can only be used between boolean values, so you have to make separate tests, x<y and x<z, and then combine the two tests with & &.

There is an alternative approach to this problem that begins by asking, "which order should x and y be printed in?" Once that's known, you only have to decide where to stick in z. This line of thought leads to different Java code:

```
if ( x < y ) {  // x comes before y
    if ( z < x )                    // z comes first
            System.out.println( z + " " + x + " " + y);
    else if ( z > y ) // z comes last
            System.out.println( x + " " + y + " " + z);
    else        // z is in the middle
            System.out.println( x + " " + z + " " + y);
}
else {          // y comes before x
    if ( z < y )                    // z comes first
            System.out.println( z + " " + y + " " + x);
    else if ( z > x )    // z comes last
            System.out.println( y + " " + x + " " + z);
    else        // z is in the middle
            System.out.println( y + " " + z + " " + x);
}
```

Once again, we see how the same problem can be solved in many different ways. The two approaches to this problem have not exhausted all the possibilities. For example, you might start by testing whether x is greater than y. If so, you could swap their values. Once you've done that, you know that x should be printed before y.

Finally, let's write a complete program that uses an if statement in an interesting way. I want a program that will convert measurements of length from one unit of measurement to another, such as miles to yards or inches to feet. So far, the problem is extremely under- specified. Let's say that the program will only deal with measurements in inches, feet, yards, and miles. It would be easy to extend it later to deal with other units. The user will type in a measurement in one of these units, such as "17 feet" or "2.73 miles". The output will show the length in terms of each of the four units of measure. (This is easier than asking the user which units to use in the output.) An outline of the process is

Read the user's input measurement and units of measure Express the measurement in inches, feet, yards, and miles Display the four results

The program can read both parts of the user's input from the same line by using TextIO.getDouble() to read the numerical measurement and TextIO.getlnWord() to read the unit of measure. The conversion into different units of measure can be simplified by first converting the user's input into inches. From there, the number of inches can easily be converted into feet, yards, and miles. Before converting into inches, we have to test the input to determine which unit of measure the user has specified:

```
Let measurement = TextIO.getDouble()
Let units = TextIO.getlnWord()
if the units are inches
    Let inches = measurement
else if the units are feet
    Let inches = measurement * 12     // 12 inches per foot
else if the units are yards
    Let inches = measurement * 36     // 36 inches per yard
else if the units are miles
    Let inches = measurement * 12 * 5280      // 5280 feet per mile
else
    The units are illegal!
    Print an error message and stop processing
Let feet = inches / 12.0
Let yards = inches / 36.0
Let miles = inches / (12.0 * 5280.0)
Display the results
```

Since units is a *String*, we can use units.equals("inches") to check whether the specified unit of measure is "inches". However, it would be nice to allow the units to be specified as "inch" or abbreviated to "in". To allow these three possibilities, we can check if (units.equals("inches") || units.equals("inch") || units.equals("in")). It would also be nice to allow upper case letters, as in "Inches" or "IN". We can do this by converting units to lower case before testing it or by substituting the function units.equalsIgnoreCase for units.equals.

In my final program, I decided to make things more interesting by allowing the user to repeat the process of entering a measurement and seeing the results of the conversion for each measurement. The program will end only when the user inputs 0. To program that, I just had to wrap the above algorithm inside a while loop, and make sure that the loop ends when the user inputs a 0. Here's the complete program:

```
import textio.TextIO;
/**
This program will convert measurements expressed in inches,
feet, yards, or miles into each of the possible units of
measure.    The measurement is input by the user, followed by
the unit of measure. For example:    "17 feet", "1 inch", or
"2.73 mi".   Abbreviations in, ft, yd, and mi are accepted.
The program will continue to read and convert measurements
until the user enters an input of 0.
*/
public class LengthConverter {
    public static void main(String[] args) {
            double measurement;    // Numerical measurement, input by user.
            String units;    // The unit of measure for the input, also
                             //        specified by the user.
            double inches, feet, yards, miles;  // Measurement expressed in
                                                //        each possible unit of
                                                //        measure.
            System.out.println("""
                    Enter measurements in inches, feet, yards, or miles. For example: 1
                    inch 17 feet 2.73 miles You can use abbreviations:  in        ft
                    yd mi I will convert your input into the other units of measure.
                    """);
    while (true) {
            /* Get the user's input, and convert units to lower case. */
            System.out.print("Enter your measurement, or 0 to end:   ");
            measurement = TextIO.getDouble();
```

```
            if (measurement == 0)
                        break;   // Terminate the while loop.
            units = TextIO.getlnWord();
            units = units.toLowerCase();          // convert units to lower case
            /* Convert the input measurement to inches. */
            if (units.equals("inch") || units.equals("inches")
                                || units.equals("in")) {
                        inches = measurement;
}
            else if (units.equals("foot") || units.equals("feet")
                                || units.equals("ft")) {
                        inches = measurement * 12;
}
            else if (units.equals("yard") || units.equals("yards")
                                || units.equals("yd")) {
                        inches = measurement * 36;
}
            else if (units.equals("mile") || units.equals("miles")
                                || units.equals("mi")) {
                        inches = measurement * 12 * 5280;
}
else {
            System.out.println("Sorry, but I don't understand \""
                                            + units + "\".");
continue;          // back to start of while loop
}
            /* Convert measurement in inches to feet, yards, and miles. */
            feet = inches / 12;
            yards = inches / 36;
            miles = inches / (12*5280);
            /* Output measurement in terms of each unit of measure. */
```

```
            System.out.printf("""
                    That's equivalent to:
                    %14.5g inches
                    %14.5g feet
                    %14.5g yards
                    %14.5g miles
                    """, inches, feet, yards, miles);
            System.out.println();
    } // end while
            System.out.println();
            System.out.println("OK! Bye for now.");
        } // end main()
    } // end class LengthConverter
```

(Note that this program uses text blocks for multiline outputs. It also uses formatted output with the "g" format specifier. In this program, we have no control over how large or how small the numbers might be. It could easily make sense for the user to enter very large or very small measurements. The "g" format will print a real number in exponential form if it is very large or very small, and in the usual decimal form otherwise. Remember that in the format specification %14.5g, the 5 is the total number of significant digits that are to be printed, so we will always get the same number of significant digits in the output, no matter what the size of the number. If we had used an "f" format specifier such as %14.5f, the output would be in decimal form with 5 digits after the decimal point. This would print the number 0.000000000745482 as 0.00000, with no significant digits at all! With the "g" format specifier, the output would be 7.4549e-10.)

3.5.4 The Empty Statement

As a final note in this section, I will mention one more type of statement in Java: the *empty statement*. This is a statement that consists simply of a semicolon and which tells the computer to do nothing. The existence of the empty statement makes the following legal, even though you would not ordinarily see a semicolon after a } :

```
if (x < 0) {
    x = -x;
};
```

The semicolon is legal after the }, but the computer considers it to be an empty statement, not part of the if statement. Occasionally, you might find yourself using the empty statement when what you mean is, in fact, "do nothing." For example, the rather contrived if statement

```
if ( done )
      ;          // Empty statement
else
      System.out.println( "Not done yet.");
```

does nothing when the boolean variable done is true, and prints out "Not done yet" when it is false. You can't just leave out the semicolon in this example, since Java syntax requires an actual statement between the if and the else. I prefer, though, to use an empty block, consisting of { and } with nothing between, for such cases.

Occasionally, stray empty statements can cause annoying, hard-to-find errors in a program.

For example, the following program segment prints out "Hello" just once, not ten times:

```
for (i = 0; i < 10; i++);
      System.out.println("Hello");
```

Why? Because the ";" at the end of the first line is a statement, and it is this empty statement that is executed ten times. The System.out.println statement is not really inside the for statement at all, so it is executed just once, after the for loop has completed. The for loop just does nothing, ten times!

3.6 THE SWITCH STATEMENT

The second branching statement in Java is the switch statement, which is introduced in this section. The switch statement is used much less often than the if statement, but it is sometimes useful for expressing a certain type of multiway branch.

3.6.1 The Basic switch Statement

A switch statement allows you to test the value of an expression and, depending on that value, to jump directly to some location within the switch statement. Only expressions of certain types can be used. The value of the expression can be one of the primitive integer types int, short, or byte. It can be the primitive char type. It can be *String*. Or it can be an enum type (see Subsection 2.3.5 for an introduction to enum types). In particular, note that the expression cannot be a double or float value.

Java has two different syntaxes for switch statements. The original switch syntax, which like other Java control structures was modeled on the C programming language, is error-prone and kind-of ugly. The new syntax, which requires Java 17, is an improvement. You still need to know the traditional syntax, since it is used in a lot of existing code, but my advice would be to use the new syntax wh en you write new code. We look at the new syntax first, and will cover the traditional syntax at the end of this section.

The positions within a switch statement to which it can jump are marked with *case labels* that take the form: "case (*constantList*)". The (*constantList*) here consists of one or more literals of the same type as the expression in the switch, separated by commas. For example:

case 2, 4, 8

or

case "Paper"

The case label is followed by ->, that is by a symbol made up of a hyphen and a greater-than character, and then by a single statement. The statement can be a subroutine call statement, a throw statement, or a block statement, containing several nested statements. A switch statement can also, optionally, have one jump point labeled with default instead of with a case label. The syntax for the statement can be specified as follows, noting that there can be at most one default case and that all the constants in the case labels must be different:

```
switch ( (expression ) ) {
    (case-label-or-default ) -> (statement )
    (case-label-or-default ) -> (statement )
        .
        .
        .
    (case-label-or-default ) -> (statement )
}
```

When the computer executes this switch statement, it evaluates the (*expression*). If the value is one of the constants in a case label, the computer executes the statement that follows that case label, and then jumps out of the switch statement. If the value of the expression does not match any of the case constants, then the computer looks for a default case, and if one is present, executes the statement that follows it.

It is probably easiest to look at an example. This is not a useful example, but it should be easy to follow:

```
switch ( N ) {          // (Assume N is an integer variable.)
    case 1 -> System.out.println("The number is 1.");
```

```
        case 2, 4, 8 -> {
                    System.out.println("The number is 2, 4, or 8.");
                    System.out.println("(That's a power of 2!)");
        }
    case 3, 6, 9 -> {
                    System.out.println("The number is 3, 6, or 9.");
                    System.out.println("(That's a multiple of 3!)");
        }
    case 5 -> System.out.println("The number is 5.");
        default ->
                    System.out.println("The number is 7 or is outside the range 1 to 9.");
        }
```

The braces, { and }, in this example are required to group multiple statements into a single block statement. Braces could also be added to the other cases, but are not required there. This switch statement has exactly the same effect as the following multiway if statement:

```
    if ( N == 1 ) {
        System.out.println("The number is 1.");
    }
    else if ( N == 2 || N == 4 || N == 8 ) {
        System.out.println("The number is 2, 4, or 8.");
        System.out.println("(That's a power of 2!)");
    }
    else if ( N == 3 || N == 6 || N == 9 ) {
        System.out.println("The number is 3, 6, or 9.");
        System.out.println("(That's a multiple of 3!)");
    }
    else if ( N == 5 ) {
        System.out.println("The number is 5.");
    }
    else {
        System.out.println("The number is 7 or is outside the range 1 to 9.");
    }
```

More generally, any switch statement could be replaced by a multiway if statement. The switch statement can be easier to read. And it might be more efficient since the computer can jump directly to the correct case instead of working through a series of tests to get to the correct case.

3.6.2 Menus and switch Statements

One application of switch statements is in processing menus. A menu is a list of options. The user selects one of the options. The computer has to respond to each possible choice in a different way. If the options are numbered 1, 2, . . . , then the number of the chosen option can be used in a switch statement to select the proper response.

In a command-line program, the menu can be presented as a numbered list of options, and the user can choose an option by typing in its number. It can be convenient to use a text block (see Subsection 2.3.4) to present the menu. Here is an example that could be used in a variation of the LengthConverter example from the previous section:

```
int optionNumber;   // Option number from menu, selected by user.
double measurement; // A numerical measurement, input by the user.
                    //      The unit of measurement depends on which
                    //      option the user has selected.
double inches;      // The same measurement, converted into inches.
/* Display menu of options, and get user's selected option number. */
System.out.println("""
    What unit of measurement does your input use?
            inches
            feet
            yards
            miles
    Enter the number of your choice:
    """);
optionNumber = TextIO.getlnInt();
/* Read user's measurement and convert to inches. */
switch ( optionNumber ) {
    case 1 -> {
            System.out.println("Enter    the    number    of    inches:    ");
```

```
                measurement = TextIO.getlnDouble();
                inches = measurement;
        }
    case 2 -> {
                System.out.println("Enter the number of feet: ")
                measurement = TextIO.getlnDouble();
                inches = measurement * 12;
        }
    case 3 -> {
                System.out.println("Enter the number of yards: ");
                measurement = TextIO.getlnDouble();
                inches = measurement * 36;
        }
    case 4 -> {
                System.out.println("Enter the number of miles: ");
                measurement = TextIO.getlnDouble();
                inches = measurement * 12 * 5280;
        }
        default -> {
                System.out.println("Error! Illegal option number! I quit!");
                System.exit(1);
        }
    } // end switch
    /* Now go on to convert inches to feet, yards, and miles... */
```

Alternatively, this example could be designed to ask the use to enter the unit of measure as a string, instead of as an option number, and then use that string directly in a switch statement:

```
String units;        // Unit of measurement, entered by user.
double measurement; // A numerical measurement, input by the user.
double inches;       // The same measurement, converted into inches.
/* Read the user's unit of measurement. */
System.out.println("What unit of measurement does your input use?");
units = TextIO.getln().toLowerCase();
/* Read user's measurement and convert to inches. */
```

```
System.out.print("Enter the number of " + units + ":        ");
measurement = TextIO.getlnDouble();
switch ( units ) {
        case "inch", "inches", "in" ->      inches = measurement;
        case "foot", "feet", "ft"   ->      inches    =    measurement    *    12;
        case "yard", "yards", "yd"      ->      inches  =  measurement  *  36;
        case "mile", "miles", "mi"      ->      inches  =  measurement  *  12  *
        5280; default -> {
        System.out.println("Wait a minute!     Illegal    unit    of    measure!
        I quit!"); System.exit(1);
    }
} // end switch
```

3.6.3 Enums in switch Statements

The type of the expression in a switch can be an enum type. In that case, the constants in the case labels must be values from the enum type. For example, suppose that the type of the expression is the enumerated type *Season* defined by

```
enum Season { SPRING, SUMMER, FALL, WINTER }
```

and that the expression in a switch statement is an expression of type *Season*. The constants in the case label must be chosen from among the values Season.SPRING, Season.SUMMER, Season.FALL, or Season.WINTER. However, there is a quirk in the syntax: when an enum constant is used in a case label, only the simple name, such as "SPRING" is used, not the full name, such as "Season.SPRING". Of course, the computer already knows that the value in the case label must belong to the enumerated type, since it can tell that from the type of expression used, so there is really no need to specify the type name in the constant. For example, assuming that currentSeason is a variable of type *Season*, then we could have the switch statement:

```
System.out.print("The months in " + currentSeason + " are: ");
switch ( currentSeason ) {
    case WINTER -> // ( NOT Season.WINTER ! )
            System.out.println("December, January, February");
case SPRING ->
            System.out.println("March, April, May");
case SUMMER ->
    System.out.println("June, July, August");
```

```
case FALL ->
    System.out.println("September, October, November");
}
```

3.6.4 Definite Assignment and switch Statements

As a somewhat more realistic example, the following switch statement makes a ran- dom choice among three possible alternatives. Recall that the value of the expression (int)(3*Math.random()) is one of the integers 0, 1, or 2, selected at random with equal probability, so the switch statement below will assign one of the values "Rock", "Paper", "Scissors" to computerMove, with probability 1/3 for each case:

```
switch ( (int)(3*Math.random()) ) {
    case 0 -> computerMove = "Rock";
    case 1 -> computerMove = "Paper";
    case 2 -> computerMove = "Scissors";
}
```

This switch statement is perfectly OK, but suppose that we use it in the following code segment:

```
String computerMove;
switch ( (int)(3*Math.random()) ) {
    case 0 -> computerMove = "Rock";
    case 1 -> computerMove = "Paper";
    case 2 -> computerMove = "Scissors";
}
System.out.println("The computer's move is " + computerMove);    // ERROR!
```

Now there is a subtle error on the last line! The problem here is due to definite assignment, the idea that the Java compiler must be able to determine that a variable has definitely been assigned a value before its value is used. Definite assignment was introduced in Subsection 3.1.5. In this example, it's true that the three cases in the switch cover all the possibilities, but the compiler is not smart enough to figure that out; it just sees that there is an integer-valued expression in the switch but not all possible integer values are covered by the given cases.

A simple solution is to replace the final case in the switch statement with default. With a default case, all possible values of the expression in the switch are certainly covered, and the compiler knows that computerMove is definitely assigned a value:

```
String computerMove;
switch ( (int)(3*Math.random()) ) {
    case 0 -> computerMove = "Rock";
    case 1 -> computerMove = "Paper";
    default -> computerMove = "Scissors";
}
System.out.println("The computer's move is " + computerMove);        // OK!
```

3.6.5 Switch Expressions

Often, the whole purpose of a switch statement is to assign a value to a variable, where the value that is to be assigned depends on the value of the expression in the switch statement. For example, this is true for the switch statement in the previous subsection.

This type of thing can be handled more elegantly by using a *switch expression* instead of a switch statement. Like any expression, a switch expression computes and returns a single value. The syntax is similar to a switch statement, but instead of a statement in each case, there is an expression (or a throw statement). For example,

```
String computerMove = switch ( (int)(3*Math.random()) ) {
    case 1 -> "Rock";
    case 2 -> "Paper";
    default -> "Scissors";
};
```

This is a single assignment statement, where the value to be assigned to computerMove is computed by the switch expression. The semicolon on the last line is the semicolon that is required at the end of the assignment statement; it is not part of the switch expression.

A switch expression must always compute a value (or throw an exception) and therefore will usually have a default case. The expression in a case can be replaced by a block containing several statements; the value for that case should then be specified by a yield statement, which takes a form such as "yield 42;". The value after the word yield is then returned as the value of the switch expression.

Of course, switch expressions are not limited to assignment statements. You can use a switch expression any place where any other kind of expression could be used, such as in an output statement or as part of a larger expression.

3.6.6 The Traditional switch Statement

The older traditional syntax for switch statements is more complicated, but you should be aware of it since it has been widely used in Java and in other programming languages. As it is most often used, the traditional switch has the form:

```
switch ((expression )) {
    case (constant-1 ):
            (statements-1 )
            break;
    case (constant-2 ):
            (statements-2 )
break;
.
.   // (more cases)
.
case (constant-N ):
    (statements-N ) break;
    default: // optional default case
            (statements-(N+1) )
} // end of switch statement
```

Note that in the traditional syntax, only one constant is allowed in a case label (but Java 17 allows a comma-separated list of constants here). A case label can be followed by any number of statements. This traditional syntax uses a colon after each case label, rather than ->. The default case is optional.

To execute this switch statement, the computer will evaluate the (*expression*) and jump to the case label that contains that constant, if there is one, or to the default case if not. The break statements in this switch are not actually required by the syntax of the switch statement. The effect of a break is to make the computer jump past the end of the switch statement, skipping over all the remaining cases. If you leave out the break statement, the computer will just forge ahead after completing one case and will execute the statements associated with the next case label. This is called "fall through"; it is rarely what you want, and it is a common source of bugs. However, it is legal and is even occasionally useful.

Note that you can leave out one of the groups of statements entirely (including the break). You then have two case labels in a row, containing two different constants. This just means that the computer will jump to the same place and perform the same action for each of the two constants.

Here is how our first example switch statement would be written using the traditional syntax:

```
switch ( N ) {          // (Assume N is an integer variable.)
    case 1:
            System.out.println("The number is 1.");
            break;
    case 2:
    case 4:
    case 8:
            System.out.println("The number is 2, 4, or 8.");
            System.out.println("(That's a power of 2!)");
            break;
    case 3:
    case 6:
    case 9:
            System.out.println("The number is 3, 6, or 9.");
            System.out.println("(That's a multiple of 3!)");
            break;
    case 5:
            System.out.println("The number is 5.");
            break;
    default:
            System.out.println("The number is 7 or is outside the range 1 to 9.");
}
```

3.7 EXCEPTIONS AND TRY..CATCH: AN INTRODUCTION

In addition to the control structures that determine the normal flow of control in a program, Java has a way to deal with "exceptional" cases that throw the flow of control off its normal track. When an error occurs during the execution of a program, the default behavior is to terminate the program and to print an error message. However, Java makes it possible to "catch" such errors and program a response different from simply letting the program crash. This is done with the *try..catch* statement. In this section, we will take a preliminary and incomplete look the try..catch statement, leaving out a lot of the rather complex syntax of this statement. Error handling is a complex topic, which we will return to in Section 8.3, and we will cover the full syntax of try..catch at that time.

3.7.1 Exceptions

The term *exception* is used to refer to the type of event that one might want to handle with a try..catch. An exception is an exception to the normal flow of control in the program. The term is used in preference to "error" because in some cases, an exception might not be considered to be an error at all. You can sometimes think of an exception as just another way to organize a program.

Exceptions in Java are represented as objects of type *Exception*. Actual exceptions are usually defined by subclasses of *Exception*. Different subclasses represent different types of exceptions. We will look at only two types of exception in this section: *NumberFormatException* and *IllegalArgumentException*.

A *NumberFormatException* can occur when an attempt is made to convert a string into a number. Such conversions are done by the functions Integer.parseInt and Double.parseDouble. (See Subsection 2.5.7.) Consider the function call Integer.parseInt(str) where str is a variable of type *String*. If the value of str is the string "42", then the function call will correctly convert the string into the int 42. However, if the value of str is, say, "fred", the function call will fail because "fred" is not a legal string representation of an int value. In this case, an exception of type *NumberFormatException* occurs. If nothing is done to handle the exception, the program will crash.

An *IllegalArgumentException* can occur when an illegal value is passed as a parameter to a subroutine. For example, if a subroutine requires that a parameter be greater than or equal to zero, an *IllegalArgumentException* might occur when a negative value is passed to the subroutine. How to respond to the illegal value is up to the person who wrote the subroutine, so we can't simply say that every illegal parameter value will result in an *IllegalArgumentException*. However, it is a common response.

3.7.2 try..catch

When an exception occurs, we say that the exception is "thrown." For example, we say that Integer.parseInt(str) *throws* an exception of type *NumberFormatException* when the value of str is illegal. When an exception is thrown, it is possible to "catch" the exception and prevent it from crashing the program. This is done with a *try..catch* statement. In simplified form, the syntax for a try..catch statement can be:

```
try {
    (statements-1 )
}
catch ( (exception-class-name ) (variable-name ) ) {
    (statements-2 )
}
```

The (*exception-class-name*) could be *NumberFormatException*, *IllegalArgumentException*, or some other exception class. When the computer executes this try..catch statement, it executes (*statements-1*), the statements inside the try part. If no exception occurs during the execution of (*statements-1*), then the computer just skips over the catch part and proceeds with the rest of the program. However, if an exception of type (*exception-class-name*) occurs during the execution of (*statements-1*), the computer immediately jumps from the point where the exception occurs to the catch part and executes (*statements-2*), skipping any remaining statements in (*statements-1*). Note that only one type of exception is caught; if some other type of exception occurs during the execution of (*statements-1*), it will crash the program as usual.

An exception is represented by an object. During the execution of (*statements-2*), the (*variable-name*) represents that exception object, so that you can, for example, print it out. The exception object contains information about the cause of the exception. This includes an error message, which will be displayed if you print out the exception object.

After the end of the catch part, the computer proceeds with the rest of the program; the exception has been caught and handled and does not crash the program.

By the way, note that the braces, { and }, are part of the syntax of the try..catch statement. They are required even if there is only one statement between the braces. This is different from the other statements we have seen, where the braces around a single statement are optional.

As an example, suppose that str is a variable of type *String* whose value might or might not represent a legal real number. Then we could say:

```
double x;
try {
    x = Double.parseDouble(str);
    System.out.println( "The number is " + x );
}
    catch ( NumberFormatException e ) {
    System.out.println( "Not a legal number." )
     x = Double.NaN;
}
```

If an error is thrown by the call to Double.parseDouble(str), then the output statement in the try part is skipped, and the statement in the catch part is executed. (In this example, I set x to be the value Double.NaN when an exception occurs. Double.NaN is the special "not-a-number" value for type double.)

It's not always a good idea to catch exceptions and continue with the program. Often that can just lead to an even bigger mess later on, and it might be better just to let the exception crash the program at the point where it occurs. However, sometimes it's possible to recover from an error.

Suppose, for example, we want a program that will find the average of a sequence of real numbers entered by the user, and we want the user to signal the end of the sequence by entering a blank line. If we use TextIO.getlnInt() to read the user's input, we will have no way of detecting the blank line, since that function simply skips over blank lines. A solution is to use TextIO.getln() to read the user's input. This allows us to detect a blank input line, and we can convert non-blank inputs to numbers using Double.parseDouble. And we can use try..catch to avoid crashing the program when the user's input is not a legal number. In this example, it makes sense to simply print an error message, ignore the bad input, and let the program continue. Here's the program:

```
import textio.TextIO;
public class ComputeAverage2 {
    public static void main(String[] args) {
            String str;        // The user's input.
            double number; // The input converted into a number.
            double total;      // The total of all numbers entered.
            double avg;        // The average of the numbers.
            int count;         // The number of numbers entered.
            total = 0;
            count = 0;
            System.out.println("Enter your numbers, press return to end.");
            while (true) {
                    System.out.print("? ");
                    str = TextIO.getln();
                    if (str.equals("")) {
                            break; // Exit the loop, since the input line was blank.
                    }
                    try {
                    number = Double.parseDouble(str);
                    // If an error occurs, the next 2 lines are skipped!
```

```
                total = total + number;
                count = count + 1;
            }
            catch (NumberFormatException e) {
                System.out.println("Not a legal number!   Try again.");
            }
        }
        avg = total/count;
        System.out.printf("The average of %d numbers is %1.6g%n", count, avg);
        }
    }
```

3.7.3 Exceptions in TextIO

When TextIO reads a numeric value from the user, it makes sure that the user's response is legal, using a technique similar to the while loop and try..catch in the previous example. However, TextIO can read data from other sources besides the user. When it is reading from a file, there is no reasonable way for TextIO to recover from an illegal value in the input, so it responds by throwing an exception. To keep things simple, TextIO only throws exceptions of type *IllegalArgumentException*, no matter what type of error it encounters. For example, an exception will occur if an attempt is made to read from a file after all the data in the file has already been read. In TextIO, the exception is of type *IllegalArgumentException*. If you have a better response to file errors than to let the program crash, you can use a try..catch to catch exceptions of type *IllegalArgumentException*.

As an example, we will look at yet another number-averaging program. In this case, we will read the numbers from a file. Assume that the file contains nothing but real numbers, and we want a program that will read the numbers and find their sum and their average. Since it is unknown how many numbers are in the file, there is the question of when to stop reading. One approach is simply to try to keep reading indefinitely. When the end of the file is reached, an exception occurs. This exception is not really an error—it's just a way of detecting the end of the data. So, we can catch the exception and finish up the program when it occurs. We can read the data in a while (true) loop and break out of the loop when an exception occurs. This is an example of the somewhat unusual technique of using an exception as part of the expected flow of control in a program.

To read from the file, we need to know the file's name. To make the program more general, we can let the user enter the file name, instead of hard-coding a fixed file name in the program. However, it is possible that the user will enter the name of a file that does not exist. When we use TextIO.readfile to open a file that does not exist, an exception of type *IllegalArgumentException* occurs. We can catch this exception and ask the user to enter a different file name. Here is a complete program that uses all these ideas:

```
import textio.TextIO;

/**

This program reads numbers from a file.        It computes the sum and

the average of the numbers that it reads.        The file should contain

nothing but numbers of type double; if this is not the case, the

output will be the sum and average of however many numbers were

successfully read from the file.            The name of the file will be

input by the user.    (The user can choose to end the program by

typing Control-C.)

*/

public class AverageNumbersFromFile {

    public static void main(String[] args) {

            while (true) {

                    String fileName; // The name of the file, to be input by the user.

                    System.out.print("Enter the name of the file: ");

                    fileName = TextIO.getln();

                    try {

                            TextIO.readFile( fileName ); // Try to open the file for input.

                            break;    // If that succeeds, break out of the loop.

                    }

                    catch ( IllegalArgumentException e ) {

                            System.out.println("Can't read from the file \"" + fileName
                            + "\".");

                            System.out.println("Please try again.\n");

                    }

            }

            /* At this point, TextIO is reading from the file. */
```

```
double number; // A number read from the data file.
double sum;      // The sum of all the numbers read so far.
int count;       // The number of numbers that were read.
sum = 0;
count = 0;
try {
        while (true) { // Loop ends when an exception occurs.
                number = TextIO.getDouble();
                count++;// This is skipped when the exception occurs
                sum += number;
        }
}
catch ( IllegalArgumentException e ) {
        // We expect this to occur when the end-of-file is encountered.
        // We don't consider this to be an error, so there is nothing to do
        // in this catch clause.   Just proceed with the rest of the program.
}
// At this point, we've read the entire file.
System.out.println();
System.out.println("Number of data values read: " + count);
System.out.println("The sum of the data values: " + sum);
if ( count == 0 )
        System.out.println("Can't compute an average of 0 values.");
else
        System.out.println("The average of the values:     " + (sum/count));
    }
}
```

3.8 ARRAYS: AN INTRODUCTION

In previous sections of this chapter, we have already covered all of Java's control structures. But before moving on to the next chapter, we will take preliminary looks at two additional topics that are at least somewhat related to control structures.

This section is an introduction to arrays. Arrays are a basic and very commonly used data structure, and array processing is often an exercise in using control structures. The next section will introduce computer graphics and will allow you to apply what you know about control structures in another context.

3.8.1 Creating and Using Arrays

A *data structure* consists of a number of data items chunked together so that they can be treated as a unit. An *array* is a data structure in which the items are arranged as a numbered sequence, so that each individual item can be referred to by its position number. In Java—but not in some other programming languages—all the items must be of the same type, and the numbering always starts at zero. You will need to learn several new terms to talk about arrays: The number of items in an array is called the *length* of the array. The type of the individual items in an array is called the *base type* of the array. And the position number of an item in an array is called the *index* of that item.

Suppose that you want to write a program that will process the names of, say, one thousand people. You will need a way to deal with all that data. Before you knew about arrays, you might have thought that the program would need a thousand variables to hold the thousand names, and if you wanted to print out all the names, you would need a thousand print statements.

Clearly, that would be ridiculous! In reality, you can put all the names into an array. The array is represented by a single variable, but it holds the entire list of names. The length of the array would be 1000, since there are 1000 individual names. The base type of the array would be *String* since the items in the array are strings. The first name would be at index 0 in the array, the second name at index 1, and so on, up to the thousandth name at index 999.

The base type of an array can be any Java type, but for now, we will stick to arrays whose base type is *String* or one of the eight primitive types. If the base type of an array is int, it is referred to as an "array of ints." An array with base type *String* is referred to as an "array of *Strings*." However, an array is not, properly speaking, a list of integers or strings or other values. It is better thought of as a list of variables of type int, or a list of variables of type *String*, or of some other type. As always, there is some potential for confusion between the two uses of a variable: as a name for a memory location and as a name for the value stored in that memory location. Each position in an array acts as a variable. Each position can hold a value of a specified type (the base type of the array), just as a variable can hold a value. The value can be changed at any time, just as the value of a variable can be changed. The items in an array—really, the individual variables that make up the array—are more often referred to as the *elements* of the array.

As I mentioned above, when you use an array in a program, you can use a variable to refer to the array as a whole. But you often need to refer to the individual elements of the array. The name for an element of an array is based on the name for the array and the index number of the element. The syntax for referring to an element looks, for example, like this: namelist[7].

Here, namelist is the variable that names the array as a whole, and namelist[7] refers to the element at index 7 in that array. That is, to refer to an element of an array, you use the array name, followed by element index enclosed in square brackets. An element name of this form can be used like any other variable: You can assign a value to it, print it out, use it in an expression, and so on.

An array also contains a kind of variable representing its length. For example, you can refer to the length of the array namelist as namelist.length. However, you cannot assign a value to namelist.length, since the length of an array cannot be changed.

Before you can use a variable to refer to an array, that variable must be declared, and it must have a type. For an array of *Strings*, for example, the type for the array variable would be String[ ], and for an array of ints, it would be int[ ]. In general, an array type consists of the base type of the array followed by a pair of empty square brackets. Array types can be used to declare variables; for example,

String[] namelist;

int[] A;

double[] prices;

and variables declared in this way can refer to arrays. However, declaring a variable does not make the actual array. Like all variables, an array variable has to be assigned a value before it can be used. In this case, the value is an array. Arrays have to be created using a special syntax. (The syntax is related to the fact that arrays in Java are actually objects, but that doesn't need to concern us here.) Arrays are created with an operator named *new* . Here are some examples:

namelist = new String[1000];

A = new int[5];

prices = new double[100];

The general syntax is

(array-variable) = new (base-type)[(array-length)];

The length of the array can be given as either an integer or an integer-valued expression. For example, after the assignment statement "A = new int[5];", A is an array containing the five integer elements A[0], A[1], A[2], A[3], and A[4]. Also, A.length would have the value 5. It's useful to have a picture in mind:

The statement A = new int[5]; creates an array that holds five elements of type int. A is a name for the whole array.

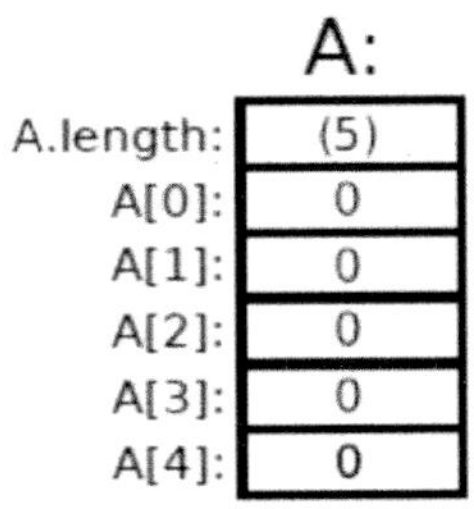

The array contains five elements, which are referred to as A[0], A[1], A[2], A[3], A[4]. Each element is a variable of type int. The array also contains A.length, whose value cannot be changed.

When you create an array of int, each element of the array is automatically initialized to zero. Any array of numbers is filled with zeros when it is created. An array of boolean is filled with the value false. And an array of char is filled with the character that has Unicode code number zero.

3.8.2 Arrays and For Loops

A lot of the real power of arrays comes from the fact that the index of an element can be given by an integer variable or even an integer-valued expression. For example, if list is an array and i is a variable of type int, then you can use list[i] and even list[2*i+1] as variable names. The meaning of list[i] depends on the value of i. This becomes especially useful when we want to process all the elements of an array, since that can be done with a for loop.

For example, to print out all the items in an array, list, we can just write

```
int i;          // the array index
for (i = 0; i < list.length; i++) {
    System.out.println( list[i] );
}
```

The first time through the loop, i is 0, and list[i] refers to list[0]. So, it is the value stored in the variable list[0] that is printed. The second time through the loop, i is 1, and the value stored in list[1] is printed. If the length of the list is 5, then the loop ends after printing the value of list[4], when i becomes equal to 5 and the continuation condition "i < list.length" is no longer true. This is a typical example of using a loop to process an array.

Let's look at a few more examples. Suppose that A is an array of double, and we want to find the average of all the elements of the array. We can use a for loop to add up the numbers, and then divide by the length of the array to get the average:

```
double total;// The sum of the numbers in the array.
double average;      // The average of the numbers.
int i;          // The array index.
total = 0;
```

```
for ( i = 0; i < A.length; i++ ) {
     total = total + A[i];          // Add element number i to the total.
}
average = total / A.length;     // A.length is the number of items
```

Another typical problem is to find the largest number in the array A. The strategy is to go through the array, keeping track of the largest number found so far. We'll store the largest number found so far in a variable called max. As we look through the array, whenever we find a number larger than the current value of max, we change the value of max to that larger value. After the whole array has been processed, max is the largest item in the array overall. The only question is, what should the original value of max be? One possibility is to start with max equal to A[0], and then to look through the rest of the array, starting from A[1], for larger items:

```
double max; // The largest number seen so far.
max = A[0];  // At first, the largest number seen is A[0]. int i;
for ( i = 1; i < A.length; i++ ) {
     if (A[i] > max) {
               max = A[i];
     }
}
// at this point, max is the largest item in A
```

Sometimes, you only want to process some elements of the array. In that case, you can use an if statement inside the for loop to decide whether or not to process a given element. Let's look at the problem of averaging the elements of an array, but this time, suppose that we only want to average the non-zero elements. In this case, the number of items that we add up can be less than the length of the array, so we will need to keep a count of the number of items added to the sum:

```
double total;// The sum of the non-zero numbers in the array.
int count;    // The number of non-zero numbers.
double average;        // The average of the non-zero numbers. int i;
total = 0;
count = 0;
for ( i = 0; i < A.length; i++ ) {
     if ( A[i] != 0 ) { // Only process non-zero elements!
```

```
            total = total + A[i]; // Add element to the total
            count = count + 1; //      and count it.
        }
    }
    if (count == 0) {
        System.out.println("There were no non-zero elements.");
    }
    else {
        average = total / count;   // Divide by number of items
        System.out.printf("Average of %d elements is %1.5g%n",
                          count, average);
    }
```

3.8.3 Random Access

So far, my examples of array processing have used *sequential access*. That is, the elements of the array were processed one after the other in the sequence in which they occur in the array. But one of the big advantages of arrays is that they allow *random access*. That is, every element of the array is equally accessible at any given time.

As an example, let's look at a well-known problem called the birthday problem: Suppose that there are N people in a room. What's the chance that there are two people in the room who have the same birthday? (That is, they were born on the same day in the same month, but not necessarily in the same year.) Most people severely underestimate the probability. We will actually look at a different version of the question: Suppose you choose people at random and check their birthdays. How many people will you check before you find one who has the same birthday as someone you've already checked? Of course, the answer in a particular case depends on random factors, but we can simulate the experiment with a computer program and run the program several times to get an idea of how many people need to be checked on average. To simulate the experiment, we need to keep track of each birthday that we find. There are 365 different possible birthdays. (We'll ignore leap years.) For each possible birthday, we need to keep track of whether or not we have already found a person who has that birthday. The answer to this question is a boolean value, true or false. To hold the data for all 365 possible birthdays, we can use an array of 365 boolean values:

```
boolean[] used;
used = new boolean[365];
```

For this problem, the days of the year are numbered from 0 to 364. The value of used[i] is true if someone has been selected whose birthday is day number i. Initially, all the values in the array are false. (Remember that this is done automatically when the array is created.) When we select someone whose birthday is day number i, we first check whether used[i] is true. If it is true, then this is the second person with that birthday. We are done. On the other hand, if used[i] is false, we set used[i] to be true to record the fact that we've encountered someone with that birthday, and we go on to the next person. Here is a program that carries out the simulated experiment (of course, in the program, there are no simulated people, only simulated birthdays):

```
/**
Simulate choosing people at random and checking the day of the year they
were born on.        If the birthday is the same as one that was seen previously,
stop, and output the number of people who were checked.
*/
public class BirthdayProblem {
    public static void main(String[] args) {
            boolean[] used;  // For recording the possible birthdays
                             //      that have been seen so far.      A value
                             //      of true in used[i] means that a person
                             //      whose birthday is the i-th day of the
                             //      year has been found.
            int count;       // The number of people who have been checked.
            used = new boolean[365]; // Initially, all entries are false. count = 0;
            while (true) {
                             // Select a birthday at random, from 0 to 364.
                             // If the birthday has already been used, quit.
                             // Otherwise, record the birthday as used.
            int birthday;    // The selected birthday.
            birthday = (int)(Math.random()*365);
            count++;
            System.out.printf("Person %d has birthday number %d%n", count, birthday);
            if ( used[birthday] ) {
                             // This day was found before; it's a duplicate. We are done.
```

```
                break;
            }
            used[birthday] = true;
        } // end while
        System.out.println();
        System.out.println("A duplicate birthday was found after "
                                + count + " tries.");
    }
} // end class BirthdayProblem
```

You should study the program to understand how it works and how it uses the array. Also, try it out! You will probably find that a duplicate birthday tends to occur sooner than you expect.

3.8.4 Partially Full Arrays

Consider an application where the number of items that we want to store in an array changes as the program runs. Since the size of the array can't be changed, a separate counter variable must be used to keep track of how many spaces in the array are in use. (Of course, every space in the array has to contain something; the question is, how many spaces contain useful or valid items?)

Consider, for example, a program that reads positive integers entered by the user and stores them for later processing. The program stops reading when the user inputs a number that is less than or equal to zero. The input numbers can be kept in an array, numbers, of type int[ ]. Let's say that no more than 100 numbers will be input. Then the size of the array can be fixed at 100. But the program must keep track of how many numbers have actually been read and stored in the array. For this, it can use an integer variable. Each time a number is stored in the array, we have to count it; that is, the value of the counter variable must be incremented by one. One question is, when we add a new item to the array, where do we put it? Well, if the number of items is count, then they would be stored in the array in positions number 0, 1, . . . , (count-1). The next open spot would be position number count, so that's where we should put the new item.

As a rather silly example, let's write a program that will read the numbers input by the user and then print them in the reverse of the order in which they were entered. Assume that an input value equal to zero marks the end of the data. (This is, at least, a processing task that requires that the numbers be saved in an array. Note that many types of processing, such as finding the sum or average or maximum of the numbers, can be done without saving the individual numbers.)

```
import textio.TextIO;
public class ReverseInputNumbers {
    public static void main(String[] args) {
            int[] numbers;  // An array for storing the input values
            int count;      // The number of numbers saved in the array.
            int num;        // One of the numbers input by the user.
            int i;   // for-loop variable.
            numbers = new int[100];  // Space for 100 ints.
            count = 0;      // No numbers have been saved yet.
            System.out.println("Enter up to 100 positive integers; enter 0 to end.");
            while (true) {   // Get the numbers and put them in the array.
                System.out.print("? ");
                num = TextIO.getlnInt();
                if (num <= 0) {
                        // Zero marks the end of input; we have all the numbers.
                break;
                }
                numbers[count] = num;   // Put num in position
                count. count++;  // Count the number
            }
            System.out.println("\nYour numbers in reverse order are:\n");
            for ( i = count - 1; i >= 0; i-- ) {
                System.out.println( numbers[i] );
            }
    } // end main();
}   // end class ReverseInputNumbers
```

It is especially important to note how the variable count plays a dual role. It is the number of items that have been entered into the array. But it is also the index of the next available spot in the array.

When the time comes to print out the numbers in the array, the last occupied spot in the array is location count - 1, so the for loop prints out values starting from location count - 1 and going down to 0. This is also a nice example of processing the elements of an array in reverse order.

You might wonder what would happen in this program if the user tries to input more than 100 numbers. The result would be an error that would crash the program. When the user enters the 101-st number, the program tries to store that number in an array element number[100]. However, there is no such array element. There are only 100 items in the array, and the index of the last item is 99. The attempt to use number[100] generates an exception of type *ArrayIndexOutOfBoundsException*. Exceptions of this type are a common source of run-time errors in programs that use arrays.

3.8.5 Two-dimensional Arrays

The arrays that we have considered so far are "one-dimensional." This means that the array consists of a sequence of elements that can be thought of as being laid out along a line. It is also possible to have *two-dimensional arrays*, where the elements can be laid out in a rectangular grid. We consider them only briefly here, but will return to the topic in Section 7.6. In a two-dimensional, or "2D," array, the elements can be arranged in rows and columns.

Here, for example, is a 2D array of int that has five rows and seven columns:

	0	1	2	3	4	5	6
0	13	7	33	54	-5	-1	92
1	-3	0	8	42	18	0	67
2	44	78	90	79	-5	72	22
3	43	-6	17	100	1	-12	12
4	2	0	58	58	36	21	87

This 5-by-7 grid contains a total of 35 elements. The rows in a 2D array are numbered 0, 1, 2, . . . , up to the number of rows minus one. Similarly, the columns are numbered from zero up to the number of columns minus one. Each individual element in the array can be picked out by specifying its row number and its column number. (The illustration shown here is not what the array actually looks like in the computer's memory, but it does show the logical structure of the array.)

In Java, the syntax for two-dimensional arrays is similar to the syntax for one-dimensional arrays, except that an extra index is involved, since picking out an element requires both a row number and a column number. For example, if A is a 2D array of int, then A[3][2] would be the element in row 3, column 2. That would pick out the number 17 in the array shown above. The type for A would be given as int[ ][ ], with two pairs of empty brackets. To declare the array variable and create the array, you could say,

```
int[][]     A;
A   =       new int[5][7];
```

The second line creates a 2D array with 5 rows and 7 columns. Two-dimensional arrays are often processed using nested for loops. For example, the following code segment will print out the elements of A in neat columns:

```
int row, col; // loop-control-variables for accessing rows and columns in A for ( row = 0;
row < 5; row++ ) {
    for ( col = 0; col < 7; col++ ) {
            System.out.printf( "%7d",          A[row][col] );
    }
    System.out.println();
}
```

The base type of a 2D array can be anything, so you can have arrays of type double[ ][ ], String[ ][ ], and so on.

There are some natural uses for 2D arrays. For example, a 2D array can be used to store the contents of the board in a game such as chess or checkers. And an example in Subsection 4.7.3 uses a 2D array to hold the colors of a grid of colored squares. But sometimes two-dimensional arrays are used in problems in which the grid is not so visually obvious. Consider a company that owns 25 stores. Suppose that the company has data about the profit earned at each store for each month in the year 2022. If the stores are numbered from 0 to 24, and if the twelve months from January 2022 through December 2022 are numbered from 0 to 11, then the profit data could be stored in an array, profit, created as follows:

```
double[][]  profit;
profit      =       new double[25][12];
```

profit[3][2] would be the amount of profit earned at store number 3 in March, and more generally, profit[storeNum][monthNum] would be the amount of profit earned in store number storeNum in month number monthNum (where the numbering, remember, starts from zero).

Let's assume that the profit array has already been filled with data. This data can be processed in a lot of interesting ways. For example, the total profit for the company—for the whole year from all its stores—can be calculated by adding up all the entries in the array:

```
double totalProfit;  // Company's total profit in 2022.
int store, month;    // variables for looping through the stores and the months totalProfit
= 0;
```

```
for ( store = 0; store < 25; store++ ) {
    for ( month = 0; month < 12; month++ )
        totalProfit += profit[store][month];
}
```

Sometimes it is necessary to process a single row or a single column of an array, not the entire array. For example, to compute the total profit earned by the company in December, that is, in month number 11, you could use the loop:

```
double decemberProfit;
int storeNum;
decemberProfit = 0.0;
for ( storeNum = 0; storeNum < 25; storeNum++ ) {
    decemberProfit += profit[storeNum][11];
}
```

Two-dimensional arrays are sometimes useful, but they are much less common than one- dimensional arrays. Java actually allows arrays of even higher dimension, but they are only rarely encountered in practice.

3.9 GUI PROGRAMMING: AN INTRODUCTION

For the past two chapters, you've been learning the sort of programming that is done inside a single subroutine, "programming in the small." In the rest of this book, we'll be more concerned with the larger scale structure of programs, but the material that you've already learned will be an important foundation for everything to come. In this section, we see how techniques that you have learned so far can be applied in the context of graphical user interface programming. GUI programs here, and in the rest of this book, are written using JavaFX, a collection of classes that form a "toolkit" for writing GUI programs. All of the classes mentioned in this section are part of JavaFX, and they must be imported into any program that uses them.

When you run a GUI program, it opens one or more windows on your computer screen. As a programmer, you can have complete control over what appears in the window and how the user can interact with it. For our first encounter, we look at one simple example: the ability of a program to display simple shapes like rectangles and lines in the window, with no user interaction. For now, the main point is to take a look at how programming-in-the-small can be used in other contexts besides text-based, command-line-style programs. You will see that a knowledge of programming-in-the-small applies to writing the guts of any subroutine, not just main().

3.9.1 Drawing Shapes

To understand computer graphics, you need to know a little about pixels and coordinate systems. The computer screen is made up of small squares called *pixels*, arranged in rows and columns, usually about 100 pixels per inch. (Many screens now have many more physical pixels per inch. On these "high-resolution" screens, a "pixel" might refer to a physical pixel, but it might also refer to a "logical pixel," which is a unit of measure somewhere close to 1/100 inch.)

The computer controls the color of the pixels, and drawing is done by changing the colors of individual pixels. Each pixel has a pair of integer coordinates, often called *x* and *y*, that specify the pixel's horizontal and vertical position. When drawing to a rectangular area on the screen, the coordinates of the pixel in the upper left corner of the rectangle are (0,0). The *x* coordinate increases from left to right, and the *y* coordinate increases from top to bottom. Shapes are specified using pixels. For example, a rectangle is specified by the *x* and *y* coordinates of its upper left corner and by its width and height measured in pixels. Here's a picture of a rectangular drawing area, showing the ranges of *x* and *y* coordinates. The "width" and "height" in this picture give the size of the drawing area, in pixels:

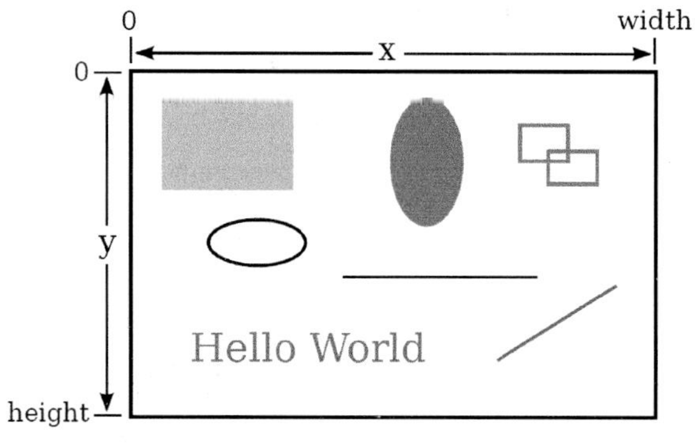

Assuming that the drawing area is 800-by-500 pixels, the rectangle in the upper left of the picture would have, approximately, width 200, height 150, and upper left corner at coordinates (50,50).

Drawing in Java is done using a *graphics context.* A graphics context is an object. As an object, it can include subroutines and data. Among the subroutines in a graphics context are routines for drawing basic shapes such as lines, rectangles, ovals, and text. (When text appears on the screen, the characters have to be drawn there by the computer, just like the computer draws any other shapes.) Among the data in a graphics context are the color and font that are currently selected for drawing. (A font determines the style and size of characters.) One other piece of data in a graphics context is the "drawing surface" on which the drawing is done. Different graphics context objects can draw to different drawing surfaces. For us, the drawing surface will be the content area of a window, not including its border or title bar.

There are two ways to draw a shape in JavaFX: You can *fill* the shape, meaning you can set the color of each of the pixels inside the shape. Or you can *stroke* the shape, meaning that you set the color of the pixels that lie along the border of the shape. Some shapes, such as a line, can only be stroked. A JavaFX graphics context actually keeps track of two separate colors, one used for filling shapes and one used for stroking shapes. Stroking a shape is like dragging a pen along the border of the shape. The properties of that pen (such as its size and whether it produces a solid line or a dashed line) are properties of the graphics context.

A graphics context is represented by a variable. The type for the variable is *GraphicsContext* (just like the type for a string variable is *String*). The variable is often named *g*, but the name of the variable is of course up to the programmer. Here are a few of the subroutines that are available in a graphics context *g*. Note that all numerical parameter values can be of type double.

- g.setFill(c) is called to set the color to be used for filling shapes. The parameter, c is an object belonging to a class named *Color*. There are many constants representing standard colors that can be used as the parameter in this subroutine. The standard colors range from common colors such as Color.BLACK, Color.WHITE, Color.RED, Color.GREEN, Color.BLUE, and Color. YELLOW, to more exotic color names such as Color.CORNFLOWERBLUE. (Later, we will see that it is also possible to create new colors.) For example, if you want to fill shapes with red, you would say "g.setFill(Color.RED);". The specified color is used for all subsequent fill operations up until the next time g.setFill() is called. Note that previously drawn shapes are not affected!
- g.setStroke(c) is called to set the color to be used for stroking shapes. It works similarly to g.setFill.
- g.setLineWidth(w) sets the size of the pen that will be used for subsequent stroke operations, where w is measured in pixels.
- g.strokeLine(x1,y1,x2,y2) draws a line from the point with coordinates (x1,y1) to the point with coordinates (x2,y2). The width of the line is 1, unless a different line width has been set by calling g.setLineWidth(), and the color is black unless a different color has been set by calling g.setStroke().
- g.strokeRect(x,y,w,h) draws the outline of a rectangle with vertical and horizontal sides. This subroutine draws the outline of the rectangle whose top-left corner is x pixels from the left edge of the drawing area and y pixels down from the top. The horizontal width of the rectangle is w pixels, and the vertical height is h pixels. Color and line width are set by calling g.setStroke() and g.setLineWidth().

- g.fillRect(x,y,w,h) is similar to g.strokeRect() except that it fills in the inside of the rectangle instead of drawing an outline, and it uses the color set by g.setFill().
- g.strokeOval(x,y,w,h) draws the outline of an oval. The oval just fits inside the rectangle that would be drawn by g.strokeRect(x,y,w,h). To get a circle, use the same values for w and for h.
- g.fillOval(x,y,w,h) is similar to g.strokeOval() except that it fills in the inside of the oval instead of drawing an outline.

This is enough information to draw some pictures using Java graphics. To start with something simple, let's say that we want to draw a set of ten parallel lines, something like this:

Let's say that the lines are 200 pixels long and that the distance from each line to the next is 10 pixels, and let's put the start of the first line at the pixel with coordinates (100,50). To draw one line, we just have to call g.strokeLine(x1,y1,x2,y2) with appropriate values for the parameters. Now, all the lines start at *x*-coordinate 100, so we can use the constant 100 as the value for x1. Since the lines are 200 pixels long, we can use the constant 300 as the value for x2. The *y*-coordinates of the lines are different, but we can see that both endpoints of a line have the same *y*-coordinates, so we can use a single variable as the value for y1 and for y2. Using y as the name of that variable, the command for drawing one of the lines becomes g.strokeLine(100,y,300,y). The value of y is 50 for the top line and increases by 10 each time we move down from one line to the next. We just need to make sure that y takes on the correct sequence of values. We can use a for loop that counts from 1 to 10:

```
int y;        // y-coordinate for the line
int i;        // loop control variable
y = 50;       // y starts at 50 for the first line
for ( i = 1; i <= 10; i++ ) {
    g.strokeLine( 100, y, 300, y );
    y = y + 10;        // increase y by 10 before drawing the next line.
}
```

Alternatively, we could use y itself as the loop control variable, noting that the value of y for the last line is 140:

```
int y;
for ( y = 50; y <= 140; y = y + 10
    g.strokeLine( 100, y, 300, y );
```

If we wanted the lines to be blue, we could do that by calling g.setStroke(Color.BLUE) before drawing them. If we just draw the lines without setting the color, they will be black. If we wanted the lines to be 3 pixels wide, we could call g.setLineWidth(3) before drawing the lines.

For something a little more complicated, let's draw a large number of randomly colored, randomly positioned, filled circles. Since we only know a few colors, I will randomly select the color to be red, green, blue, or yellow. That can be done with a simple switch statement:

```
switch ( (int)(4*Math.random()) ) {
    case 0 -> g.setFill( Color.RED );
    case 1 -> g.setFill( Color.GREEN );
    case 2 -> g.setFill( Color.BLUE );
    case 3 -> g.setFill( Color.YELLOW );
}
```

I will choose the center points of the circles at random. Let's say that the width of the drawing area is given by a variable, width. Then we want a random value in the range 0 to width-1 for the horizontal position of the center. Similarly, the vertical position of the center will be a random value in the range 0 to height-1. That leaves the size of the circle to be determined; I will make the radius of each circle equal to 50 pixels. We can draw the circle with a statement of the form g.fillOval(x,y,w,h). However, in this command, x and y are not the coordinates of the center of the circle; they are the upper left corner of a rectangle drawn around the circle. To get values for x and y, we have to move back from the center of the circle by 50 pixels, an amount equal to the radius of the circle. The parameters w and h give the width and height of the rectangle, which have to be twice the radius, or 100 pixels in this case. Taking all this into account, here is a code segment for drawing a random circle:

```
centerX = (int)(width*Math.random());
centerY = (int)(height*Math.random());
g.fillOval( centerX - 50, centerY - 50, 100, 100 );
```

This code comes after the color-setting code given above. In the end, I found that the picture looks better if I also draw a black outline around each filled circle, so I added this code at the end:

```
g.setStroke( Color.BLACK );
g.strokeOval( centerX - 50, centerY - 50, 100, 100 );
```

Finally, to get a large number of circles, I put all of the above code into a for loop that runs for 500 executions. Here's a typical drawing from the program, shown at reduced size:

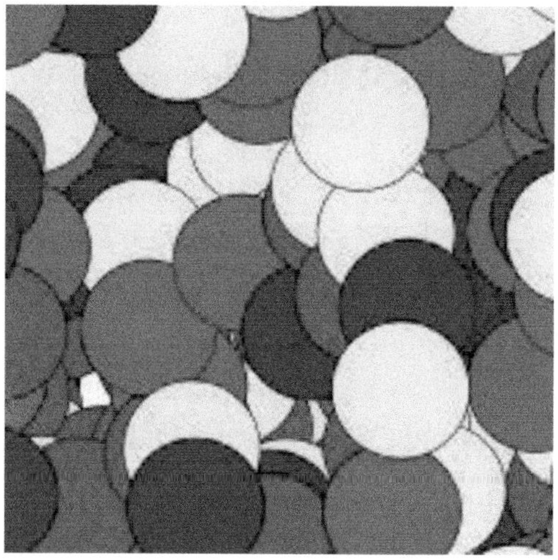

3.9.2 Drawing in a Program

Now, as you know, you can't just have a bunch of Java code standing by itself. The code has to be inside a subroutine definition that is itself inside a class definition. In fact, for my circle-drawing program, the complete subroutine for drawing the picture looks like this:

```
public void drawPicture(GraphicsContext g, int width, int height) {
    g.setFill(Color.WHITE);
    g.fillRect(0, 0, width, height); // First, fill  with a background color.
    // As an example, draw a large number of colored disks.
    // To get a different picture, erase this code, and substitute your own.
    int centerX; // The x-coord of the center of a disk.
    int centerY; // The y-coord of the center of a disk.
    int colorChoice; // Used to select a random color.
    int count;          // Loop control variable for counting disks
```

```
        for (count = 0; count < 500; count++) {
                centerX = (int)(width*Math.random());
                centerY = (int)(height*Math.random());
                colorChoice = (int)(4*Math.random());
                switch (colorChoice) {
                        case 0 -> g.setFill( Color.RED );
                        case 1 -> g.setFill( Color.GREEN );
                        case 2 -> g.setFill( Color.BLUE );
                        case 3 -> g.setFill( Color.YELLOW );
                }
                g.fillOval( centerX - 50, centerY - 50, 100, 100 );
                g.setStroke(Color.BLACK);
                g.strokeOval( centerX - 50, centerY - 50, 100, 100 );
        }
    } // end drawPicture()
```

This is the first subroutine definition that you have seen, other than main, but you will learn all about defining subroutines in the next chapter. The first line of the definition makes available certain values that are used in the subroutine: the graphics context g and the width and height of the drawing area. These values come from outside the subroutine, but the subroutine can use them. The point here is that to draw something, you just have to fill in the inside of the subroutine, just as you write a program by filling in the inside of main.

The subroutine definition still has to go inside a class that defines the program. In this case, the class is named *SimpleGraphicsStarter*, and the complete program is available in the sample source code file SimpleGraphicsStarter.java. You can run that program to see the drawing. You can use this sample program as a starting point for drawing your own pictures.

There's a lot in the program that you won't understand. To make your own drawing, all you have to do is erase the inside of the drawPicture routine in the source code and substitute your own drawing code. You don't need to understand the rest.

(By the way, you might notice that the main subroutine uses the word static in its definition, but drawPicture does not. This has to do with the fact that drawPicture is a subroutine in an object rather than in a class. The difference between static and non-static subroutines is important but not something that we need to worry about for the time being.

3.9.3 Animation

We can extend the idea of drawing pictures to making *animations*. A computer animation is simply a sequence of individual pictures, displayed quickly one after the other. If the change from each picture to the next is small, the user will perceive the sequence of images as a continuous animation. Each picture in the animation is called a *frame*. The sample program SimpleAnimationStarter.java can be used as a starting point for writing animations. It contains a subroutine named drawFrame() that draws one frame in an animation. You can create an animation by filling in the definition of this subroutine. In addition to the graphics context and the width and height of the drawing area, you can use the value of two other variables in your code: frameNumber and elapsedSeconds. The drawFrame subroutine will automatically be called about 60 times per second. The variable frameNumber takes on the values 0, 1, 2, 3, . . . in successive calls to the subroutine, and the value of elapsedSeconds is the number of seconds that the animation has been running. By using either of these variables in your code, you can draw a different picture each time drawFrame() is called, and the user will see the series of pictures as an animation.

As an example of animation, we look at drawing a set of nested rectangles. The rectangles will shrink towards the center of the drawing, giving an illusion of infinite motion. One frame from the animation looks like this:

Consider how to draw a picture like this one. The rectangles can be drawn with a while loop, which draws the rectangles starting from the one on the outside and moving in. Think about what variables will be needed and how they change from one iteration of the while loop to the next. Each time through the loop, the rectangle that is drawn is smaller than the previous one and is moved down and over a bit. The difference between two rectangles is in their sizes and in the coordinates of their upper left corners. We need variables to represent the width and height of the rectangle, which I call rectWidth and rectHeight. The x and y-coordinates of the upper left corner are the same, and they can be represented by the same variable. I call that variable inset, since it is the amount by which the edges of the rectangle are inset from the edges of the drawing area. The width and height decrease from one rectangle to the next, while the inset increases. The while loop ends when either the width or the height becomes less than or equal to zero. In general outline, the algorithm for drawing the rectangles in one frame is

Set the amount of inset for the first rectangle

Set the width and height for the first rectangle

Set the stroke color to black

while the width and height are both greater than zero:

> *draw a rectangle (using the g.strokeRect subroutine)*
>
> *increase the inset (to move the next rectangle over and down)*
>
> *decrease the width and height (to make the next rectangle smaller)*

In my program, each rectangle is 15 pixels away from the rectangle that surrounds it, so the inset is increased by 15 each time through the while loop. The rectangle shrinks by 15 pixels on the left and by 15 pixels on the right, so the width of the rectangle shrinks by 30 before drawing the next rectangle. The height also shrinks by 30 pixels each time through the loop.

The pseudocode is then easy to translate into Java, except that we need to know what initial values to use for the inset, width, and height of the first rectangle. To figure that out, we have to think about the fact that the picture is animated, so that what we draw will depend in some way on the frame number. From one frame to the next frame of the animation, the top-left corner of the outer rectangle moves over and down; that is, the inset for the outer rectangle increases from one frame to the next. We can make this happen by setting the inset for frame number 0 to 0, the inset for frame number 1 to 1, and so on. But that can't go on forever, or eventually all the rectangles would disappear. In fact, when the animation gets to frame 15, a new rectangle should appear at the outside of the drawing area—but it's not really a "new rectangle," it's just that the inset for the outer rectangle goes back to zero. So, as the animation proceeds, the inset should go through the sequence of values 0, 1, 2, . . . , 14 over and over. We can accomplish that very easily by setting

inset = frameNumber % 15;

Finally, note that the first rectangle that is drawn in a frame fills the drawing area except for a border of size inset around the outside of the rectangle. This means that the width of the first rectangle is the width of the drawing area minus two times the inset, and similarly for the height. Here, then is the drawFrame() subroutine for the moving rectangle example:

```
public void drawFrame(GraphicsContext g, int frameNumber,
            double elapsedSeconds, int width, int height) {
    g.setFill(Color.WHITE);
    g.fillRect(0,0,width,height);          // Fill drawing area with white.
    double inset; // Gap between edges of drawing area and outer rectangle.
    double rectWidth, rectHeight;     // The size of one of the rectangles.
    g.setStroke(Color.BLACK);          // Draw the rectangle outlines in black.
    inset = frameNumber % 15 + 0.5;   // (The 0.5 is a technicality that gives
                                      //        a sharper picture.)
    rectWidth = width - 2*inset;
    rectHeight = height - 2*inset;
    while (rectWidth >= 0 && rectHeight >= 0) {
            g.strokeRect(inset, inset, rectWidth, rectHeight);
            inset += 15;        // rectangles are 15 pixels apart
            rectWidth -= 30;
            rectHeight -= 30;
    }
}
```

You can find the full source code for the program is in the sample program MovingRects.java. Take a look! It's a neat effect. For another example of animation, see the sample program RandomCircles.java. That program adds one random colored disk to the picture in each frame; it illustrates the fact that the image from one frame is not automatically erased before the next frame is drawn.

Chapter 4 HOW TO PROGRAM IN THE LARGE I: SUBROUTINES

A method to decompose a complex program into manageable components is through the utilization of subroutines. A subroutine comprises a collection of instructions designated for executing a certain task, organized collectively and assigned a name. In other parts of the program, that name can serve as a substitute for the entire set of instructions. When a computer runs a program and discovers a subroutine name, it executes all instructions required to perform the task linked to that subroutine. Subroutines can be utilized repeatedly at various locations within the program. A subroutine may be utilized within another subroutine. This enables the creation of basic subroutines that can subsequently assist in the development of more intricate subroutines, which may then be utilized in more subroutines. Thus, intricate programs can be developed incrementally, with each phase of building being relatively straightforward. Java subroutines can be classified as either static or non-static. This chapter addresses static subroutines. The subsequent chapter will address non-static subroutines utilized in authentic object-oriented programming.

4.1 BLACK BOXES AND PROCEDURAL ABSTRACTION

A subroutine consists of instructions for performing some task, chunked together and given a name. "Chunking" allows you to deal with a potentially very complicated task as a single concept. Instead of worrying about the many, many steps that the computer might have to go though to perform that task, you just need to remember the name of the subroutine. Whenever you want your program to perform the task, you just call the subroutine. Subroutines are a major tool for dealing with complexity.

A subroutine is sometimes said to be a "black box" because you can't see what's "inside" it (or, to be more precise, you usually don't want to see inside it, because then you would have to deal with all the complexity that the subroutine is meant to hide). Of course, a black box that has no way of interacting with the rest of the world would be pretty useless. A black box needs some kind of *interface* with the rest of the world, which allows some interaction between what's inside the box and what's outside. A physical black box might have buttons on the outside that you can push, dials that you can set, and slots that can be used for passing information back and forth. Since we are trying to hide complexity, not create it, we have the first rule of black boxes:

> *The interface of a black box should be fairly straight- forward, well-defined, and easy to understand.*

Are there any examples of black boxes in the real world? Yes; in fact, you are surrounded by them. Your television, your car, your mobile phone, your refrigerator. . . . You can turn your television on and off, change channels, and set the volume by using elements of the television's interface—on/off switch, remote control, don't forget to plug in the power—without understanding anything about how the thing actually works. The same goes for a mobile phone, although the interface in that case is a lot more complicated.

Now, a black box does have an inside—the code in a subroutine that actually performs the task, or all the electronics inside your television set. The inside of a black box is called its *implementation* . The second rule of black boxes is that:

> *To use a black box, you shouldn't need to know anything about its implementation; all you need to know is its interface.*

In fact, it should be possible to change the implementation, as long as the behavior of the box, as seen from the outside, remains unchanged. For example, when the insides of TV sets went from using vacuum tubes to using transistors, the users of the sets didn't need to know about it—or even know what it means. Similarly, it should be possible to rewrite the inside of a subroutine, to use more efficient code for example, without affecting the programs that use that subroutine.

Of course, to have a black box, someone must have designed and built the implementation in the first place. The black box idea works to the advantage of the implementor as well as the user of the black box. After all, the black box might be used in an unlimited number of different situations. The implementor of the black box doesn't need to know about any of that. The implementor just needs to make sure that the box performs its assigned task and interfaces correctly with the rest of the world. This is the third rule of black boxes:

The implementor of a black box should not need to know anything about the larger systems in which the box will be used.

In a way, a black box divides the world into two parts: the inside (implementation) and the outside. The interface is at the boundary, connecting those two parts.

By the way, you should not think of an interface as just the physical connection between the box and the rest of the world. The interface also includes a *specification* of what the box does and how it can be controlled by using the elements of the physical interface. It's not enough to say that a TV set has a power switch; you need to specify that the power switch is used to turn the TV on and off!

To put this in computer science terms, the interface of a subroutine has a semantic as well as a syntactic component. The syntactic part of the interface tells you just what you have to type in order to call the subroutine. The semantic component specifies exactly what task the subroutine will accomplish. To write a legal program, you need to know the syntactic specification of the subroutine. To understand the purpose of the subroutine and to use it effectively, you need to know the subroutine's semantic specification. I will refer to both parts of the interface—syntactic and semantic—collectively as the *contract* of the subroutine.

The contract of a subroutine says, essentially, "Here is what you have to do to use me, and here is what I will do for you, guaranteed." When you write a subroutine, the comments that you write for the subroutine should make the contract very clear. (I should admit that in practice, subroutines' contracts are often inadequately specified, much to the regret and annoyance of the programmers who have to use them.)

For the rest of this chapter, I turn from general ideas about black boxes and subroutines in general to the specifics of writing and using subroutines in Java. But keep the general ideas and principles in mind. They are the reasons that subroutines exist in the first place, and they are your guidelines for using them, where I will discuss subroutines as a tool in program development.

You should keep in mind that subroutines are not the only example of black boxes in programming. For example, a class is also a black box. We'll see that a class can have a "public" part, representing its interface, and a "private" part that is entirely inside its hidden implementation. All the principles of black boxes apply to classes as well as to subroutines.

Introduced the idea of "control abstraction" to express the fact that a Java control structure lets the user work on a higher level than machine language, hiding the details of the process in the CPU that implements the control structure.

In a similar way, we say that a subroutine is a *procedural abstraction* . The interface of a subroutine is an abstraction that you can use to carry out some procedure without worrying about the details of how the procedure is actually implemented. This is just another, fancier way of saying that the subroutine can be used as a black box, but it brings us back to abstraction as a central concept in computer science.

An important aspect of abstraction in general is *information hiding* . An abstraction hides information about what is behind the abstraction, in its implementation. Information hiding by control abstractions is what makes it possible to use the same Java control structures on different types of CPU, with different underlying machine language implementations. Information hiding by procedural abstractions is what makes it possible for the inside of a subroutine to be changed without affecting the programs in which the subroutine is used. Again, this is just another term for the black box principle.

4.2 STATIC SUBROUTINES AND STATIC VARIABLES

Every subroutine in Java must be defined inside some class. This makes Java rather unusual among programming languages, since most languages allow free-floating, independent subroutines. One purpose of a class is to group together related subroutines and variables. Perhaps the designers of Java felt that everything must be related to something. As a less philosophical motivation, Java's designers wanted to place firm controls on the ways things are named, since a Java program potentially has access to a huge number of subroutines created by many different programmers. The fact that those subroutines are grouped into named classes (and classes are grouped into named "packages," as we will see later) helps control the confusion that might result from so many different names.

There is a basic distinction in Java between *static* and *non-static* subroutines. A class definition can contain the source code for both types of subroutine, but what's done with them when the program runs is very different. Static subroutines are easier to understand: In a running program, a static subroutine is a member of the class itself. Non-static subroutine definitions, on the other hand, are only there to be used when objects are created, and the subroutines themselves become members of the objects. Non-static subroutines only become relevant when you are working with objects. The distinction between static and non-static also applies to variables and to other things that can occur in class definitions. This chapter will deal with static subroutines and static variables almost exclusively. We'll turn to non-static stuff and to object-oriented programming in the next chapter.

A subroutine that is in a class or object is often called a *method* , and "method" is the term that most people prefer for subroutines in Java. I will start using the term "method" occasionally, but I will continue to prefer the more general term "subroutine" in this chapter, at least for static subroutines. However, you should start thinking of the terms "method" and "subroutine" as being essentially synonymous as far as Java is concerned. Other terms that you might see used to refer to subroutines are "procedures" and "functions." (I generally use the term "function" only for subroutines that compute and return a value, but in some programming languages, it is used to refer to subroutines in general.)

4.2.1 Subroutine Definitions

A subroutine must be defined somewhere. The definition has to include the name of the subroutine, enough information to make it possible to call the subroutine, and the code that will be executed each time the subroutine is called. A subroutine definition in Java takes the form:

(modifiers) (return-type) (subroutine-name) ((parameter-list)) {

(statements)

}

It will take us a while—most of the chapter—to get through what all this means in detail. Of course, you've already seen examples of subroutines in previous chapters, such as the main() routine of a program and the drawFrame() routine of the animation programs in Section 3.9. So you are familiar with the general format.

The (*statements*) between the braces, { and }, in a subroutine definition make up the *body* of the subroutine. These statements are the inside, or implementation part, of the "black box," as discussed in the previous section. They are the instructions that the computer executes when the method is called. Subroutines can contain any of the statements.

The (*modifiers*) that can occur at the beginning of a subroutine definition are words that set certain characteristics of the subroutine, such as whether it is static or not. The modifiers that you've seen so far are "static" and "public". There are only about a half-dozen possible modifiers altogether.

If the subroutine is a function, whose job is to compute some value, then the (*return-type*) is used to specify the type of value that is returned by the function. It can be a type name such as *String* or int or even an array type such as double[ ]. If the subroutine is not a function, then the (*return-type*) is replaced by the special value void, which indicates that no value is returned. The term "void" is meant to indicate that the return value is empty or non-existent.

Finally, we come to the (*parameter-list*) of the method. Parameters are part of the interface of a subroutine. They represent information that is passed into the subroutine from outside, to be used by the subroutine's internal computations. For a concrete example, imagine a class named *Television* that includes a method named changeChannel(). The immediate question is: What channel should it change to? A parameter can be used to answer this question. If a channel number is an integer, the type of the parameter would be int, and the declaration of the changeChannel() method might look like

public void changeChannel(int channelNum) { ... }

This declaration specifies that changeChannel() has a parameter named channelNum of type int. However, channelNum does not yet have any particular value. A value for channelNum is provided when the subroutine is called; for example: changeChannel(17);

The parameter list in a subroutine can be empty, or it can consist of one or more parameter declarations of the form (*type*) (*parameter-name*). If there are several declarations, they are separated by commas. Note that each declaration can name only one parameter. For example, if you want two parameters of type double, you have to say "double x, double y", rather than "double x, y".

Parameters are covered in more detail in the next section.

Here are a few examples of subroutine definitions, leaving out the statements that define what the subroutines do:

```
public static void playGame() {
    // "public" and "static" are modifiers; "void" is the
    // return-type; "playGame" is the subroutine-name;
    // the parameter-list is empty.
    ...      // Statements that define what playGame does go here.
}
int getNextN(int N) {
    // There are no modifiers; "int" is the return-type;
    // "getNextN" is the subroutine-name; the parameter-list
    // includes one parameter whose name is "N" and whose
    // type is "int".
    ...      // Statements that define what getNextN does go here.
}
static boolean lessThan(double x, double y) {
    // "static" is a modifier; "boolean" is the
    // return-type; "lessThan" is the subroutine-name;
    // the parameter-list includes two parameters whose names are
    // "x" and "y", and the type of each of these parameters
    // is "double".
    ...      // Statements that define what lessThan does go here.
}
```

In the second example given here, getNextN is a non-static method, since its definition does not include the modifier "static"—and so it's not an example that we should be looking at in this chapter! The other modifier shown in the examples is "public". This modifier indicates that the method can be called from anywhere in a program, even from outside the class where the method is defined. There is another modifier, "private", which indicates that the method can be called only from inside the same class. The modifiers public and private are called *access specifiers*. If no access specifier is given for a method, then by default, that method can be called from anywhere in the package that contains the class, but not from outside that package. (You will learn more about packages later in this chapter, in Section 4.6.) There is one other access modifier, protected, which will only become relevant when we turn to object-oriented programming.

Note, by the way, that the main() routine of a program follows the usual syntax rules for a subroutine. In

public static void main(String[] args) { ... }

the modifiers are public and static, the return type is void, the subroutine name is main, and the parameter list is "String[] args". In this case, the type for the parameter is the array type String[ ].

You've already had some experience with filling in the implementation of a subroutine. In this chapter, you'll learn all about writing your own complete subroutine definitions, including the interface part.

4.2.2 Calling Subroutines

When you define a subroutine, all you are doing is telling the computer that the subroutine exists and what it does. The subroutine doesn't actually get executed until it is called. (This is true even for the main() routine in a class—even though you don't call it, it is called by the system when the system runs your program.) For example, the playGame() method given as an example above could be called using the following subroutine call statement:

playGame();

This statement could occur anywhere in the same class that includes the definition of playGame(), whether in a main() method or in some other subroutine. Since playGame() is a public method, it can also be called from other classes, but in that case, you have to tell the computer which class it comes from. Since playGame() is a static method, its full name includes the name of the class in which it is defined. Let's say, for example, that playGame() is defined in a class named Poker. Then to call playGame() from outside the Poker class, you would have to say

Poker.playGame();

The use of the class name here tells the computer which class to look in to find the method. It also lets you distinguish between Poker.playGame() and other potential playGame() methods defined in other classes, such as Roulette.playGame() or Blackjack.playGame().

More generally, a *subroutine call statement* for a static subroutine takes the form (*subroutine-name*)((*parameters*));

if the subroutine that is being called is in the same class, or

(class-name).(subroutine-name)((parameters));

if the subroutine is defined elsewhere, in a different class. (Non-static methods belong to objects rather than classes, and they are called using objects instead of class names. More on that later.) Note that the parameter list can be empty, as in the playGame() example, but the parentheses must be there even if there is nothing between them. The number of parameters that you provide when you call a subroutine must match the number specified in the parameter list in the subroutine definition, and the types of the parameters in the call statement must match the types in the subroutine definition.

4.2.3 Subroutines in Programs

It's time to give an example of what a complete program looks like, when it includes other subroutines in addition to the main() routine. Let's write a program that plays a guessing game with the user. The computer will choose a random number between 1 and 100, and the user will try to guess it. The computer tells the user whether the guess is high or low or correct.

If the user gets the number after six guesses or fewer, the user wins the game. After each game, the user has the option of continuing with another game.

Since playing one game can be thought of as a single, coherent task, it makes sense to write a subroutine that will play one guessing game with the user. The main() routine will use a loop to call the playGame() subroutine over and over, as many times as the user wants to play. We approach the problem of designing the playGame() subroutine the same way we write a main() routine: Start with an outline of the algorithm and apply stepwise refinement. Here is a short pseudocode algorithm for a guessing game routine:

Pick a random number

while the game is not over:

Get the user's guess

Tell the user whether the guess is high, low, or correct.

The test for whether the game is over is complicated, since the game ends if either the user makes a correct guess or the number of guesses is six. As in many cases, the easiest thing to do is to use a "while (true)" loop and use break to end the loop whenever we find a reason to do so. Also, if we are going to end the game after six guesses, we'll have to keep track of the number of guesses that the user has made. Filling out the algorithm gives:

```
Let computersNumber be a random number between 1 and 100
Let guessCount = 0
while (true):
    Get the user's guess
    Count the guess by adding 1 to guess count
    if the user's guess equals computersNumber:
            Tell the user he won
            break out of the loop
if the number of guesses is 6:
    Tell the user he lost
    break out of the loop
if the user's guess is less than computersNumber:
    Tell the user the guess was low
else if the user's guess is higher than computersNumber:
    Tell the user the guess was high
```

With variable declarations added and translated into Java, this becomes the definition of the playGame() routine. A random integer between 1 and 100 can be computed as (int)(100 * Math.random()) + 1. I've cleaned up the interaction with the user to make it flow better.

```
static void playGame() {
    int computersNumber; // A random number picked by the computer.
    int usersGuess;  // A number entered by user as a guess.
    int guessCount;  // Number of guesses the user has made.
    computersNumber = (int)(100 * Math.random()) + 1;
                // The value assigned to computersNumber is a randomly
                //       chosen integer between 1 and 100, inclusive.
    guessCount = 0;
    System.out.println();
    System.out.print("What is your first guess? ");
    while (true) {
    usersGuess = TextIO.getInt();      // Get the user's guess.
    guessCount++;
```

```
        if (usersGuess == computersNumber) {
                System.out.println("You got it in " + guessCount
                        + " guesses!     My number was " + computersNumber);
                break;   // The game is over; the user has won.
        }
        if (guessCount == 6) {
                System.out.println("You didn't get the number in 6 guesses.");
                System.out.println("You lose.     My number was " + computersNumber);
                break;   // The game is over; the user has lost.
        }
        // If we get to this point, the game continues.
        // Tell the user if the guess was too high or too low.
        if (usersGuess < computersNumber)
                System.out.print("That's too low. Try again: ");
        else if (usersGuess > computersNumber)
                System.out.print("That's too high.       Try again: ");
        }
        System.out.println();
    } // end of playGame()
```

Now, where exactly should you put this? It should be part of the same class as the main() routine, but not inside the main routine. It is not legal to have one subroutine physically nested inside another. The main() routine will call playGame(); it will not contain the definition of playGame. You can put the definition of playGame() either before or after the main() routine. Java is not very picky about having the subroutine definitions in a class in any particular order. It's pretty easy to write the main routine. You've done things like this before. Here's what the complete program looks like (except that a serious program needs more comments than I've included here).

```
    import textio.TextIO;
    public class GuessingGame {
        public static void main(String[] args) {
                System.out.println("Let's play a game.     I'll pick a number between");
                System.out.println("1 and 100, and you try to guess it.");
```

```
        boolean playAgain;
        do {
                playGame();      // call subroutine to play one game
                System.out.print("Would you like to play again? ");
                playAgain = TextIO.getlnBoolean();
        } while (playAgain);
        System.out.println("Thanks for playing.   Goodbye.");
    } // end of main()
    static void playGame() {
        int computersNumber; // A random number picked by the computer
        int usersGuess;  // A number entered by user as a guess.
        int guessCount;  // Number of guesses the user has made.
        computersNumber = (int)(100 * Math.random()) + 1;
                    // The value assigned to computersNumber is a randomly
                    //        chosen integer between 1 and 100, inclusive.
        guessCount = 0;
        System.out.println();
        System.out.print("What is your first guess? ");
        while (true) {
            usersGuess = TextIO.getInt();        // Get the user's guess.
            guessCount++;
            if (usersGuess == computersNumber) {
                System.out.println("You got it in "+ guessCount
                        + " guesses!        My number was " +
                        computersNumber);
                break;   // The game is over; the user has won.
            }
            if (guessCount == 6) {
                System.out.println("You didn't get the number in 6
                guesses.");
                System.out.println("You lose.       My number was " +
                computersNumber);
```

```
                break;   // The game is over; the user has lost.
            }
            // If we get to this point, the game continues.
            // Tell the user if the guess was too high or too low.
            if (usersGuess < computersNumber)
                System.out.print("That's too low. Try again: ");
            else if (usersGuess > computersNumber)
                System.out.print("That's too high.         Try again: ");
            }
            System.out.println();
        } // end of playGame()
    } // end of class GuessingGame
```

Take some time to read the program carefully and figure out how it works. And try to convince yourself that even in this relatively simple case, breaking up the program into two methods makes the program easier to understand and probably made it easier to write each piece.

4.2.4 Member Variables

A class can include other things besides subroutines. In particular, it can also include variable declarations. Of course, you can declare variables inside subroutines. Those are called *local variables.* However, you can also have variables that are not part of any subroutine. To distinguish such variables from local variables, we call them *member variables,* since they are members of a class. Another term for them is *global variable.*

Just as with subroutines, member variables can be either static or non-static. In this chapter, we'll stick to static variables. A static member variable belongs to the class as a whole, and it exists as long as the class exists. Memory is allocated for the variable when the class is first loaded by the Java interpreter. Any assignment statement that assigns a value to the variable changes the content of that memory, no matter where that assignment statement is located in the program. Any time the variable is used in an expression, the value is fetched from that same memory, no matter where the expression is located in the program. This means that the value of a static member variable can be set in one subroutine and used in another subroutine. Static member variables are "shared" by all the static subroutines in the class. A local variable in a subroutine, on the other hand, exists only while that subroutine is being executed, and is completely inaccessible from outside that one subroutine.

The declaration of a member variable looks just like the declaration of a local variable except for two things: The member variable is declared outside any subroutine (although it still has to be inside a class), and the declaration can be marked with modifiers such as static, public, and private. Since we are only working with static member variables for now, every declaration of a member variable in this chapter will include the modifier static. They might also be marked as public or private. For example:

static String usersName;

public static int numberOfPlayers;

private static double velocity, time;

A static member variable that is not declared to be private can be accessed from outside the class where it is defined, as well as inside. When it is used in some other class, it must be referred to with a compound identifier of the form (*class-name*).(*variable-name*). For example, the *System* class contains the public static member variable named out, and you use this variable in your own classes by referring to System.out. Similarly, Math.PI is a public static member variable in the *Math* class. If numberOfPlayers is a public static member variable in a class named Poker, then code in the Poker class would refer to it simply as numberOfPlayers, while code in another class would refer to it as Poker.numberOfPlayers.

As an example, let's add a couple of static member variables to the GuessingGame class that we wrote earlier in this section. We add a variable named gamesPlayed to keep track of how many games the user has played and another variable named gamesWon to keep track of the number of games that the user has won. The variables are declared as static member variables:

static int gamesPlayed;

static int gamesWon;

In the playGame() routine, we always add 1 to gamesPlayed, and we add 1 to gamesWon if the user wins the game. At the end of the main() routine, we print out the values of both variables. It would be impossible to do the same thing with local variables, since both subroutines need to access the variables, and local variables exist in only one subroutine. Furthermore, global variables keep their values between one subroutine call and the next. Local variables do not; a local variable gets a new value each time that the subroutine that contains it is called.

When you declare a local variable in a subroutine, you have to assign a value to that variable before you can do anything with it. Member variables, on the other hand are automatically initialized with a default value. The default values are the same as those that are used when initializing the elements of an array: For numeric variables, the default value is zero; for boolean variables, the default is false; for char variables, it's the character that has Unicode code number zero; and for objects, such as *Strings*, the default initial value is the special value null. Since they are of type int, the static member variables gamesPlayed and gamesWon automatically get zero as their initial value. This happens to be the correct initial value for a variable that is being used as a counter. You can, of course, assign a value to a variable at the beginning of the main() routine if you are not satisfied with the default initial value, or if you want to make the initial value more explicit.

Here's the revised version of GuessingGame.java. The changes from the above version are shown in italic:

```
import textio.TextIO;
public class GuessingGame2 {
    static int gamesPlayed;  // The number of games played.
    static int gamesWon;     // The number of games won.
    public static void main(String[] args) {
            gamesPlayed = 0;
            gamesWon = 0;  // This is actually redundant, since 0 is
                           //       the default initial value.
            System.out.println("Let's play a game.    I'll pick a number between");
            System.out.println("1 and 100, and you try to guess it.");
            boolean playAgain;
            do {
                    playGame();      // call subroutine to play one game
                    System.out.print("Would you like to play again? ");
                    playAgain = TextIO.getlnBoolean();
            } while (playAgain);
            System.out.println();
            System.out.println("You played " + gamesPlayed + " games,");
            System.out.println("and you won " + gamesWon + " of those games.");
            System.out.println("Thanks for playing.   Goodbye.");
    } // end of main()
    static void playGame() {
            int computersNumber; // A random number picked by the computer.
            int usersGuess;            // A number entered by user as a guess.
```

```
int guessCount;             // Number of guesses the user has made.
gamesPlayed++; // Count this game.
computersNumber = (int)(100 * Math.random()) + 1;
        // The value assigned to computersNumber is a randomly
        //      chosen integer between 1 and 100, inclusive.
guessCount = 0;
System.out.println();
System.out.print("What is your first guess? ");
while (true) {
        usersGuess = TextIO.getInt();       // Get the user's guess.
        guessCount++;
        if (usersGuess == computersNumber) {
                System.out.println("You got it in " + guessCount
                        + " guesses!        My number was " +
                        computersNumber);
                gamesWon++;     // Count this win.
                break;  // The game is over; the user has won.
        }
        if (guessCount == 6) {
                System.out.println("You didn't get the number in 6
                guesses.");
                System.out.println("You lose.       My number was " +
                computersNumber);
                break;  // The game is over; the user has lost.
        }
        // If we get to this point, the game continues.
        // Tell the user if the guess was too high or too low.
        if (usersGuess < computersNumber)
                System.out.print("That's too low. Try again: ");
        else if (usersGuess > computersNumber)
                System.out.print("That's too high.         Try again: ");
}
```

```
        System.out.println();
    } // end of playGame()
} // end of class GuessingGame2
```

(By the way, notice that in my example programs, I didn't mark the static subroutines or variables as being public or private. You might wonder what it means to leave out both modifiers. Recall that global variables and subroutines with no access modifier can be used anywhere in the same package as the class where they are defined, but not in other packages. Classes that don't declare a package are in the default package. So, any class in the default package would have access to gamesPlayed, gamesWon, and playGame()—and that includes most of the classes in this book. In fact, it is considered to be good practice to make member variables and subroutines private, unless there is a reason for doing otherwise. (But then again, it's also considered good practice to avoid using the default package.))

4.3 PARAMETERS

If a subroutine is a black box, then a parameter is something that provides a mechanism for passing information from the outside world into the box. Parameters are part of the interface of a subroutine. They allow you to customize the behavior of a subroutine to adapt it to a particular situation.

As an analogy, consider a thermostat—a black box whose task it is to keep your house at a certain temperature. The thermostat has a parameter, namely the dial that is used to set the desired temperature. The thermostat always performs the same task: maintaining a constant temperature. However, the exact task that it performs—that is, which temperature it maintains—is customized by the setting on its dial.

4.3.1 Using Parameters

As an example, let's go back to the "3N+1" problem that was discussed in Subsection 3.2.2. (Recall that a 3N+1 sequence is computed according to the rule, "if N is odd, multiply it by 3 and add 1; if N is even, divide it by 2; continue until N is equal to 1." For example, starting from N=3 we get the sequence: 3, 10, 5, 16, 8, 4, 2, 1.) Suppose that we want to write a subroutine to print out such sequences. The subroutine will always perform the same task: Print out a 3N+1 sequence. But the exact sequence it prints out depends on the starting value of N. So, the starting value of N would be a parameter to the subroutine. The subroutine can be written like this:

```
/**
This subroutine prints a 3N+1 sequence to standard output, using
startingValue as the initial value of N.        It also prints the number
```

```
of terms in the sequence. The value of the parameter, startingValue,
must        be a positive integer.
*/
static void print3NSequence(int startingValue) {
    int N;   // One of the terms in the sequence.
    int count;         // The number of terms.
    N = startingValue;         // The first term is whatever value
                               //        is passed to the subroutine as
                               //        a parameter.
count = 1; // We have one term, the starting value, so far.
System.out.println("The 3N+1 sequence starting from " + N);
System.out.println();
System.out.println(N);         // print initial term of sequence
while (N > 1) {
    if (N % 2 == 1)    // is N odd?
            N = 3 * N + 1;
    else
                N = N / 2;
            count++;// count this term
            System.out.println(N);   // print this term
    }
    System.out.println();
    System.out.println("There were " + count + " terms in the sequence.");
}   // end print3NSequence
```

The parameter list of this subroutine, "(int startingValue)", specifies that the subroutine has one parameter, of type int. Within the body of the subroutine, the parameter name can be used in the same way as a variable name. But notice that there is nothing in the subroutine definition that gives a value to the parameter! The parameter gets its initial value from outside the subroutine. When the subroutine is called, a value must be provided for the parameter in the subroutine call statement. This value will be assigned to startingValue before the body of the subroutine is executed. For example, the subroutine could be called using the subroutine call statement "print3NSequence(17);". When the computer executes this statement, the computer first assigns the value 17 to startingValue and then executes the statements in the subroutine. This prints the 3N+1 sequence starting from 17. If K is a variable of type int, then the subroutine can be called by saying "print3NSequence(K);". When the computer executes this subroutine call statement, it takes the value of the variable K, assigns that value to startingValue, and then executes the body of the subroutine.

The class that contains print3NSequence can contain a main() routine (or other subrou- tines) that call print3NSequence. For example, here is a main() program that prints out 3N+1 sequences for various starting values specified by the user:

```
public static void main(String[] args) {
System.out.println("This program will print out 3N+1 sequences");
System.out.println("for starting values that you specify.");
System.out.println();
int K;          // Input from user; loop ends when K < 0.
do {
          System.out.println("Enter a starting value.");
          System.out.print("To end the program, enter 0: ");
          K = TextIO.getInt();       // Get starting value from user.
          if (K > 0)// Print sequence, but only if K is > 0.
                    print3NSequence(K);
  } while (K > 0);   // Continue only if K > 0.
} // end main
```

Remember that before you can use this program, the definitions of main and of print3NSequence must both be wrapped inside a class definition.

4.3.2 Formal and Actual Parameters

Note that the term "parameter" is used to refer to two different, but related, concepts. There are parameters that are used in the definitions of subroutines, such as startingValue in the above example. And there are parameters that are used in subroutine call statements, such as the K in the statement "print3NSequence(K);". Parameters in a subroutine definition are called *formal parameters* or *dummy parameters.* The parameters that are passed to a subroutine when it is called are called *actual parameters* or *arguments.* When a subroutine is called, the actual parameters in the subroutine call statement are evaluated and the values are assigned to the formal parameters in the subroutine's definition. Then the body of the subroutine is executed.

A formal parameter must be a name, that is, a simple identifier. A formal parameter is very much like a variable, and—like a variable—it has a specified type such as int, boolean, *String*, or double[ ]. An actual parameter is a value, and so it can be specified by any expression, provided that the expression computes a value of the correct type. The type of the actual parameter must be one that could legally be assigned to the formal parameter with an assignment statement. For example, if the formal parameter is of type double, then it would be legal to pass an int as the actual parameter since ints can legally be assigned to doubles. When you call a subroutine, you must provide one actual parameter for each formal parameter in the subroutine's definition.

Consider, for example, a subroutine

```
static void doTask(int N, double x, boolean test) {
    // statements to perform the task go here
}
```

This subroutine might be called with the statement

```
doTask(17, Math.sqrt(z+1), z >= 10);
```

When the computer executes this statement, it has essentially the same effect as the block of statements:

```
{
int N;            // Allocate memory locations for the formal parameters.
double x; boolean test;
N = 17;           // Assign 17 to the first formal parameter, N.
x = Math.sqrt(z+1);  // Compute Math.sqrt(z+1), and assign it to
                     //       the second formal parameter, x.
test = (z >= 10);    // Evaluate "z >= 10" and assign the resulting
                     //       true/false value to the third formal
                     //       parameter, test.
                     // statements to perform the task go here
}
```

(There are a few technical differences between this and "doTask(17,Math.sqrt(z+1),z>=10);" – besides the amount of typing—because of questions about scope of variables and what happens when several variables or parameters have the same name.)

Beginning programming students often find parameters to be surprisingly confusing. Calling a subroutine that already exists is not a problem—the idea of providing information to the subroutine in a parameter is clear enough. Writing the subroutine definition is another matter. A common beginner's mistake is to assign values to the formal parameters at the beginning of the subroutine, or to ask the user to input their values. This represents a fundamental misunderstanding. By the time the computer starts executing the statements in the subroutine, the formal parameters have already been assigned initial values! The computer automatically assigns values to the formal parameters before it starts executing the code inside the subroutine. The values come from the actual parameters in the subroutine call statement. Remember that a subroutine is not independent. It is called by some other routine, and it is the subroutine call statement's responsibility to provide appropriate values for the parameters.

4.3.3 Overloading

In order to call a subroutine legally, you need to know its name, you need to know how many formal parameters it has, and you need to know the type of each parameter. This information is called the subroutine's *signature*. The signature of the subroutine doTask, used as an example above, can be expressed as: doTask(int,double,boolean). Note that the signature does not include the names of the parameters; in fact, if you just want to use the subroutine, you don't even need to know what the formal parameter names are, so the names are not part of the interface.

Java is somewhat unusual in that it allows two different subroutines in the same class to have the same name, provided that their signatures are different. When this happens, we say that the name of the subroutine is *overloaded* because it has several different meanings. The computer doesn't get the subroutines mixed up. It can tell which one you want to call by the number and types of the actual parameters that you provide in the subroutine call statement. You have already seen overloading used with *System.out*. This object includes many different methods named println, for example. These methods all have different signatures, such as:

println(int) *println(double)*

println(char) *println(boolean)*

println()

The computer knows which of these subroutines you want to use based on the type of the actual parameter that you provide. System.out.println(17) calls the subroutine with signature println(int), while System.out.println('A') calls the subroutine with signature println(char). Of course all these different subroutines are semantically related, which is why it is acceptable programming style to use the same name for them all. But as far as the computer is concerned, printing out an int is very different from printing out a char, which is different from printing out a boolean, and so forth—so that each of these operations requires a different subroutine.

Note, by the way, that the signature does not include the subroutine's return type. It is illegal to have two subroutines in the same class that have the same signature but that have different return types. For example, it would be a syntax error for a class to contain two subroutines defined as:

int getln() { ... }

double getln() { ... }

This is why in the *TextIO* class, the subroutines for reading different types are not all named getln(). In a given class, there can only be one routine that has the name getln with no parameters. So, the input routines in *TextIO* are distinguished by having different names, such as getlnInt() and getlnDouble().

4.3.4 Subroutine Examples

Let's do a few examples of writing small subroutines to perform assigned tasks. Of course, this is only one side of programming with subroutines. The task performed by a subroutine is always a subtask in a larger program. The art of designing those programs—of deciding how to break them up into subtasks—is the other side of programming with subroutines. We'll return to the question of program design in Section 4.7.

As a first example, let's write a subroutine to compute and print out all the divisors of a given positive integer. The integer will be a parameter to the subroutine. Remember that the syntax of any subroutine is:

(modifiers) (return-type) (subroutine-name) ((parameter-list)) {

(statements)

}

Writing a subroutine always means filling out this format. In this case, the statement of the problem implies that there is one parameter, of type int, that represents the "given integer" whose divisors are to be printed. And it tells us what the statements in the body of the subroutine should do. Since we are only working with static subroutines for now, we'll need to use static as a modifier. We could add an access modifier (public or private), but in the absence of any instructions, I'll leave it out. Since we are not told to return a value, the return type is void. Since no names are specified, we'll have to make up names for the formal parameter and for the subroutine itself. I'll use N for the parameter and printDivisors for the subroutine name. The subroutine will look like

```
static void printDivisors( int N ) {
    (statements )
}
```

and all we have left to do is to write the statements that make up the body of the routine. This is not difficult. Just remember that you have to write the body assuming that N already has a value! The algorithm is: "For each possible divisor D in the range from 1 to N, if D evenly divides N, then print D." Written in Java, this becomes:

```
/**
Print all the divisors of N.
We assume that N is a positive integer.
*/
static void printDivisors( int N ) {
    int D;    // One of the possible divisors of N.
    System.out.println("The divisors of " + N + " are:");
    for ( D = 1; D <= N; D++ ) {
            if ( N % D == 0 )  // Does D evenly divide N?
                    System.out.println(D);
    }
}
```

I've added a comment before the subroutine definition indicating the contract of the subroutine—that is, what it does and what assumptions it makes. The contract includes the assumption that N is a positive integer. It is up to the caller of the subroutine to make sure that this assumption is satisfied.

As a second short example, consider the problem: Write a private subroutine named printRow. It should have a parameter ch of type char and a parameter N of type int. The subroutine should print out a line of text containing N copies of the character ch.

Here, we are told the name of the subroutine and the names of the two parameters, and we are told that the subroutine is private, so we don't have much choice about the first line of the subroutine definition. The task in this case is pretty simple, so the body of the subroutine is easy to write. The complete subroutine is given by

```
/**
Write one line of output containing N copies of the
character ch.        If N <= 0, an empty line is output.
```

```
*/
private static void printRow( char ch, int N ) {
    int i;    // Loop-control variable for counting off the copies.
    for ( i = 1; i <= N; i++ ) {
            System.out.print( ch );
    }
    System.out.println();
}
```

Note that in this case, the contract makes no assumption about N, but it makes it clear what will happen in all cases, including the unexpected case that N <= 0.

Finally, let's do an example that shows how one subroutine can build on another. Let's write a subroutine that takes a *String* as a parameter. For each character in the string, it should print a line of output containing 25 copies of that character. It should use the printRow() subroutine defined above to produce the output.

Again, we get to choose a name for the subroutine and a name for the parameter. I'll call the subroutine printRowsFromString and the parameter str. The algorithm is pretty clear: For each position i in the string str, call printRow(str.charAt(i),25) to print one line of the output that contains 25 copies of character number i from the string. So, we get:

```
/**
For each character in str, write a line of output
containing 25 copies of that character.
*/
private static void printRowsFromString( String str ) {
    int i;    // Loop-control variable for counting off the chars.
    for ( i = 0; i < str.length(); i++ ) {
            printRow( str.charAt(i), 25 );
    }
}
```

We could then use printRowsFromString in a main() routine such as

```
public static void main(String[] args) {
    String inputLine;          // Line of text input by user.
    System.out.print("Enter a line of text: ");
    inputLine = TextIO.getln();
```

```
        System.out.println();
        printRowsFromString( inputLine );
    }
```

Of course, the three routines, main(), printRowsFromString(), and printRow(), would have to be collected together inside the same class. The program is rather useless, but it does demonstrate the use of subroutines. You'll find the program in the file RowsOfChars.java, if you want to take a look.

4.3.5 Array Parameters

It's possible for the type of a parameter to be an array type. This means that an entire array of values can be passed to the subroutine as a single parameter. For example, we might want a subroutine to print all the values in an integer array in a neat format, separated by commas and enclosed in a pair of square brackets. To tell it which array to print, the subroutine would have a parameter of type int[ ]:

```
    static void printValuesInList( int[] list ) {
        System.out.print('[');
        int i;
        for ( i = 0; i < list.length; i++ ) {
              if ( i > 0 )
                    System.out.print(','); // No comma in front of list[0]
              System.out.print(list[i]);
        }
        System.out.println(']');
    }
```

To use this subroutine, you need an actual array. Here is a legal, though not very realistic, code segment that creates an array just to pass it as an argument to the subroutine:

```
    int[] numbers;
    numbers = new int[3];
    numbers[0] = 42;
    numbers[1] = 17;
    numbers[2] = 256;
    printValuesInList( numbers );
```

The output produced by the last statement would be [42,17,256].

4.3.6 Command-line Arguments

The main routine of a program has a parameter of type String[ ]. When the main routine is called, some actual array of *String* must be passed to main() as the value of the parameter. The system provides the actual parameter when it calls main(), so the values come from outside the program. Where do the strings in the array come from, and what do they mean? The strings in the array are *command-line arguments* from the command that was used to run the program. When using a command-line interface, the user types a command to tell the system to execute a program. The user can include extra input in this command, beyond the name of the program. This extra input becomes the command-line arguments. The system takes the command-line arguments, puts them into an array of strings, and passes that array to main(). For example, if the name of the program is myProg, then the user can type "java myProg"

to execute the program. In this case, there are no command-line arguments. But if the user types the command java myProg one two three then the command-line arguments are the strings "one", "two", and "three". The system puts these strings into an array of *Strings* and passes that array as a parameter to the main() routine. Here, for example, is a short program that simply prints out any command line arguments entered by the user:

```
public class CLDemo {
    public static void main(String[] args) {
            System.out.println("You entered " + args.length
                            + " command-line arguments");
            if (args.length > 0) {
                    System.out.println("They were:");
                    int i;
                    for ( i = 0; i < args.length; i++ )
                            System.out.println("      " + args[i]);
                    }
            } // end main()
    } // end class CLDemo
```

Note that the parameter, args, can be an array of length zero. This just means that the user did not include any command-line arguments when running the program.

In practice, command-line arguments are often used to pass the names of files to a program. For example, consider the following program for making a copy of a text file. It does this by copying one line at a time from the original file to the copy, using TextIO. The function TextIO.eof() is a boolean-valued function that is true if the end of the input file has been reached.

```
input textio.TextIO;
/**
Requires two command line arguments, which must be file names.       The
first must be the name of an existing file.       The second is the name
of a file to be created by the program. The contents of the first file
are copied into the second.    WARNING:        If the second file already
exists when the program is run, its previous contents will be lost!
This program only works for plain text files.
*/
public class CopyTextFile {
    public static void main( String[] args ) {
            if (args.length < 2 ) {
                    System.out.println("Two command-line arguments are required!");
                    System.exit(1);
    }
    TextIO.readFile( args[0] );          // Open the original file for reading.
    TextIO.writeFile( args[1] );         // Open the copy file for writing.
    int lineCount;    // Number of lines copied
    lineCount = 0;
    while ( TextIO.eof() == false ) {
                    // Read one line from the original file and write it to the copy.
                    String line;
                    line = TextIO.getln();
                    TextIO.putln(line);
                    lineCount++;
            }
            System.out.printf( "%d lines copied from %s to %s%n",
                                    lineCount, args[0], args[1] );
    }
}
```

Since most programs are run in a GUI environment these days, command-line arguments aren't as important as they used to be. But at least they provide a nice example of how array parameters can be used.

4.3.7 Throwing Exceptions

I have been talking about the "contract" of a subroutine. The contract says what the subroutine will do, provided that the caller of the subroutine provides acceptable values for the subroutine's parameters. The question arises, though, what should the subroutine do when the caller violates the contract by providing bad parameter values?

We've already seen that some subroutines respond to bad parameter values by throwing exceptions. For example, the contract of the built-in subroutine

Double.parseDouble says that the parameter should be a string representation of a number of type double; if this is true, then the subroutine will convert the string into the equivalent numeric value. If the caller violates the contract by passing an invalid string as the actual parameter, the subroutine responds by throwing an exception of type *NumberFormatException*. Many subroutines throw *IllegalArgumentExceptions* in response to bad parameter values.

You might want to do the same in your own subroutines. This can be done with a *throw statement*. An exception is an object, and in order to throw an exception, you must create an exception object. You won't officially learn how to do this until Chapter 5, but for now, you can use the following syntax for a throw statement that throws an *IllegalArgumentException*:

throw new IllegalArgumentException((error-message));

where (*error-message*) is a string that describes the error that has been detected. (The word "new" in this statement is what creates the object.) To use this statement in a subroutine, you would check whether the values of the parameters are legal. If not, you would throw the exception. For example, consider the print3NSequence subroutine from the beginning of this section. The parameter of print3NSequence is supposed to be a positive integer. We can modify the subroutine definition to make it throw an exception when this condition is violated:

```
static void print3NSequence( int startingValue) {
    if (startingValue <= 0)    // The contract is violated!
            throw new IllegalArgumentException( "Starting value must be positive." );

    .
    .       // (The rest of the subroutine is the same as before.)
    .
```

If the start value is bad, the computer executes the throw statement. This will immediately terminate the subroutine, without executing the rest of the body of the subroutine. Furthermore, the program as a whole will crash unless the exception is "caught" and handled elsewhere in the program by a try..catch statement, as discussed. For this to work, the subroutine call would have to be in the "try" part of the statement.

4.3.8 Global and Local Variables

I'll finish this section on parameters by noting that we now have three different sorts of variables that can be used inside a subroutine: local variables declared in the subroutine, formal parameter names, and static member variables that are declared outside the subroutine.

Local variables have no connection to the outside world; they are purely part of the internal working of the subroutine.

Parameters are used to "drop" values into the subroutine when it is called, but once the subroutine starts executing, parameters act much like local variables. Changes made inside a subroutine to a formal parameter have no effect on the rest of the program (at least if the type of the parameter is one of the primitive types—things are more complicated in the case of arrays and objects, as we'll see later).

Things are different when a subroutine uses a variable that is defined outside the subroutine. That variable exists independently of the subroutine, and it is accessible to other parts of the program as well. Such a variable is said to be *global* to the subroutine, as opposed to the local variables defined inside the subroutine. A global variable can be used in the entire class in which it is defined and, if it is not private, in other classes as well. Changes made to a global variable can have effects that extend outside the subroutine where the changes are made.

You've seen how this works in the last example in the previous section, where the values of the global variables, gamesPlayed and gamesWon, are computed inside a subroutine and are used in the main() routine.

It's not always bad to use global variables in subroutines, but you should realize that the global variable then has to be considered part of the subroutine's interface. The subroutine uses the global variable to communicate with the rest of the program. This is a kind of sneaky, back-door communication that is less visible than communication done through parameters, and it risks violating the rule that the interface of a black box should be straightforward and easy to understand. So before you use a global variable in a subroutine, you should consider whether it's really necessary.

I don't advise you to take an absolute stand against using global variables inside subroutines. There is at least one good reason to do it: If you think of the class as a whole as being a kind of black box, it can be very reasonable to let the subroutines inside that box be a little sneaky about communicating with each other, if that will make the class as a whole look simpler from the outside.

4.4 RETURN VALUES

A subroutine that returns a value is called a *function* . A given function can only return a value of a specified type, called the *return type* of the function. A function call generally occurs in a position where the computer is expecting to find a value, such as the right side of an assignment statement, as an actual parameter in a subroutine call, or in the middle of some larger expression. A boolean-valued function can even be used as the test condition in an if, while, for or do..while statement.

(It is also legal to use a function call as a stand-alone statement, just as if it were a regular subroutine. In this case, the computer ignores the value computed by the subroutine. Sometimes this makes sense. For example, the function TextIO.getln(), with a return type of *String*, reads and returns a line of input typed in by the user. Usually, the line that is returned is assigned to a variable to be used later in the program, as in the statement "name = TextIO.getln();". However, this function is also useful as a subroutine call statement "TextIO.getln();", which still reads all input up to and including the next carriage return. Since the return value is not assigned to a variable or used in an expression, it is simply discarded. So, the effect of the subroutine call is to read and discard some input. Sometimes, discarding unwanted input is exactly what you need to do.)

4.4.1 The return statement

You've already seen how functions such as Math.sqrt() and TextIO.getInt() can be used. What you haven't seen is how to write functions of your own. A function takes the same form as a regular subroutine, except that you have to specify the value that is to be returned by the subroutine. This is done with a *return statement* , which has the following syntax:

return *(expression)* ;

Such a return statement can only occur inside the definition of a function, and the type of the (*expression*) must match the return type that was specified for the function. (More exactly, it must be an expression that could legally be assigned to a variable whose type is specified by the return type of the function.) When the computer executes this return statement, it evaluates the expression, terminates execution of the function, and uses the value of the expression as the returned value of the function.

For example, consider the function definition

```
static double pythagoras(double x, double y) {
            // Computes the length of the hypotenuse of a right
            // triangle, where the sides of the triangle are x and y.
    return  Math.sqrt( x*x + y*y );
}
```

Suppose the computer executes the statement "totalLength = 17 + pythagoras(12,5);". When it gets to the term pythagoras(12,5), it assigns the actual parameters 12 and 5 to the formal parameters x and y in the function. In the body of the function, it evaluates Math.sqrt(12.0*12.0 + 5.0*5.0), which works out to 13.0. This value is "returned" by the function, so the 13.0 essentially replaces the function call in the assignment statement, which then has the same effect as the statement "totalLength = 17+*13.0* ". The return value is added to 17, and the result, 30.0, is stored in the variable, totalLength.

Note that a return statement does not have to be the last statement in the function definition. At any point in the function where you know the value that you want to return, you can return it. Returning a value will end the function immediately, skipping any subsequent statements in the function. However, a function must definitely return some value (or throw an exception), no matter what path the execution of the function takes through the code.

You can use a return statement inside an ordinary subroutine, one with declared return type "void". Since a void subroutine does not return a value, the return statement does not include an expression; it simply takes the form "return;". The effect of this statement is to terminate execution of the subroutine and return control back to the point in the program from which the subroutine was called. This can be convenient if you want to terminate execution somewhere in the middle of the subroutine, but return statements are optional in non-function subroutines. In a function, on the other hand, a return statement, with expression, is always required.

Note that a return inside a loop will end the loop as well as the subroutine that contains it. Similarly, a return in a switch statement breaks out of the switch statement as well as the subroutine. So, you will sometimes use return in contexts where you are used to seeing a break.

4.4.2 Function Examples

Here is a very simple function that could be used in a program to compute 3N+1 sequences. (The 3N+1 sequence problem is one we've looked at several times already, including in the previous section.) Given one term in a 3N+1 sequence, this function computes the next term of the sequence:

```
static int nextN(int currentN) {
    if (currentN % 2 == 1)    // test if current N is odd
            return 3*currentN + 1;    // if so, return this value
    else
            return currentN / 2;      // if not, return this instead
}
```

This function has two return statements. Exactly one of the two return statements is executed to give the value of the function. Some people prefer to use a single return statement at the very end of the function when possible. This allows the reader to find the return statement easily. You might choose to write nextN() like this, for example:

```
static int nextN
    int currentN) {int answer;          // answer will be the value returned
    if (currentN % 2 == 1)    // test if current N is odd
            answer = 3*currentN+1; // if so, this is the answer
    else
            answer = currentN / 2; // if not, this is the answer
    return answer;  // (Don't forget to return the answer!)
}
```

Here is a subroutine that uses this nextN function. In this case, the improvement from the version of the subroutine in Section 4.3 is not great, but if nextN() were a long function that performed a complex computation, then it would make a lot of sense to hide that complexity inside a function:

```
static void print3NSequence(int startingValue) {
    int N;  // One of the terms in the sequence.
    int count;          // The number of terms found.
    N = startingValue;          // Start the sequence with startingValue.
    count = 1;
    System.out.println("The 3N+1 sequence starting from " + N);
    System.out.println();
    System.out.println(N);   // print initial term of sequence
    while (N > 1) {
```

```
            N = nextN( N );   // Compute next term, using the function nextN.
            count++;// Count this term.
            System.out.println(N);    // Print this term.
        }
        System.out.println();
        System.out.println("There were " + count + " terms in the sequence.");
    }
```

Here are a few more examples of functions. The first one computes a letter grade corresponding to a given numerical grade, on a typical grading scale:

```
    /**
    Returns the letter grade corresponding to the numerical
    grade that is passed to this function as a parameter.
    */
    static char letterGrade(int numGrade) {
        if (numGrade >= 90)
                return 'A';        // 90 or above gets an A
        else if (numGrade >= 80)
                return 'B';        // 80 to 89 gets a B
        else if (numGrade >= 65)
                return 'C';        // 65 to 79 gets a C
        else if (numGrade >= 50)
                return 'D';        // 50 to 64 gets a D
        else
                return 'F';        // anything else gets an F
    }  // end of function letterGrade
```

The type of the return value of letterGrade() is char. Functions can return values of any type at all. Here's a function whose return value is of type boolean. It demonstrates some interesting programming points, so you should read the comments:

```
    /**
    This function returns true if N is a prime number.     A prime number
    is an integer greater than 1 that is not divisible by any positive
```

```
integer, except itself and 1.   If N has any divisor, D, in the range
1 < D < N, then it has a divisor in the range 2 to Math.sqrt(N), namely
either D itself or N/D.          So we only test possible divisors from 2 to
Math.sqrt(N).
*/
static boolean isPrime(int N) {
    int divisor;        // A number we will test to see whether it evenly divides N.
    if (N <= 1)
            return false;       // No number <= 1 is a prime.
    int maxToTry;   // The largest divisor that we need to test.
    maxToTry = (int)(Math.sqrt(N) + 0.001);
            // We will try to divide N by numbers between 2 and maxToTry.
            // If N is not evenly divisible by any of these numbers, then
            // N is prime.     (Note that since Math.sqrt(N) is defined to
            // return a value of type double, the value must be typecast
            // to type int before it can be assigned to maxToTry.        I added
            // the 0.001 because computations with double values are not
            // exact, and I worry that, for example, Math.sqrt(49) might
            // be computed as 6.999... instead of as 7.0.)
    for (divisor = 2; divisor <= maxToTry; divisor++) {
            if ( N % divisor == 0 )      // Test if divisor evenly divides N.
                    return false;        // If so, we know N is not prime.
                                         // No need to continue testing!
    }
    // If we get to this point, N must be prime.          Otherwise,
    // the function would already have been terminated by
    // a return statement in the previous loop.
    return true;      // Yes, N is prime.
}   // end of function isPrime
```

Finally, here is a function with return type *String*. This function has a *String* as parameter. The returned value is a reversed copy of the parameter. For example, the reverse of "Hello World" is "dlroW olleH". The algorithm for computing the reverse of a string, str, is to start with an empty string and then to append each character from str, starting from the last character of str and working backwards to the first:

```
static String reverse(String str) {
    String copy;              // The reversed copy.
    int i;                    // One of the positions in str,
                              //      from str.length() - 1 down to 0.
    copy = "";                // Start with an empty string.
    for ( i = str.length() - 1;  i >= 0;  i-- ) {
                      // Append i-th char of str to copy.
        copy = copy + str.charAt(i);
    }
    return copy;
}
```

A *palindrome* is a string that reads the same backwards and forwards, such as "radar". The reverse() function could be used to check whether a string, word, is a palindrome by testing "if (word.equals(reverse(word)))".

By the way, a typical beginner's error in writing functions is to print out the answer, instead of returning it. This represents a fundamental misunderstanding. The task of a function is to compute a value and return it to the point in the program where the function was called. That's where the value is used. Maybe it will be printed out. Maybe it will be assigned to a variable. Maybe it will be used in an expression. But it's not for the function to decide.

4.4.3 3N+1 Revisited

I'll finish this section with a complete new version of the 3N+1 program. This will give me a chance to show the function nextN(), which was defined above, used in a complete program. I'll also take the opportunity to improve the program by getting it to print the terms of the sequence in columns, with five terms on each line. This will make the output more presentable. The idea is this: Keep track of how many terms have been printed on the current line; when that number gets up to 5, start a new line of output. To make the terms line up into neat columns, I use formatted output.

```
import textio.TextIO;
/**
A program that computes and displays several 3N+1 sequences. Starting
```

```
values for the sequences are input by the user.Terms in the sequence
are printed in columns, with five terms on each line of output.
After a sequence has been displayed, the number of terms in that
sequence is reported to the user.
*/
public class ThreeN2 {
    public static void main(String[] args) {
            System.out.println("This program will print out 3N+1 sequences");
            System.out.println("for starting values that you specify.");
            System.out.println();
            int K;   // Starting point for sequence, specified by the user.
            do {
                    System.out.println("Enter a starting value;");
                    System.out.print("To end the program, enter 0: ");
                    K = TextIO.getlnInt();      // get starting value from user
                    if (K > 0)// print sequence, but only if K is > 0
                            print3NSequence(K);
            } while (K > 0);   // continue only if K > 0
    } // end main
    /**
    print3NSequence prints a 3N+1 sequence to standard output, using
    startingValue as the initial value of N.     It also prints the number
    of terms in the sequence. The value of the parameter, startingValue,
    must be a positive integer.
    */
    static void print3NSequence(int startingValue) {
            int N;   // One of the terms in the sequence.
            int count;          // The number of terms found.
            int onLine;         // The number of terms that have been output
                                //       so far on the current line.
            N = startingValue;          // Start the sequence with startingValue;
            count = 1;          // We have one term so far.
```

```
        System.out.println("The 3N+1 sequence starting from " + N);
        System.out.println();
        System.out.printf("%8d", N);      // Print initial term, using 8 characters.
        onLine = 1;       // There's now 1 term on current output line.
        while (N > 1) {
                N = nextN(N);    // compute next term
                count++;// count this term
                if (onLine == 5) { // If current output line is full
                System.out.println();      // ...then output a carriage return
                onLine = 0;         // ...and note that there are no terms
                                    //         on the new line.
                }
                System.out.printf("%8d", N);// Print this term in an 8-char column.
                onLine++;           // Add 1 to the number of terms on this line.
        }
        System.out.println();      // end current line of output
        System.out.println();      // and then add a blank line
        System.out.println("There were " + count + " terms in the sequence.");
}       // end of print3NSequence
/**
nextN computes and returns the next term in a 3N+1 sequence,
given that the current term is currentN.
*/
static int nextN(int currentN) {
        if (currentN % 2 == 1)
                return 3 * currentN + 1;
        else
                return currentN / 2;
}       // end of nextN()
} // end of class ThreeN2
```

You should read this program carefully and try to understand how it works.

4.5 LAMBDA EXPRESSIONS

In a running program, a subroutine is just a bunch of binary numbers (representing instructions) stored somewhere in the computer's memory. Considered as a long string of zeros and ones, a subroutine doesn't seem all that different from a data value such as, for example, as an integer, a string, or an array, which is also represented as a string of zeros and ones in memory. We are used to thinking of subroutines and data as very different things, but inside the computer, a subroutine is just another kind of data. Some programming languages make it possible to work with a subroutine as a kind of data value. In Java 8, that ability was added to Java in the form of something called *lambda expressions.*

Lambda expressions are becoming more and more common in Java programs. They are especially useful for working with the stream API and with the JavaFX GUI toolkit. It will definitely be useful to know about them before we cover GUI programming in Chapter 6. However, so you can skip this section for now if you want.

4.5.1 First-class Functions

Lambda is a letter in the Greek alphabet that was used by the mathematician Alonzo Church in his study of computable functions. His lambda notation makes it possible to define a function without giving it a name. For example, you might think that the notation x^2 is a perfectly good way of representing a function that squares a number, but in fact, it's an expression that represents the result of squaring *x*, which leaves open the question of what *x* represents. We can define a function with *x* as a dummy parameter:

```
static double square( double x ) {
    return x*x;
}
```

but to do that, we had to name the function *square*, and that name becomes a permanent part of the program—which is overkill if we just want to use the function once. Alonzo Church introduced the notation *lambda(x).x* ^{2} to represent "the function of *x* that is given by x^2" (except using the Greek letter instead of the word "lambda"). This notation is a kind of function literal that represents a value of type "function" in the same way that 42 is an integer literal that represents a value of type int.

Having function literals is the starting point for thinking of a function as just another kind of data value. Once we do that, we should be able to do the same things with functions that we can do with other values, such as assign a function to a variable, pass a function as a parameter to a subroutine, return a function as the value of subroutine, or even make an array of functions. A programming language that allows you to do all those things with functions is said to have "first-class functions" or "functions as first-class objects."

In fact, you can do all of those things with Java lambda expressions. Java's notation is different from the one used by Alonzo Church, and in spite of the name "lambda expression" it does not even use the word lambda. In Java, the lambda expression for a squaring function like the one above can be written

```
x -> x*x
```

The operator -> is what makes this a lambda expression. The dummy parameter for the function is on the left of the operator, and the expression that computes the value of the function is on the right. You might see an expression like this one being passed as an actual parameter to a subroutine, assigned to a variable, or returned by a function.

So are functions now first-class in Java? I'm not quite sure. There are some cool things that can be done in other languages but can't be done in Java. For example, in Java we can assign the above expression to a variable named, say, *sqr*, but we can't then use *sqr* as if it actually is a function. For example, we can't say *sqr* (42). The problem, really, is that Java is a strongly typed language; to have a variable named *sqr*, we must declare that variable and give it a type. But what sort of type would be appropriate for a value that is a function? The answer in Java is something called a *functional interface*, which we turn to next.

But first one more note: Lambda expressions in Java can actually represent arbitrary subroutines, not just functions. Nevertheless, it is the term "function" that is usually associated with them, rather than "subroutine" or "method."

4.5.2 Functional Interfaces

To know how a subroutine can be legally used, you need to know its name, how many parameters it requires, their types, and the return type of the subroutine. A functional interface specifies this information about one subroutine. A functional interface is similar to a class, and it can be defined in a .java file, just like a class. However, its content is just a specification for a single subroutine. Here is an example:

```
public interface FunctionR2R {
    double valueAt( double x );
}
```

This code would be in a file named *FunctionR2R.java*. It specifies a function named *valueAt* with one parameter of type double and a return type of double. (The name of the parameter, *x*, is not really part of the specification, and it's a little annoying that it has to be there.) Here is another example:

```
public interface ArrayProcessor {
    void process( String[] array, int count );
}
```

Java comes with many standard functional interfaces. One of the most important is a very simple one named *Runnable*, which is already defined in Java as

```
public interface Runnable {
    public void run();
}
```

I will use these three functional interfaces for examples in this section.

"Interfaces" in Java can be much more complicated than functional interfaces. You will learn more about them in Section 5.7. But it is only functional interfaces that are relevant to lambda expressions: a functional interface provides a template for a subroutine that might be represented by a lambda expression. The name of a functional interface is a type, just as *String* and double are types. That is, it can be used to declare variables and parameters and to specify the return type of a function. When a type is a functional interface, a value for that type can be given as a lambda expression.

4.5.3 Lambda Expressions

A lambda expression represents an anonymous subroutine, that is, one without a name. But it does have a formal parameter list and a definition. The full syntax is:

((parameter-list)) -> *{ (statements) }*

As with a regular subroutine, the (*parameter-list*) can be empty, or it can be a list of parameter declarations, separated by commas, where each declaration consists of a type followed by a parameter name. However, the syntax can often be simplified. First of all, the parameter types can be omitted, as long as they can be deduced from the context. For example, if the lambda expression is known to be of type *FunctionR2R*, then the parameter type must be double, so it is unnecessary to specify the parameter type in the lambda expression. Next, if there is exactly one parameter and if its type is not specified, then the parentheses around the parameter list can be omitted. On the right-hand side of the ->, if the only thing between the braces, { and }, is a single subroutine call statement, then the braces can be omitted. And if the right-hand side has the form { return (*expression*); }, then you can omit everything except the (*expression*). For example, suppose that we want a lambda expression to represent a function that computes the square of a double value. The type of such a function can be the *FunctionR2R* interface given above. If *sqr* is a variable of type *FunctionR2R*, then the value of the function can be a lambda expression, which can be written in any of the following forms:

```
sqr = (double x) -> { return x*x; }; // The full lambda expression syntax!
sqr = (x) -> { return x*x; };
sqr = x -> { return x*x; };
sqr = x -> x*x;
sqr = (double fred) -> fred*fred;
sqr = (z) -> z*z;
```

The last two statements are there to emphasize that the parameters in a lambda expression are dummy parameters; their names are irrelevant. The six lambda expressions in these statements all define exactly the same function. Note that the parameter type double can be omitted because the compiler knows that sqr is of type *FunctionR2R*, and a *FunctionR2R* requires a parameter of type double. A lambda expression can only be used in a context where the compiler can deduce its type, and the parameter type has to be included only in a case where leaving it out would make the type of the lambda expression ambiguous.

Now, in Java, the variable *sqr* as defined here is not quite a function. It is a value of type *FunctionR2R*, which means that it contains a function named *valueAt*, as specified in the definition of interface *FunctionR2R*. The full name of that function is *sqr.valueAt*, and we must use that name to call the function. For example: sqr.valueAt(42) or sqr.valueAt(x) + sqr.valueAt(y).

When a lambda expression has two parameters, the parentheses are not optional. Here is an example of using the *ArrayProcessor* interface, which also demonstrates a lambda expression with a multiline definition:

```
ArrayProcessor concat;
concat = (A,n) -> { // parentheses around (A,n) are required!
    String str;
    str = "";
    for (int i = 0; i < n; i++)
            str += A[i];
    System.out.println(str);
};  // The semicolon marks the end of the assignment statement;
    //        it is not part of the lambda expression.
String[] nums;
nums = new String[4]; nums[0] = "One";
nums[1] = "Two";
```

```
nums[2] = "Three";
nums[3] = "Four";
for (int i = 1; i < nums.length; i++) {
    concat.process( nums, i );
}
```

This will print out

```
One
OneTwo
OneTwoThree
OneTwoThreeFour
```

Things get more interesting when a lambda expression is used as an actual parameter, which is the most common use in practice. For example, suppose that the following function is defined:

```
/**
For a function f, compute f(start) + f(start+1) + ... + f(end).
The value of end should be >= the value of start.
*/
static double sum( FunctionR2R f, int start, int end ) {
    double total = 0;
    for (int n = start; n <= end; n++) {
            total = total + f.valueAt( n );
    }
    return total;
}
```

Note that since *f* is a value of type *FunctionR2R*, the value of *f* at *n* is actually written as *f.valueAt* (*n*). When the function *sum* is called, the first parameter can be given as a lambda expression that matches the type *FunctionR2R*. For example:

```
System.out.print("The sum of n squared for n from 1 to 100 is ");
System.out.println( sum( x -> x*x, 1, 100 ) );
System.out.print("The sum of 2 raised to the power n, for n from 1 to 10 is ");
System.out.println( sum( num -> Math.pow(2,num), 1, 10 ) );
```

As another example, suppose that we have a subroutine that performs a given task several times. The task can be specified as a value of type *Runnable*:

```
static void doSeveralTimes( Runnable task, int repCount ) {
    for (int i = 0; i < repCount; i++) {
            task.run();        // Perform the task!
    }
}
```

We could then say "Hello World" ten times by calling

```
doSeveralTimes( () -> System.out.println("Hello World"), 10 );
```

Note that for a lambda expression of type *Runnable*, the parameter list is given as an empty pair of parentheses. Here is an example in which the syntax is getting rather complicated:

```
doSeveralTimes( () -> {
            // count from 1 up to some random number between 5 and 25
    int count = 5 + (int)(21*Math.random());
    for (int i = 1; i <= count; i++) { System.out.print(i + " ");
    }
    System.out.println();
}, 100);
```

This is a single subroutine call statement in which the first parameter is a lambda expression that extends over multiple lines. The second parameter is 100, and the semicolon on the last line ends the subroutine call statement.

We have seen examples of assigning a lambda expression to a variable and of using one as an actual parameter. Here is an example in which a lambda expression is the return value of a function:

```
static FunctionR2R makePowerFunction( int n ) {
    return x -> Math.pow(x,n);
}
```

Then *makePowerFunction*(2) returns a *FunctionR2R* that computes the square of its parameter, while *makePowerFunction*(10) returns a *FunctionR2R* that computes the 10-th power of its parameter. This example also illustrates the fact that a lambda expression can use other variables in addition to its parameter, such as *n* in this case (although there are some restrictions on when that can be done).

4.5.4 Method References

Suppose that we want a lambda expression to represent the square root function as a value of type *FunctionR2R*. We could write it as x -> Math.sqrt(x). However, this lambda expression is a simple wrapper for a *Math.sqrt* function that already exists. Instead of writing out the lambda expression, that function can be written as a *method reference*, which takes the form= Math::sqrt. (Recall that in Java, "method" is another word for "subroutine.") This method reference is just a shorthand for the lambda expression, and it can be used wherever that lambda expression could be used, such as in the *sum* function defined above:

```
System.out.print("The sum of the square root of n for n from 1 to 100 is ");
System.out.println( sum( Math::sqrt, 1, 100 ) );
```

It would be nice if we could simply use the name *Math.sqrt* here instead of introducing a new notation with ::, but the notation *Math.sqrt* was already defined to mean a variable named *sqrt* in the *Math* class.

More generally, a lambda expression that simply calls an existing static method can be written as a method reference of the form

(classname) :: (method-name)

Furthermore, this notation extends to methods that are in objects rather than classes. For example, if *str* is a *String*, then *str* contains the method *str.length()*. The method reference str::length could be used as a lambda expression of type *SupplyInt*, where *SupplyInt* is the functional interface

```
public interface SupplyInt {
    int get( );
}
```

4.6 APIS, PACKAGES, MODULES, AND JAVADOC

As computers and their user interfaces have become easier to use, they have also become more complex for programmers to deal with. You can write programs for a simple console-style user interface using just a few subroutines that write output to the console and read the user's typed replies. A modern graphical user interface, with windows, buttons, scroll bars, menus, text-input boxes, and so on, might make things easier for the user, but it forces the programmer to cope with a hugely expanded array of possibilities. The programmer sees this increased complexity in the form of great numbers of subroutines that are provided for managing the user interface, as well as for other purposes.

4.6.1 Toolboxes

Someone who wanted to program for the original Macintosh computers—and to produce programs that look and behave the way users expected them to—had to deal with the "Macintosh Toolbox," a collection of well over a thousand different subroutines. There were routines for opening and closing windows, for drawing geometric figures and text to windows, for adding buttons to windows, and for responding to mouse clicks on the window. There were other routines for creating menus and for reacting to user selections from menus. Aside from the user interface, there were routines for opening files and reading data from them, for communicating over a network, for sending output to a printer, for handling communication between programs, and in general for doing all the standard things that a computer has to do. Microsoft Windows provides its own set of subroutines for programmers to use, and they are quite a bit different from the subroutines used on the Mac. Linux has several different GUI toolboxes for the programmer to choose from.

The analogy of a "toolbox" is a good one to keep in mind. Every programming project involves a mixture of innovation and reuse of existing tools. A programmer is given a set of tools to work with, starting with the set of basic tools that are built into the language: things like variables, assignment statements, if statements, and loops. To these, the programmer can add existing toolboxes full of routines that have already been written for performing certain tasks. These tools, if they are well-designed, can be used as true black boxes: They can be called to perform their assigned tasks without worrying about the particular steps they go through to accomplish those tasks. The innovative part of programming is to take all these tools and apply them to some particular project or problem (word-processing, keeping track of bank accounts, processing image data from a space probe, Web browsing, computer games, . . .). This is called *applications programming* .

A software toolbox is a kind of black box, and it presents a certain interface to the programmer. This interface is a specification of what routines are in the toolbox, what parameters they use, and what tasks they perform. This information constitutes the *API* , or *Application Programming Interface*, associated with the toolbox. The API is the abstraction through which you access the functionality of the software in the toolbox. The Macintosh API is a specification of all the routines available in the Macintosh Toolbox. A company that makes some hardware device—say a card for connecting a computer to a network—might publish an API for that device consisting of a list of routines that programmers can call in order to communicate with and control the device. Scientists who write a set of routines for doing some kind of complex computation—such as solving "differential equations," say—would provide an API to allow others to use those routines without understanding the details of the computations they perform.

The Java programming language is supplemented by a large, standard API. You've seen part of this API already, in the form of mathematical subroutines such as Math.sqrt(), the *String* data type and its associated routines, and the System.out.print() routines. The standard Java API includes routines for working with graphical user interfaces, for network communication, for reading and writing files, and more.

It's tempting to think of these routines as being part of the Java language, but they are technically subroutines that have been written and made available for use in Java programs.

Java is platform-independent. That is, the same program can run on platforms as diverse as MacOS, Windows, Linux, and others. The same Java API must work on all these platforms. But notice that it is the interface that is platform-independent; the implementation of some parts of the API varies from one platform to another. A Java system on a particular computer includes implementations of all the standard API routines. A Java program includes only calls to those routines. When the Java interpreter executes a program and encounters a call to one of the standard routines, it will pull up and execute the implementation of that routine which is appropriate for the particular platform on which it is running. This is a very powerful idea. It is the power of abstraction. It means that you only need to learn one API to program for a wide variety of platforms.

4.6.2 Java's Standard Packages

Like all subroutines in Java, the routines in the standard API are grouped into classes. To provide larger-scale organization, classes in Java can be grouped into *packages*, which were introduced briefly in Subsection 2.6.5. You can have even higher levels of grouping, since packages can also contain other packages. In fact, the entire standard Java API is implemented in several packages. One of these, which is named "java", contains several non-GUI packages as well as the original AWT graphical user interface classes. Another package, "javax", contains the classes used by the Swing graphical user interface, as well as many other classes. And "javafx," which is not a standard part of Java, contains the JavaFX API that is used for GUI programming in this textbook.

A package can contain both classes and other packages. A package that is contained in another package is sometimes called a "subpackage." The java and javafx packages both contain subpackages. One of the subpackages of java, for example, is named "util". Since util is contained within java, its full name is actually java.util. This package contains a variety of utility classes, including the *Scanner* class that was discussed. The java package includes several other subpackages, such as java.io, which provides facilities for input/output, and java.net, which deals with network communication. The most basic package is called java.lang. This package contains fundamental classes such as *String*, *Math*, *Integer*, and *Double.*

It might be helpful to look at a graphical representation of the levels of nesting in the java package, its subpackages, the classes in those subpackages, and the subroutines in those classes. This is not a complete picture, since it shows only a very few of the many items in each element:

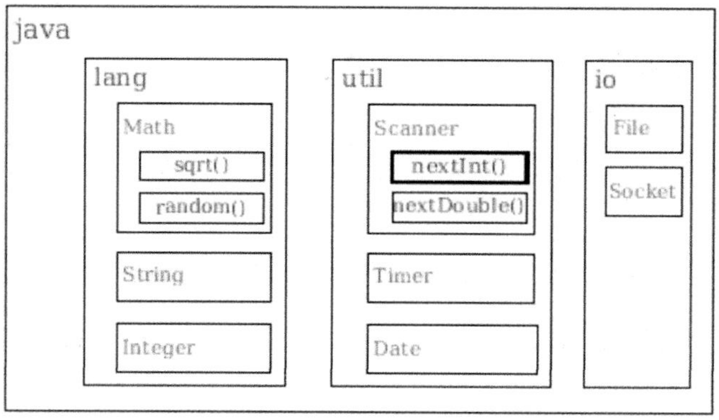

Subroutines nested in classes nested in two layers of packages.
The full name of sqrt() is java.lang.Math.sqrt().

Similarly, the package javafx contains a package javafx.scene, which in turn contains javafx.scene.control. This package contains classes that represent GUI components such as buttons and input boxes. Another subpackage, javafx.scene.paint, contains class *Color* and other classes that define ways to fill and stroke a shape.

The standard Java API includes thousands of classes in hundreds of packages. Many of the classes are rather obscure or very specialized, but you might want to browse through the documentation to see what is available. As I write this, the documentation for the complete basic API for Java 8 can be found at

https://docs.oracle.com/javase/8/docs/api/

and for JavaFX 8 at

https://docs.oracle.com/javase/8/javafx/api/toc.htm

See the subsection about "modules," below, for a discussion of changes that were made the language after Java 8 and for links to the documentation for Java 17. However, for the purposes of this textbook, you will probably find that the Java 8 documentation is easier to use, and the information that it provides is still relevant.

Even an expert programmer won't be familiar with the entire Java API, or even a majority of it. In this book, you'll only encounter several dozen classes, and those will be sufficient for writing a wide variety of programs.

4.6.3 Using Classes from Packages

Let's say that you want to use the class javafx.scene.paint.Color in a program that you are writing. This is the full name of class *Color* in package javafx.scene.paint. Like any class, javafx.scene.paint.Color is a type, which means that you can use it to declare variables and parameters and to specify the return type of a function. One way to do this is to use the full name of the class as the name of the type. For example, suppose that you want to declare a variable named rectColor of type

Color. You could say:

javafx.scene.paint.Color rectColor;

This is just an ordinary variable declaration of the form "(*type-name*) (*variable-name*);". Of course, using the full name of every class can get tiresome, and you will hardly ever see full names like this used in a program. Java makes it possible to avoid using the full name of a class by *importing* the class. If you put

import javafx.scene.paint.Color;

at the beginning of a Java source code file, then, in the rest of the file, you can abbreviate the full name javafx.scene.paint.Color to just the simple name of the class, which is Color. Note that the import line comes at the start of a file (after the package statement, if there is one) and is not inside any class. Although it is sometimes referred to as a statement, it is more properly called an *import directive* since it is not a statement in the usual sense. The import directive "import javafx.scene.paint.Color" would allow you to say

Color rectColor;

to declare the variable. Note that the only effect of the import directive is to allow you to use simple class names instead of full "package.class" names. You aren't really importing anything substantial; if you leave out the import directive, you can still access the class—you just have to use its full name. There is a shortcut for importing all the classes from a given package. For example, you can import all the classes from java.util by saying

import java.util.;*

The "*" is a *wildcard* that matches every class in the package. (However, it does not match subpackages; for example, you cannot import the entire contents of all the subpackages of the java package by saying import java.*.)

Some programmers think that using a wildcard in an import statement is bad style, since it can make a large number of class names available that you are not going to use and might not even know about. They think it is better to explicitly import each individual class that you want to use. In my own programming, I often use wildcards to import all the classes from the most relevant packages, and use individual imports when I am using just one or two classes from a given package.

A program that works with networking might include the line "import java.net.*;", while one that reads or writes files might use "import java.io.*;". But when you start importing lots of packages in this way, you have to be careful about one thing: It's possible for two classes that are in different packages to have the same name. For example, both the java.awt package and the java.util package contain a class named List. If you import both java.awt.* and java.util.*, the simple name List will be ambiguous. If you try to declare a variable of type List, you will get a compiler error message about an ambiguous class name. You can still use both classes in your program: Use the full name of the class, either java.awt.List or java.util.List. Another solution, of course, is to use import to import the individual classes you need, instead of importing entire packages.

Because the package java.lang is so fundamental, all the classes in java.lang are automatically imported into every program. It's as if every program began with the statement "import java.lang.*;". This is why we have been able to use the class name *String* instead of java.lang.String, and Math.sqrt() instead of java.lang.Math.sqrt(). It would still, however, be perfectly legal to use the longer forms of the names.

Programmers can create new packages. Suppose that you want some classes that you are writing to be in a package named utilities. Then the source code files that defines those classes must begin with the line

package utilities;

This would come even before any import directive in that file. Furthermore, the source code file would be placed in a folder with the same name as the package, "utilities" in this example. And a class that is in a subpackage must be in a subfolder. For example, a class in a package named utilities.net would be in folder named "net" inside a folder named "utilities". A class that is in a package automatically has access to other classes in the same package; that is, a class doesn't have to import classes from the package in which it is defined.

In projects that define large numbers of classes, it makes sense to organize those classes into packages. It also makes sense for programmers to create new packages as toolboxes that provide functionality and APIs for dealing with areas not covered in the standard Java API. (And in fact such "toolmaking" programmers often have more prestige than the applications programmers who use their tools.)

However, with just a couple of exceptions such as class *TextIO* in package textio, the classes written for this book are not in packages. For the purposes of this book, you need to know about packages mainly so that you will be able to import *TextIO* and classes from the standard packages. The standard packages are always available to the programs that you write. You might wonder where the standard classes are actually located. Again, that can depend to some extent on the version of Java that you are using, but they will be part of the installed JDK.

Although we won't be creating packages explicitly, every class is actually part of a package. If a class is not specifically placed in a package, then it is put in something called the *default package*, which has no name. Almost all the examples that you see in this book are in the default package.

4.6.2 About Modules

Starting with Java 9, a major change was made to the large-scale structure of Java with the introduction of *modules.* A module is a collection of packages, so it represents yet another level of containment: Modules contain packages which contain classes which contain variables and methods. A package does not have to be in a module to be used, but all of the standard classes in Java and in JavaFX have been divided into a set of modules.

Modules were introduced for several reasons. A major reason is to provide better access control. Before modules, a class that is declared public can be used anywhere, from any class in any package, as can its public variables and methods. For a class that is defined in a module, on the other hand, "public" only automatically means public within the module where it is defined. However, a module can explicitly *export* a package. Exporting a package from a module makes the public classes in the package accessible from anywhere, including from other modules and from classes that are not part of any module. (It is even possible to export a package just to certain specified modules, providing an even finer level of access control.) The upshot is that it is now possible to have entire packages that are essentially private: They provide services to other packages in the same module, but are invisible from outside that module. So a module is another kind of black box, and a non-exported package is part of its hidden implementation. Of course, modularity on this scale is really only important for very large-scale applications.

Another motivation for modules is the sheer size of the standard JRE (Java Runtime Environment), which includes all of the standard classes. A given application will use only a small part of the standard runtime. Modularization makes it possible to construct smaller, custom JREs that contain only the modules that are required by an application. The JDK includes a *jlink* command for making custom runtimes, which can include modules that define an application as well as the standard modules that are required to run that application.

That runtime can then be distributed as a standalone application that can be executed even by people who have not installed a JDK on their computer. But just as for the JDK itself, different versions of the custom runtime will be needed for Windows, for MacOS, and for Linux. Furthermore, when security updates are made to the JDK, they are not automatically applied to custom runtimes, so the application developer takes on the responsibility of updating custom runtimes. Once again, this is really only useful for fairly large applications.

In a JDK for Java 9 or later, compiled class files from the standard modules are stored together in a file named *modules* inside a directory named *lib* in the main JDK directory. This is a so-called "jimage file," and there is a command-line tool named *jimage* for working with such files. If you use the *jlink* tool to create a custom runtime, part of what it does is to create a custom *modules* file containing just the modules that are needed by the runtime. In the JDK 17 on my Linux computer, *modules* is a 127 megabyte file containing 26401 classes in 835 packages in 70 modules. The JDK directory also has a subdirectory named *jmods* that contains the modules in another form. However, it is not required for compiling and running programs and, as far as I can tell, is meant mostly for use by *jlink*.

Modules in the JDK include, for example, *java.base* (which contains the basic modules such as java.lang and java.util) and java.desktop (which include packages for the Swing GUI toolkit). JavaFX packages include *javafx.base*, *javafx.control*, *javafx.graphics*, and a few that are less generally useful. The API documentation for modular versions of Java is divided into modules, then into packages, and finally into classes. This makes the documentation harder to browse than in older versions of Java. However, the documentation web site does have an effective search feature. As I write this, the documentation for Java 17 and for JavaFX 17 is available at:

https://docs.oracle.com/en/java/javase/17/docs/api/index.html https://openjfx.io/javadoc/17/

A class can be defined outside of any module, and it is possible for that class to use packages from modules, provided that those packages are exported by the modules where they are defined. In particular, a programmer can use classes from the JDK without ever thinking about modules or knowing that they exist. This applies to all the command-line programs in this book. However, when using Java 9 or later, things are different for GUI programs that use JavaFX, which has been removed from the JDK and is distributed as a separate set of modules. when you compile or run a JavaFX program, you need to specify a module path that includes the JavaFX modules, and you need to provide an --add-modules option.

The value for --add-modules was given as ALL-MODULE-PATH, which lets the program access any modules that are found on the module path. An alternative is to specify a list of names of just those modules that are actually used by the program.)

Aside from using modules with JavaFX and the basic background information in this section, this textbook does not cover modules.

4.6.5 Javadoc

To use an API effectively, you need good documentation for it. The documentation for most Java APIs is prepared using a system called *Javadoc*. For example, this system is used to prepare the documentation for Java's standard packages. And almost everyone who creates a toolbox in Java publishes Javadoc documentation for it.

Javadoc documentation is prepared from special comments that are placed in the Java source code file. Recall that one type of Java comment begins with /* and ends with */. A Javadoc comment takes the same form, but it begins with /** rather than simply /*. You have already seen comments of this form in many of the examples in this book.

Note that a Javadoc comment must be placed just before the subroutine that it is commenting on. This rule is always followed. You can have Javadoc comments for subroutines, for member variables, and for classes. The Javadoc comment always immediately precedes the thing it is commenting on.

Like any comment, a Javadoc comment is ignored by the computer when the file is compiled. But there is a tool called javadoc that reads Java source code files, extracts any Javadoc comments that it finds, and creates a set of Web pages containing the comments in a nicely formatted, interlinked form. By default, javadoc will only collect information about public classes, subroutines, and member variables, but it allows the option of creating documentation for non-public things as well. If javadoc doesn't find any Javadoc comment for something, it will construct one, but the comment will contain only basic information such as the name and type of a member variable or the name, return type, and parameter list of a subroutine. This is syntactic information. To add information about semantics and pragmatics, you have to write a Javadoc comment.

As an example, you can look at the documentation Web page for *TextIO*. The documentation page was created by applying the javadoc tool to the source code file, TextIO.java. If you have downloaded the on-line version of this book, the documentation can be found in the TextIO Javadoc directory, or you can find a link to it in the on-line version of this section.

In a Javadoc comment, the *'s at the start of each line are optional. The javadoc tool will remove them. In addition to normal text, the comment can contain certain special codes. For one thing, the comment can contain *HTML mark-up* commands. HTML is the language that is used to create web pages, and Javadoc comments are meant to be shown on web pages.

The javadoc tool will copy any HTML commands in the comments to the web pages that it creates. The book will not teach you HTML, but as an example, you can add <p> to indicate the start of a new paragraph. (Generally, in the absence of HTML commands, blank lines and extra spaces in the comment are ignored. Furthermore, the characters & and < have special meaning in HTML and should not be used in Javadoc comments except with those meanings; they can be written as & and <.)

In addition to HTML commands, Javadoc comments can include *doc tags*, which are processed as commands by the javadoc tool. A doc tag has a name that begins with the character @. I will only discuss four tags: @author, @param, @return, and @ throws. The @author tag can be used only for a class, and should be followed by the name of the author. The other three tags are used in Javadoc comments for a subroutine to provide information about its parameters, its return value, and the exceptions that it might throw. These tags must be placed at the end of the comment, after any description of the subroutine itself. The syntax for using them is:

@param (parameter-name) (description-of-parameter)

@return (description-of-return-value)

@throws (exception-class-name) (description-of-exception)

The (*descriptions*) can extend over several lines. The description ends at the next doc tag or at the end of the comment. You can include a @param tag for every parameter of the subroutine and a @throws for as many types of exception as you want to document. You should have a @return tag only for a non-void subroutine. These tags do not have to be given in any particular order.

Here is an example that doesn't do anything exciting but that does use all three types of doc tag:

```
/**
This subroutine computes the area of a rectangle, given its width
and its height.          The length and the width should be positive numbers.
@param width the length of one side of the rectangle
@param height the length the second side of the rectangle
@return the area of the rectangle
@throws IllegalArgumentException if either the width or the height
is a negative number.
*/
public static double areaOfRectangle( double length, double width ) {
    if ( width < 0      ||       height < 0 )
            throw new IllegalArgumentException("Sides must have positive length.");
    double area;
    area = width * height;
    return area;
}
```

I use Javadoc comments for many of my examples. I encourage you to use them in your own code, even if you don't plan to generate Web page documentation of your work, since it's a standard format that other Java programmers will be familiar with.

If you do want to create Web-page documentation, you need to run the javadoc tool. This tool is available as a command in the Java Development Kit that was discussed in Section 2.6. You can use the javadoc tool in a command line interface similarly to the way that the javac and java commands are used. Javadoc can also be applied in the integrated development environments. I won't go into any of the details here; consult the documentation for your programming environment.

4.6.6 Static Import

Before ending this section, I will mention an extension of the import directive. We have seen that import makes it possible to refer to a class such as java.util.Scanner using its simple name, *Scanner*. But you still have to use compound names to refer to static member variables such as System.out and to static methods such as Math. sqrt.

There is another form of the import directive that can be used to import static members of a class in the same way that the ordinary import directive imports classes from a package. That form of the directive is called a *static import*, and it has syntax

import static (package-name).(class-name).(static-member-name);

to import one static member name from a class, or

import static (package-name).(class-name).;*

to import all the public static members from a class. For example, if you preface a class definition with

import static java.lang.System.out;

then you can use the simple name out instead of the compound name System.out. This means you can say out.println instead of System.out.println. If you are going to work extensively with the *Math* class, you might preface your class definition with

import static java.lang.Math.;*

This would allow you to say sqrt instead of Math.sqrt, log instead of Math.log, PI instead of Math.PI, and so on. And you could import the *getlnInt* function from *TextIO* using

import static textio.TextIO.getlnInt;

Note that the static import directive requires a (*package-name*), even for classes in the standard package java.lang. One consequence of this is that you can't do a static import from a class in the default package.

4.7 FURTHER INSIGHTS ON PROGRAM DESIGN

Understanding how programs work is one thing. Designing a program to perform some particular task is another thing altogether. In Section 3.2, I discussed how pseudocode and stepwise refinement can be used to methodically develop an algorithm. We can now see how subroutines can fit into the process.

Stepwise refinement is inherently a top-down process, but the process does have a "bottom," that is, a point at which you stop refining the pseudocode algorithm and translate what you have directly into proper program code. In the absence of subroutines, the process would not bottom out until you get down to the level of assignment statements and very primitive input/output operations. But if you have subroutines lying around to perform certain useful tasks, you can stop refining as soon as you've managed to express your algorithm in terms of those tasks.

This allows you to add a bottom-up element to the top-down approach of stepwise refinement. Given a problem, you might start by writing some subroutines that perform tasks relevant to the problem domain. The subroutines become a toolbox of ready-made tools that you can integrate into your algorithm as you develop it. (Alternatively, you might be able to buy or find a software toolbox written by someone else, containing subroutines that you can use in your project as black boxes.)

Subroutines can also be helpful even in a strict top-down approach. As you refine your algorithm, you are free at any point to take any sub-task in the algorithm and make it into a subroutine. Developing that subroutine then becomes a separate problem, which you can work on separately. Your main algorithm will merely call the subroutine. This, of course, is just a way of breaking your problem down into separate, smaller problems. It is still a top-down approach because the top-down analysis of the problem tells you what subroutines to write. In the bottom-up approach, you start by writing or obtaining subroutines that are relevant to the problem domain, and you build your solution to the problem on top of that foundation of subroutines.

4.7.1 Preconditions and Postconditions

When working with subroutines as building blocks, it is important to be clear about how a subroutine interacts with the rest of the program. This interaction is specified by the *contract* of the subroutine. A convenient way to express the contract of a subroutine is in terms of *preconditions* and *postconditions*.

A precondition of a subroutine is something that must be true when the subroutine is called, if the subroutine is to work correctly. For example, for the built-in function Math.sqrt(x), a precondition is that the parameter, x, is greater than or equal to zero, since it is not possible to take the square root of a negative number. In terms of a contract, a precondition represents an obligation of the *caller* of the subroutine. If you call a subroutine without meeting its precondition, then there is no reason to expect it to work properly. The program might crash or give incorrect results, but you can only blame yourself, not the subroutine, because you haven't lived up to your side of the deal.

A postcondition of a subroutine represents the other side of the contract. It represents an obligation of the subroutine. It is something that will be true after the subroutine has run (assuming that its preconditions were met—and that there are no bugs in the subroutine). The postcondition of the function Math.sqrt() is that the square of the value that is returned by this function is equal to the parameter that is provided when the subroutine is called.

Of course, this will only be true if the precondition—that the parameter is greater than or equal to zero—is met. A postcondition of the built-in subroutine System. out.print(x) is that the value of the parameter has been displayed on the screen.

Preconditions most often give restrictions on the acceptable values of parameters, as in the example of Math.sqrt(x). However, they can also refer to global variables that are used in the subroutine. Or, if it only makes sense to call the subroutine at certain times, the precondition might refer to the state that the program must be in when the subroutine is called.

The postcondition of a subroutine, on the other hand, specifies the task that it performs.

For a function, the postcondition should specify the value that the function returns.

Subroutines are sometimes described by comments that explicitly specify their preconditions and postconditions. When you are given a pre-written subroutine, a statement of its preconditions and postconditions tells you how to use it and what it does. When you are assigned to write a subroutine, the preconditions and postconditions give you an exact specification of what the subroutine is expected to do. I will use this approach in the example that constitutes the rest of this section. The comments are given in the form of Javadoc comments, but I will explicitly label the preconditions and postconditions. (Many computer scientists think that new doc tags @precondition and @postcondition should be added to the Javadoc system for explicit labeling of preconditions and postconditions, but that has not yet been done.)

4.7.2 A Design Example

Let's work through an example of program design using subroutines. In this example, we will use pre-written subroutines as building blocks and we will also design new subroutines that we need to complete the project. The API that I will use here is defined in two classes that I have written: Mosaic.java, which in turn depends on MosaicCanvas.java. To compile and run a program that uses the API, the classes *Mosaic* and *MosaicCanvas* must be available. That is, the files Mosaic.java and MosaicCanvas.java, or the corresponding compiled class files, must be in the same folder as the class that defines the program.

So, suppose that I have access to an already-written class called Mosaic. This class allows a program to work with a window that displays little colored rectangles arranged in rows and columns. The window can be opened, closed, and otherwise manipulated with static member subroutines defined in the Mosaic class. In fact, the class defines a toolbox or API that can be used for working with such windows. Here are some of the available routines in the API, with Javadoc-style comments. (Remember that a Javadoc comment comes before the thing that it is commenting on.)

```
/**
Opens a "mosaic" window on the screen      This subroutine should be called
before any of the other Mosaic subroutines are used.    The program will end
when the user closes the window.
*
Precondition:        The parameters rows, cols, h, and w are positive integers.
Postcondition:       A window is open on the screen that can display rows and columns
                     of colored rectangles. Each rectangle is w pixels wide and h pixels
                     high. The number of rows is given by the first parameter and the
                     number of columns by the second. Initially, all rectangles are black.
*
Note:        The rows are numbered from 0 to rows - 1, and the columns are
numbered from 0 to cols - 1.
*/
public static void open(int rows, int cols, int w, int h)
/**
Sets the color of one of the rectangles in the window.
*
```

Precondition: *row and col are in the valid range of row and column numbers, and r, g, and b are in the range 0 to 255, inclusive.*

Postcondition: *The color of the rectangle in row number row and column number col has been set to the color specified by r, g, and b. r gives the amount of red in the color with 0 representing no red and 255 representing the maximum possible amount of red. The larger the value of r, the more red in the color. g and b work similarly for the green and blue color components.*

*/

public static void set Color(int row, int col, int r, int g, int b)

/**

Gets the red component of the color of one of the rectangles.

*

Precondition: *row and col are in the valid range of row and column numbers.*

Postcondition: *The red component of the color of the specified rectangle is returned as an integer in the range 0 to 255 inclusive.*

*/

public static int getRed(int row, int col)

/**

Like getRed, but returns the green component of the color.

*/

public static int getGreen(int row, int col)

/**

Like getRed, but returns the blue component of the color.

*/

public static int getBlue(int row, int col)

/**

Inserts a delay in the program (to regulate the speed at which the colors are changed, for example).

*

Precondition: *milliseconds is a positive integer.*

Postcondition: *The program has paused for at least the specified number of milliseconds, where one second is equal to 1000 milliseconds.*

*/

public static void delay(int milliseconds)

Remember that these subroutines are static members of the Mosaic class, so when they are called from outside Mosaic, the name of the class must be included as part of the name of the routine. For example, we'll have to use the name Mosaic.open rather than simply open.

You'll notice that the comments on the subroutine don't specify what happens when the preconditions are not met. Although a subroutine is not really obligated by its contract to do anything particular in that case, it would be good to know what happens. For example, if the precondition, "row and col are in the valid range of row and column numbers," on the setColor() or getRed() routine is violated, an *IllegalArgumentException* will be thrown. Knowing that fact would allow you to write programs that catch and handle the exception, and it would be good to document it with a @throws doc tag in the Javadoc comment. Other questions remain about the behavior of the subroutines. For example, what happens if you call Mosaic.open() and there is already a mosaic window open on the screen? (In fact, the second call will simply be ignored.) It's difficult to fully document the behavior of a piece of software—sometimes, you just have to experiment or look at the full source code.

My idea for a program is to use the Mosaic class as the basis for a neat animation. I want to fill the window with randomly colored squares, and then randomly change the colors in a loop that continues as long as the window is open. "Randomly change the colors" could mean a lot of different things, but after thinking for a while, I decide it would be interesting to have a "disturbance" that wanders randomly around the window, changing the color of each square that it encounters. Here's a picture showing what the contents of the window might look like at one point in time:

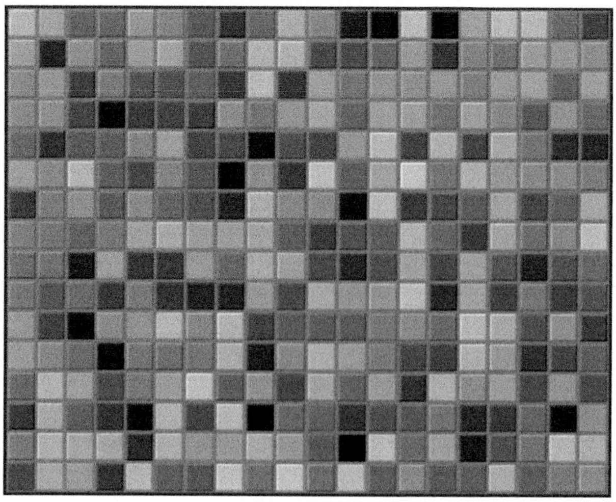

With basic routines for manipulating the window as a foundation, I can turn to the specific problem at hand. A basic outline for my program is

Open a Mosaic window

Fill window with random colors

Move around, changing squares at random

Filling the window with random colors seems like a nice coherent task that I can work on separately, so let's decide to write a separate subroutine to do it. The third step can be expanded a bit more, into the steps: Start in the middle of the window, then keep moving to new squares and changing the color of those squares. This should continue as long as the mosaic window is still open. Thus we can refine the algorithm to:

Open a Mosaic window

Fill window with random colors

Set the current position to the middle square in the window

As long as the mosaic window is open:

Randomly change color of the square at the current position

Move current position up, down, left, or right, at random

I need to represent the current position in some way. That can be done with two int variables named currentRow and currentColumn that hold the row number and the column number of the square where the disturbance is currently located. I'll use 16 rows and 20 columns of squares in my mosaic, so setting the current position to be in the center means setting currentRow to 8 and currentColumn to 10. I already have a subroutine, Mosaic.open(), to open the window. To keep the main routine simple, I decide that I will write two more subroutines of my own to carry out the two tasks in the while loop. The algorithm can then be written in Java as:

```
Mosaic.open(16,20,25,25)
fillWithRandomColors();
currentRow = 8;       // Middle row, halfway down the window.
currentColumn = 10; // Middle column.
while ( true ) { // Program ends when user closes the window.
    changeToRandomColor(currentRow, currentColumn);
    randomMove();
}
```

With the proper wrapper, this is essentially the main() routine of my program. It turns out I decided to make one small modification after running the completed program: To prevent the animation from running too fast, I added the line "Mosaic. delay(10);" to the while loop.

The main() routine is taken care of, but to complete the program, I still have to write the subroutines fillWithRandomColors(), changeToRandomColor(int,int), and randomMove(). Writing each of these subroutines is a separate, small task. The fillWithRandomColors() routine is defined by the postcondition that "each of the rectangles in the mosaic has been changed to a random color." Pseudocode for an algorithm to accomplish this task can be given as:

```
For each row:
    For each column:
            set the square in that row and column to a random color
```

"For each row" and "for each column" can be implemented as for loops. We've already planned to write a subroutine changeToRandomColor that can be used to set the color. (The possibility of reusing subroutines in several places is one of the big payoffs of using them!) So, fillWithRandomColors() can be written in proper Java as:

```
static void fillWithRandomColors() {
    int row, column;
    for ( row = 0; row < 16; row++ )
            for ( column = 0; column < 20; column++ )
            changeToRandomColor(row,column);
}
```

Turning to the changeToRandomColor subroutine, we already have a method in the Mosaic class, Mosaic.setColor(), that can be used to change the color of a square. If we want a random color, we just have to choose random values for r, g, and b. According to the precondition of the Mosaic.setColor() subroutine, these random values must be integers in the range from 0 to 255. A formula for randomly selecting such an integer is "(int)(256*Math.random())". So the random color subroutine becomes:

```
static void changeToRandomColor(int rowNum, int colNum) {
    int red = (int)(256*Math.random());
    int green = (int)(256*Math.random());
    int blue = (int)(256*Math.random());
    Mosaic.setColor(rowNum,colNum,red,green,blue);
}
```

Finally, consider the randomMove subroutine, which is supposed to randomly move the disturbance up, down, left, or right. To make a random choice among four directions, we can choose a random integer in the range 0 to 3. If the integer is 0, move in one direction; if it is 1, move in another direction; and so on. The position of the disturbance is given by the variables currentRow and currentColumn. To "move up" means to subtract 1 from currentRow. This leaves open the question of what to do if currentRow becomes -1, which would put the disturbance above the window (which would violate a precondition of several of the *Mosaic* subroutines). Rather than let this happen, I decide to move the disturbance to the opposite edge of the grid by setting currentRow to 15. (Remember that the 16 rows are numbered from 0 to 15.) An alternative to jumping to the opposite edge would be to simply do nothing in this case. Moving the disturbance down, left, or right is handled similarly. If we use a switch statement to decide which direction to move, the code for randomMove becomes:

```
int directionNum;
directionNum = (int)(4*Math.random());
switch (directionNum) {
    case 0 -> {         // move up
            currentRow--;
            if (currentRow < 0)        // CurrentRow is outside the mosaic;
            currentRow = 15;// move it to the opposite edge.
    }
    case 1 -> {         // move right
            currentColumn++;
            if (currentColumn >= 20)
            currentColumn = 0;
    }
    case 2 -> {         // move down
            currentRow++;
            if (currentRow >= 16)
            currentRow = 0;
    }
    case 3 -> {         // move left
            currentColumn--;
```

```
            if (currentColumn < 0)
            currentColumn = 19;
        }
    }
```

4.7.3 The Program

Putting this all together, we get the following complete program. Note that I've added Javadoc- style comments for the class itself and for each of the subroutines. The variables currentRow and currentColumn are defined as static members of the class, rather than local variables, because each of them is used in several different subroutines. You can find a copy of the source code in RandomMosaicWalk.java. Remember that this program actually depends on two other files, Mosaic.java and MosaicCanvas.java.

```
/**
This program opens a window full of randomly colored squares.      A "disturbance"
moves randomly around in the window, randomly changing the color of each
square that it visits. The program runs until the user closes the window.
*/
public class RandomMosaicWalk {
    static int currentRow;     // Row currently containing the disturbance.
    static int currentColumn; // Column currently containing disturbance.
    /**
    The main program creates the window, fills it with random colors,
    and then moves the disturbance in a random walk around the window
    as long as the window is open.
    */
public static void main(String[] args) {
    Mosaic.open(16,20,25,25);
    fillWithRandomColors();
    currentRow = 8; // start at center of window
    currentColumn = 10;
    while ( true ) {
            changeToRandomColor(currentRow, currentColumn);
            randomMove();
```

```
            Mosaic.delay(10);         // Remove this line to speed things up!
        }
    }   // end main
    /**
    Fills the window with randomly colored squares.
    Precondition:       The mosaic window is open.
    Postcondition:      Each square has been set to a random color.
    */
    static void fillWithRandomColors() {
        int row, column;
        for ( row=0; row < 16; row++ ) {
            for ( column=0; column < 20; column++ ) {
                changeToRandomColor(row, column);
            }
        }
    }   // end fillWithRandomColors
    /**
    Changes one square to a new randomly selected color.
    Precondition:       The specified rowNum and colNum are in the valid range of row and
                        column numbers.
    Postcondition:      The square in the specified row and column has been set to a random
                        color.
    @param rowNum the row number of the square, counting rows down
        from 0 at the top
    @param colNum the column number of the square, counting columns over
        from 0 at the left
    */
    static void changeToRandomColor(int rowNum, int colNum) {
        int red = (int)(256*Math.random());       // Choose random levels in range
        int green = (int)(256*Math.random());     //      0 to 255 for red, green,
        int blue = (int)(256*Math.random());      //      and blue color components.
        Mosaic.setColor(rowNum,colNum,red,green,blue);
```

```
} // end changeToRandomColor
/**
Move the disturbance.
Precondition:     The global variables currentRow and current Column are within the
                  legal range of row and column numbers.
Postcondition:    currentRow or currentColumn is changed to one of the neighboring
                  positions in the grid -- up, down, left, or right from the current
                  position. If this moves the position outside of the grid, then it is
                  moved to the opposite edge of the grid.
*/
static void randomMove() {
    int directionNum; // Randomly set to 0, 1, 2, or 3 to choose direction.
    directionNum = (int)(4*Math.random());
    switch (directionNum) {
            case 0 -> {        // move up
                currentRow--;
                if (currentRow < 0)        // CurrentRow is outside the mosaic;
                        currentRow = 15;// move it to the opposite edge.
                }
            case 1 -> {        // move right
                currentColumn++;
                if (currentColumn >= 20)
                        currentColumn = 0;
                }
            case 2 -> {        // move down currentRow++;
                if (currentRow >= 16)
                currentRow = 0;
                }
            case 3 -> {        // move left
                currentColumn--;
                if (currentColumn < 0)
                        currentColumn = 19;
```

```
            }
        }
    }        // end randomMove
} // end class RandomMosaicWalk
```

4.8 THE TRUTH ABOUT DECLARATIONS

Names are fundamental to programming, as I said a few chapters ago. There are a lot of details involved in declaring and using names. I have been avoiding some of those details. In this section, I'll reveal most of the truth (although still not the full truth) about declaring and using variables in Java. The material in the subsections "Initialization in Declarations" and "Named Constants" is particularly important, since I will be using it regularly from now on.

4.8.1 Initialization in Declarations

When a variable declaration is executed, memory is allocated for the variable. This memory must be initialized to contain some definite value before the variable can be used in an expression. In the case of a local variable, the declaration is often followed closely by an assignment statement that does the initialization. For example,

```
int count;    // Declare a variable named count. count = 0;        // Give count its initial value.
```

However, the truth about declaration statements is that it is legal to include the initialization of the variable in the declaration statement. The two statements above can therefore be abbreviated as

```
int count = 0;          // Declare count and give it an initial value.
```

The computer still executes this statement in two steps: Declare the variable count, then assign the value 0 to the newly created variable. The initial value does not have to be a constant. It can be any expression. It is legal to initialize several variables in one declaration statement. For example,

```
char firstInitial = 'D', secondInitial = 'E';
int x, y = 1;  // OK, but only y has been initialized!
int N = 3, M = N+2;    // OK, N is initialized
                       //        before its value is used.
```

This feature is especially common in for loops, since it makes it possible to declare a loop control variable at the same point in the loop where it is initialized. Since the loop control variable generally has nothing to do with the rest of the program outside the loop, it's reasonable to have its declaration in the part of the program where it's actually used. For example:

```
for ( int i = 0;        i < 10;   i++ ) {
    System.out.println(i);
}
```

You should remember that this is simply an abbreviation for the following, where I've added an extra pair of braces to show that i is considered to be local to the for statement and no longer exists after the for loop ends:

```
{
    int i;
    for ( i = 0;        i < 10;   i++ ) {
        System.out.println(i);
    }
}
```

A member variable can also be initialized at the point where it is declared, just as for a local variable. For example:

```
public class Bank {
    private static double interestRate = 0.05;
    private static int maxWithdrawal = 200;
          .
          .        // More variables and subroutines.
          .
}
```

A static member variable is created as soon as the class is loaded by the Java interpreter, and the initialization is also done at that time. In the case of member variables, this is not simply an abbreviation for a declaration followed by an assignment statement. Declaration statements are the only type of statement that can occur outside of a subroutine. Assignment statements cannot, so the following is illegal:

```
public class Bank {
    private static double interestRate;
    interestRate = 0.05;        // ILLEGAL:
              .                 //      Can't be outside a subroutine!:
              .
              .
```

Because of this, declarations of member variables often include initial values. In fact, as mentioned in Subsection 4.2.4, if no initial value is provided for a member variable, then a default initial value is used. For example, when declaring an integer member variable, count, "static int count;" is equivalent to "static int count = 0;".

Even array variables can be initialized. An array contains several elements, not just a single value. To initialize an array variable, you can provide a list of values, separated by commas, and enclosed between a pair of braces. For example:

```
int[] smallPrimes = { 2, 3, 5, 7, 11, 13, 17, 19, 23, 29 };
```

In this statement, an array of int of length 10 is created and filled with the values in the list. The length of the array is determined by the number of items in the list.

Note that this syntax for initializing arrays cannot be used in assignment statements. It can only be used in a declaration statement at the time when the array variable is declared.

It is also possible to initialize an array variable with an array created using the new operator (which can also be used in assignment statements). For example:

```
String[] nameList = new String[100];
```

but in that case, of course, all the array elements will have their default value.

4.8.2 Declaring Variables with var

In Java 11 and later, there is a new way of declaring variables, using the word "var" instead of specifying an explicit type for the variable. The new syntax for declarations can only be used for local variables, that is for variables that are declared inside subroutines (see Subsection 4.2.4). Furthermore a variable that is declared using var must be given an initial value. A variable that is declared with var has a defined type, just like any other variable. The Java compiler uses the type of the initial value to define the type for the variable. For example, the declaration statement

```
var interestRate = 0.05;
```

can be used to define a local variable named interestRate with initial value 0.05. The variable is of type double, since 0.05 is a value of type double. And a local variable named nameList of type String[ ] can be declared as

```
var nameList = new String[100];
```

In particular, var can be used to declare the loop control variable in a for loop. For example,

```
for ( var i = 0;          i < 10;    i++ ) {
     System.out.println(i);
```

}

All this might not seem particularly useful, but it becomes more useful for the more complicated "parameterized types"

4.8.3 Named Constants

Sometimes, the value of a variable is not supposed to change after it is initialized. For example, in the above example where interestRate is initialized to the value 0.05, it's quite possible that 0.05 is meant to be the value throughout the entire program. In that case, the programmer is probably defining the variable, interestRate, to give a meaningful name to the otherwise meaningless number, 0.05. It's easier to understand what's going on when a program says "principal += principal*interestRate;" rather than "principal += principal*0.05;". In Java, the modifier "final" can be applied to a variable declaration to ensure that the value stored in the variable cannot be changed after the variable has been initialized. For example, if the member variable interestRate is declared with

public final static double interestRate = 0.05;

then it would be impossible for the value of interestRate to change anywhere else in the program. Any assignment statement that tries to assign a value to interestRate will be rejected by the computer as a syntax error when the program is compiled. (A "final" modifier on a public interest rate makes a lot of sense—a bank might want to publish its interest rate, but it certainly wouldn't want to let random people make changes to it!)

It is legal to apply the final modifier to local variables and to formal parameters (and even to classes and subroutines), but it is probably most useful for member variables. I will often refer to a static member variable that is declared to be final as a *named constant*, since its value remains constant for the whole time that the program is running. The readability of a program can be greatly enhanced by using named constants to give meaningful names to important quantities in the program. A recommended style rule for named constants is to give them names that consist entirely of upper case letters, with underscore characters to separate words if necessary. For example, the preferred style for the interest rate constant would be

public final static double INTEREST RATE = 0.05;

This is the style that is generally used in Java's standard classes, which define many named constants. For example, we have already seen that the *Math* class contains a variable Math.PI. This variable is declared in the *Math* class as a "public final static" variable of type double. Similarly, the Color class contains named constants such as Color.RED and Color.YELLOW which are public final static variables of type Color.

Enumerated type constants (see Subsection 2.3.3) are also examples of named constants. The enumerated type definition

enum Alignment { LEFT, RIGHT, CENTER }

defines the constants Alignment.LEFT, Alignment.RIGHT, and Alignment.CENTER. Technically, *Alignment* is a class, and the three constants are public final static members of that class. Defining the enumerated type is similar to defining three constants of type, say, int:

public static final int ALIGNMENT LEFT = 0;

public static final int ALIGNMENT RIGHT = 1;

public static final int ALIGNMENT CENTER = 2;

In fact, this is how things had to be done before the introduction of enumerated types, and it is what is still done in many cases. Using the integer constants, you could define a variable of type int and assign it the values ALIGNMENT LEFT, ALIGNMENT RIGHT, or ALIGNMENT CENTER to represent different types of alignment. The only problem with this is that the computer has no way of knowing that you intend the value of the variable to represent an alignment, and it will not raise any objection if the value that is assigned to the variable is not one of the three valid alignment values. With the enumerated type, on the other hand, the only values that can be assigned to a variable of type *Alignment* are the constant values that are listed in the definition of the enumerated type. Any attempt to assign an invalid value to the variable is a syntax error which the computer will detect when the program is compiled. This extra safety is one of the major advantages of enumerated types.

Curiously enough, one of the main reasons to use named constants is that it's easy to change the value of a named constant. Of course, the value can't change while the program is running. But between runs of the program, it's easy to change the value in the source code and recompile the program. Consider the interest rate example. It's quite possible that the value of the interest rate is used many times throughout the program. Suppose that the bank changes the interest rate and the program has to be modified. If the literal number 0.05 were used throughout the program, the programmer would have to track down each place where the interest rate is used in the program and change the rate to the new value. (This is made even harder by the fact that the number 0.05 might occur in the program with other meanings besides the interest rate, as well as by the fact that someone might have, say, used 0.025 to represent half the interest rate.) On the other hand, if the named constant INTEREST RATE is declared and used consistently throughout the program, then only the single line where the constant is initialized needs to be changed.

As an extended example, I will give a new version of the RandomMosaicWalk program from the previous section. This version uses named constants to represent the number of rows in the mosaic, the number of columns, and the size of each little square. The three constants are declared as final static member variables with the lines:

```
final static int ROWS = 20;      // Number of rows in mosaic.
final static int COLUMNS = 30;          // Number of columns in mosaic.
final static int SQUARE SIZE = 15; // Size of each square in mosaic.
```

The rest of the program is carefully modified to use the named constants. For example, in the new version of the program, the Mosaic window is opened with the statement

```
Mosaic.open(ROWS, COLUMNS, SQUARE SIZE, SQUARE SIZE);
```

Sometimes, it's not easy to find all the places where a named constant needs to be used. If you don't use the named constant consistently, you've more or less defeated the purpose. It's always a good idea to run a program using several different values for any named constant, to test that it works properly in all cases.

Here is the complete new program, RandomMosaicWalk2, with all modifications from the previous version shown in italic. Note in particular how the constants ROWS and COLUMNS are used in randomMove() when moving the disturbance from one edge of the mosaic to the opposite edge. I've left out most of the comments to save space.

```
public class RandomMosaicWalk2 {
    final static int ROWS = 20;          // Number of rows in mosaic.
    final static int COLUMNS = 30;     // Number of columns in mosaic.
    final static int SQUARE SIZE = 15; // Size of each square in mosaic.
    static int currentRow;      // Row currently containing the disturbance.
    static int currentColumn; // Column currently containing the disturbance.
    public static void main(String[] args) {
            Mosaic.open( ROWS, COLUMNS, SQUARE SIZE, SQUARE SIZE );
            fillWithRandomColors();
            currentRow = ROWS / 2;  // start at center of window
            currentColumn = COLUMNS / 2;
            while ( true ) {
                    changeToRandomColor(currentRow, currentColumn);
                    randomMove();
```

```
                Mosaic.delay(5);
            }
        }       // end main
        static void fillWithRandomColors() {
            for (int row=0; row < ROWS; row++) {
                for (int column=0; column < COLUMNS; column++) {
                    changeToRandomColor(row, column);
                }
            }
    }   // end fillWithRandomColors
    static void changeToRandomColor(int rowNum, int colNum) {
        int red = (int)(256*Math.random());       // Choose random levels in range
        int green = (int)(256*Math.random());     //     0 to 255 for red, green,
        int blue = (int)(256*Math.random());      //     and blue color components.
        Mosaic.setColor(rowNum,colNum,red,green,blue);
    }   // end changeToRandomColor
    static void randomMove() {
        int directionNum; // Randomly set to 0, 1, 2, or 3 to choose direction.
        directionNum = (int)(4*Math.random());
        switch (directionNum) {
            case 0 -> {        // move up
                currentRow--;
                if (currentRow < 0)
                    currentRow = ROWS - 1;
                }
            case 1 -> {        // move right
                currentColumn++;
                if (currentColumn >= COLUMNS)
                    currentColumn = 0;
                }
            case 2 -> {        // move down
```

```
                currentRow++;
                if (currentRow >= ROWS)
                        currentRow = 0;
                }
            case 3 -> {         // move left
                currentColumn--;
                if (currentColumn < 0)
                        currentColumn = COLUMNS - 1;
                }
            }
    }       // end randomMove
} // end class RandomMosaicWalk2
```

4.8.4 Naming and Scope Rules

When a variable declaration is executed, memory is allocated for that variable. The variable name can be used in at least some part of the program source code to refer to that memory or to the data that is stored in the memory. The portion of the program source code where the variable is valid is called the *scope* of the variable. Similarly, we can refer to the scope of subroutine names and formal parameter names.

For static member subroutines, scope is straightforward. The scope of a static subroutine is the entire source code of the class in which it is defined. That is, it is possible to call the subroutine from any point in the class, including at a point in the source code before the point where the definition of the subroutine appears. It is even possible to call a subroutine from within itself. This is an example of something called "recursion," a fairly advanced topic that we will return to in Section 9.1. If the subroutine is not private, it can also be accessed from outside the class where it is defined, using its full name.

For a variable that is declared as a static member variable in a class, the situation is similar, but with one complication. It is legal to have a local variable or a formal parameter that has the same name as a member variable. In that case, within the scope of the local variable or parameter, the member variable is *hidden* . Consider, for example, a class named Game that has the form:

```
public class Game {
    static int count; // member variable
    static void playGame() {
```

```
            int count;        // local variable
            .
            .        // Some statements to define playGame()
            .
    }
    .
    .        // More variables and subroutines.
    .
} // end Game
```

In the statements that make up the body of the playGame() subroutine, the name "count" refers to the local variable. In the rest of the Game class, "count" refers to the member variable (unless hidden by other local variables or parameters named count). However, the member variable named count can also be referred to by the full name Game.count. Usually, the full name is only used outside the class where count is defined. However, there is no rule against using it inside the class. The full name, Game.count, can be used inside the playGame() subroutine to refer to the member variable instead of the local variable. So, the full scope rule is that the scope of a static member variable includes the entire class in which it is defined, but where the simple name of the member variable is hidden by a local variable or formal parameter name, the member variable must be referred to by its full name of the form ⟨*className*⟩.⟨*variableName*⟩. (Scope rules for non-static members are similar to those for static members, except that, as we shall see, non-static members cannot be used in static subroutines.)

The scope of a formal parameter of a subroutine is the block that makes up the body of the subroutine. The scope of a local variable extends from the declaration statement that defines the variable to the end of the block in which the declaration occurs. As noted above, it is possible to declare a loop control variable of a for loop in the for statement, as in "for (int i=0; i < 10; i++)". The scope of such a declaration is considered as a special case: It is valid only within the for statement and does not extend to the remainder of the block that contains the for statement.

It is not legal to redefine the name of a formal parameter or local variable within its scope, even in a nested block. For example, this is not allowed:

```
void badSub(int y) {
    int x;
    while (y > 0) {
        int x;   // ERROR:   x is already defined.
```

```
            .
            .
            .
        }
    }
```

In many languages, this would be legal; the declaration of x in the while loop would hide the original declaration. It is not legal in Java; however, once the block in which a variable is declared ends, its name does become available for reuse in Java. For example:

```
    void goodSub(int y) {
        while (y > 10) {
            int x;
            .
            .
            .
            // The scope of x ends here.
        }
    while (y > 0) {
            int x;    // OK: Previous declaration of x has expired.
            .
            .
            .
        }
    }
```

You might wonder whether local variable names can hide subroutine names. This can't happen, for a reason that might be surprising. There is no rule that variables and subroutines have to have different names. The computer can always tell whether a name refers to a variable or to a subroutine, because a subroutine name is always followed by a left parenthesis. It's perfectly legal to have a variable called count and a subroutine called count in the same class. (This is one reason why I often write subroutine names with parentheses, as when I talk about the main() routine. It's a good idea to think of the parentheses as part of the name.) Even more is true: It's legal to reuse class names to name variables and subroutines. The syntax rules of Java guarantee that the computer can always tell when a name is being used as a class name. A class name is a type, and so it can be used to declare variables and formal parameters and to specify the return type of a function. This means that you could legally have a class called Insanity in which you declare a function

static Insanity Insanity(Insanity Insanity) { ... }

The first Insanity is the return type of the function. The second is the function name, the third is the type of the formal parameter, and the fourth is the name of the formal parameter. However, please remember that not everything that is possible is a good idea!

5 Chapter INTRODUCTION TO PROGRAMMING IN THE LARGE: OBJECTS AND CLASSES

A subroutine denotes a singular task, but an object can encompass both data (as instance variables) and several activities or "behaviors" associated with that data (as instance methods). Consequently, objects offer a more refined form of structure that aids in managing the intricacies of extensive applications. The initial four sections of this chapter present the fundamental concepts necessary for object manipulation and the definition of basic classes. The subsequent parts address more complex subjects; you may not comprehend them all at first review. Specifically addresses the fundamental concepts of object-oriented programming: inheritance and polymorphism. In this chapter, we will primarily employ these concepts in a restricted manner, by establishing independent classes and augmenting existing classes instead of constructing complete class hierarchies from the ground up.

5.1 OBJECTS, INSTANCE METHODS, AND INSTANCE VARIABLES

Object-oriented programming (OOP) seeks to align programming with human cognitive processes and interactions with the world. In traditional programming paradigms, a programmer confronted with a problem must ascertain a computational task necessary for its resolution. Programming entails identifying a sequence of instructions that will achieve the desired job. At the core of object-oriented programming, rather than tasks, we encounter objects—entities that possess actions, retain information, and may interact with one another. Programming involves the creation of a collection of objects that effectively represent the topic being addressed. Software objects within the program can symbolize tangible or intangible items in the problem domain. This aims to render the program's design more intuitive, hence facilitating accuracy and comprehension.

To some extent, OOP is just a change in point of view. We can think of an object in standard programming terms as nothing more than a set of variables together with some subroutines for manipulating those variables. In fact, it is possible to use object-oriented techniques in any programming language. However, there is a big difference between a language that makes OOP possible and one that actively supports it. An object-oriented programming language such as Java includes a number of features that make it very different from a standard language. In order to make effective use of those features, you have to "orient" your thinking correctly.

As I have mentioned before, in the context of object-oriented programming, subroutines are often referred to as *methods*. Now that we are starting to use objects, I will be using the term "method" more often than "subroutine."

5.1.1 Objects, Classes, and Instances

Objects are closely related to classes. We have already been working with classes for several chapters, and we have seen that a class can contain variables and methods (that is, subroutines). If an object is also a collection of variables and methods, how do they differ from classes? And why does it require a different type of thinking to understand and use them effectively? In the one section where we worked with objects rather than classes, it didn't seem to make much difference: We just left the word "static" out of the subroutine definitions!

I have said that classes "describe" objects, or more exactly that the non-static portions of classes describe objects. But it's probably not very clear what this means. The more usual terminology is to say that objects *belong to* classes, but this might not be much clearer. (There is a real shortage of English words to properly distinguish all the concepts involved. An object certainly doesn't "belong" to a class in the same way that a member variable "belongs" to a class.) From the point of view of programming, it is more exact to say that classes are used to create objects. A class is a kind of factory—or blueprint—for constructing objects. The non-static parts of the class specify, or describe, what variables and methods the objects will contain. This is part of the explanation of how objects differ from classes: Objects are created and destroyed as the program runs, and there can be many objects with the same structure, if they are created using the same class.

Consider a simple class whose job is to group together a few static member variables. For example, the following class could be used to store information about the person who is using the program:

```
class UserData {
    static String name;
    static int age;
}
```

In a program that uses this class, there is only one copy of each of the variables UserData.name and UserData.age. When the class is loaded into the computer, there is a section of memory devoted to the class, and that section of memory includes space for the values of the variables name and age. We can picture the class in memory as looking like this:

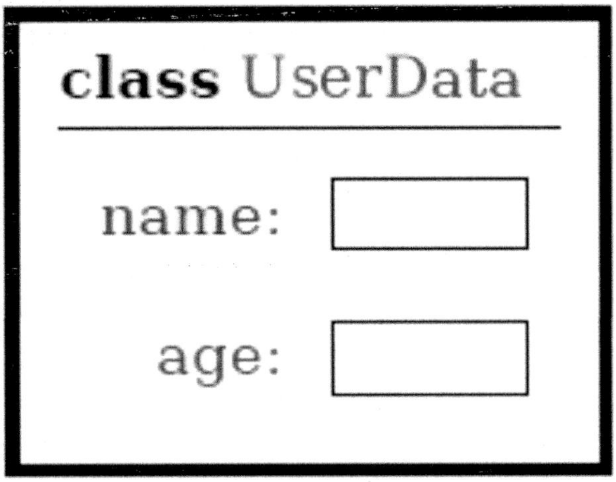

An important point is that the static member variables are part of the representation of the class in memory. Their full names, UserData.name and UserData.age, use the name of the class, since they are part of the class. When we use class *UserData* to represent the user of the program, there can only be one user, since we only have memory space to store data about one user. Note that the class, UserData, and the variables it contains exist as long as the program runs. (That is essentially what it means to be "static.") Now, consider a similar class that includes some non-static variables:

```
class PlayerData {
    static int playerCount;
    String name;
    int age;
}
```

I've also included a static variable in the *PlayerData* class. Here, the static variable playerCount is stored as part of the representation of the class in memory. Its full name is PlayerData.playerCount, and there is only one of it, which exists as long as the program runs. However, the other two variables in the class definition are non-static. There is no such variable as PlayerData.name or PlayerData.age, since non-static variables do not become part of the class itself. But the *PlayerData* class can be used to create objects. There can be many objects created using the class, and each one will have its own variables called name and age. This is what it means for the non-static parts of the class to be a template for objects: Every object gets its own copy of the non-static part of the class. We can visualize the situation in the computer's memory after several objects have been created like this:

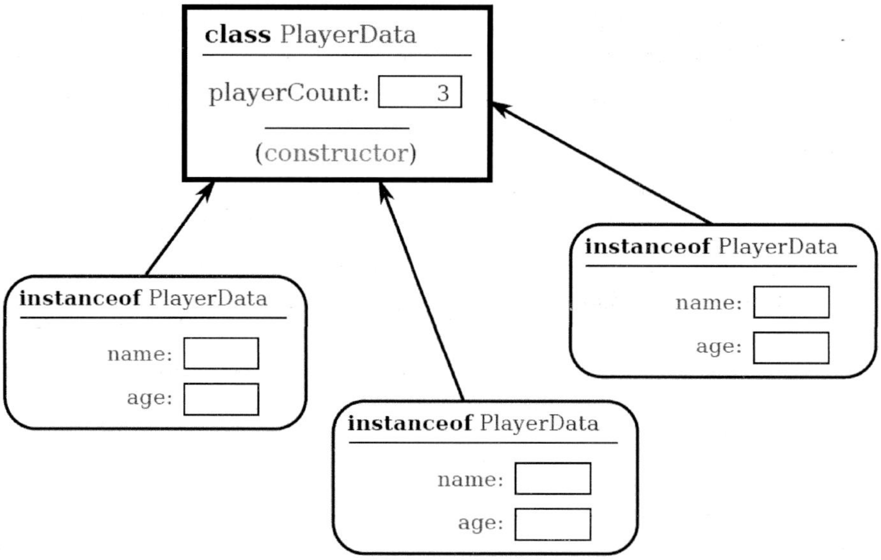

Note that the static variable playerCount is part of the class, and there is only one copy. On the other hand, every object contains a name and an age. An object that is created from a class is called an *instance* of that class, and as the picture shows, every object "knows" which class was used to create it. I've shown class *PlayerData* as containing something called a "constructor;" the constructor is a subroutine that creates objects.

Now there can be many "players," because we can make new objects to represent new players on demand. A program might use the *PlayerData* class to store information about multiple players in a game. Each player has a name and an age. When a player joins the game, a new PlayerData object can be created to represent that player. If a player leaves the game, the PlayerData object that represents that player can be destroyed. A system of objects in the program is being used to *dynamically* model what is happening in the game. You can't do this with static variables! "Dynamic" is the opposite of "static."

An object that is created using a class is said to be an *instance* of that class. We will sometimes say that the object *belongs* to the class. The variables that the object contains are called *instance variables*. The methods (that is, subroutines) that the object contains are called *instance methods*. For example, if the PlayerData class, as defined above, is used to create an object, then that object is an instance of the PlayerData class, and name and age are instance variables in the object.

My examples here don't include any methods, but methods work similarly to variables. Static methods are part of the class; non-static, or instance, methods become part of objects created from the class. It's not literally true that each object contains its own copy of the actual compiled code for an instance method. But logically an instance method is part of the object, and I will continue to say that the object "contains" the instance method.

Note that you should distinguish between the source code for the class, and the class itself (in memory). The source code determines both the class and the objects that are created from that class. The "static" definitions in the source code specify the things that are part of the class itself (in the computer's memory), whereas the non-static definitions in the source code specify things that will become part of every instance object that is created from the class. By the way, static member variables and static member subroutines in a class are sometimes called *class variables* and *class methods*, since they belong to the class itself, rather than to instances of that class.

As you can see, the static and the non-static portions of a class are very different things and serve very different purposes. Many classes contain only static members, or only non-static, and we will see only a few examples of classes that contain a mixture of the two.

5.1.2 Fundamentals of Objects

So far, I've been talking mostly in generalities, and I haven't given you much of an idea about what you have to put in a program if you want to work with objects. Let's look at a specific example to see how it works. Consider this extremely simplified version of a Student class, which could be used to store information about students taking a course:

```
public class Student {

    public String name;         // Student's name.

    public double test1, test2, test3;   // Grades on three tests.

    public double getAverage() {       // compute average test grade

            return (test1 + test2 + test3) / 3;

    }

}   // end of class Student
```

None of the members of this class are declared to be static, so the class exists only for creating objects. This class definition says that any object that is an instance of the *Student* class will include instance variables named name, test1, test2, and test3, and it will include an instance method named getAverage(). The names and test grades in different objects will generally have different values. When called for a particular student, the method getAverage() will compute an average using that student's test grades. Different students can have different averages. (Again, this is what it means to say that an instance method belongs to an individual object, not to the class.)

In Java, a class is a type, similar to the built-in types such as int and boolean. So, a class name can be used to specify the type of a variable in a declaration statement, or the type of a formal parameter, or the return type of a function. For example, a program could define a variable named std of type Student with the statement

Student std;

However, declaring a variable does not create an object! This is an important point, which is related to this Very Important Fact:

In Java, no variable can ever hold an object.

A variable can only hold a reference to an object.

You should think of objects as floating around independently in the computer's memory. In fact, there is a special portion of memory called the *heap* where objects live. Instead of holding an object itself, a variable holds the information necessary to find the object in memory. This information is called a *reference* or *pointer* to the object. In effect, a reference to an object is the address of the memory location where the object is stored. When you use a variable of object type, the computer uses the reference in the variable to find the actual object.

In a program, objects are created using an operator called new, which creates an object and returns a reference to that object. (In fact, the new operator calls a special subroutine called a "constructor" in the class.) For example, assuming that std is a variable of type Student, declared as above, the assignment statement

std = new Student();

would create a new object which is an instance of the class Student, and it would store a reference to that object in the variable std. The value of the variable is a reference, or pointer, to the object. The object itself is somewhere in the heap. It is not quite true, then, to say that the object is the "value of the variable std" (though sometimes it is hard to avoid using this terminology). It is certainly not at all true to say that the object is "stored in the variable std." The proper terminology is that "the variable std *refers to* or *points to* the object," and I will try to stick to that terminology as much as possible. If I ever say something like "std is an object," you should read it as meaning "std is a variable that refers to an object."

So, suppose that the variable std refers to an object that is an instance of class Student. That object contains instance variables name, test1, test2, and test3. These instance variables can be referred to as std.name, std.test1, std.test2, and std.test3. This follows the usual naming convention that when B is part of A, then the full name of B is A.B. For example, a program might include the lines

System.out.println("Hello, " + std.name + ". Your test grades are:");

System.out.println(std.test1);

System.out.println(std.test2);

System.out.println(std.test3);

This would output the name and test grades from the object to which std refers. Similarly, std can be used to call the getAverage() instance method in the object by saying std.getAverage(). To print out the student's average, you could say:

System.out.println("Your average is " + std.getAverage());

More generally, you could use std.name any place where a variable of type *String* is legal. You can use it in expressions. You can assign a value to it. You can even use it to call subroutines from the *String* class. For example, std.name.length() is the number of characters in the student's name.

It is possible for a variable like std, whose type is given by a class, to refer to no object at all. We say in this case that std holds a *null pointer* or *null reference*. The null pointer is written in Java as: null. You can store a null reference in the variable std by saying

std = null;

null is an actual value that is stored in the variable, not a pointer to something else. It is not correct to say that the variable "points to null"; in fact, the variable is null. For example, you can test whether the value of std is null by testing

if (std == null) . . .

If the value of a variable is null, then it is, of course, illegal to refer to instance variables or instance methods through that variable—since there is no object, and hence no instance variables to refer to! For example, if the value of the variable std is null, then it would be illegal to refer to std.test1. If your program attempts to use a null pointer illegally in this way, the result is an error called a *null pointer exception* . When this happens while the program is running, an exception of type *NullPointerException* is thrown.

Let's look at a sequence of statements that work with objects:

```
Student std, std1,      // Declare four variables of
std2, std3;  //         type Student.
std = new Student(); // Create a new object belonging
                     //      to the class Student, and
                     //      store a reference to that
                     //      object in the variable std.
std1 = new Student();// Create a second Student object
                     //      and store a reference to
                     //      it in the variable std1.
```

std2 = std1; // Copy the reference value in std1
// into the variable std2.

std3 = null; // Store a null reference in the
// variable std3.

std.name = "John Smith"; // Set values of some instance variables.

std1.name = "Mary Jones";

// (Other instance variables have default

// initial values of zero.)

After the computer executes these statements, the situation in the computer's memory looks like this:

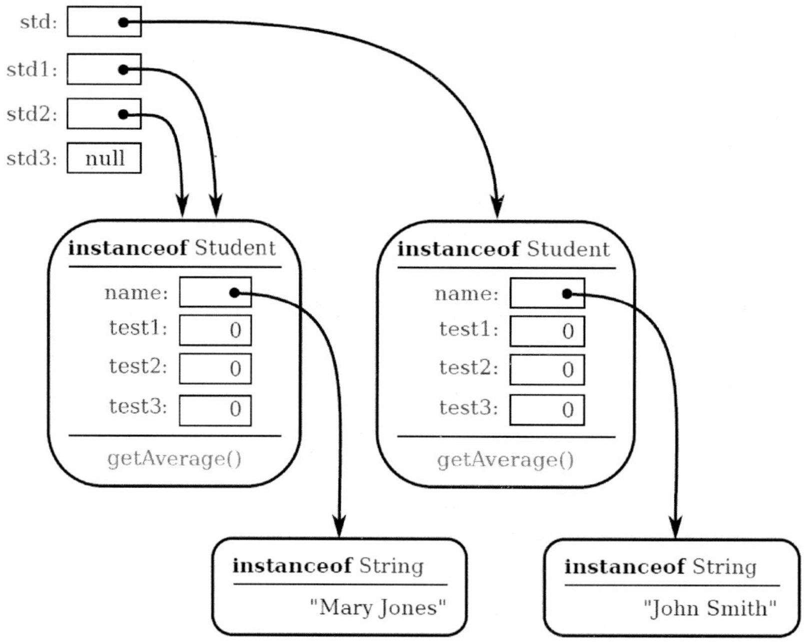

In this picture, when a variable contains a reference to an object, the value of that variable is shown as an arrow pointing to the object. Note, by the way, that the *Strings* are objects! The variable std3, with a value of null, doesn't point anywhere. The arrows from std1 and std2 both point to the same object. This illustrates a Very Important Point:

> *When one object variable is assigned to another, only a reference is copied. The object referred to is not copied.*

When the assignment "std2 = std1;" was executed, no new object was created. Instead, std2 was set to refer to the very same object that std1 refers to. This is to be expected, since the assignment statement just copies the value that is stored in std1 into std2, and that value is a pointer, not an object. But this has some consequences that might be surprising. For example, std1.name and std2.name are two different names for the same variable, namely the instance variable in the object that both std1 and std2 refer to. After the string "Mary Jones" is assigned to the variable std1.name, it is also true that the value of std2.name is "Mary Jones". There is a potential for a lot of confusion here, but you can help protect yourself from it if you keep telling yourself, "The object is not in the variable. The variable just holds a pointer to the object."

You can test objects for equality and inequality using the operators == and !=, but here again, the semantics are different from what you are used to. When you make a test "if (std1 == std2)", you are testing whether the values stored in std1 and std2 are the same. But the values that you are comparing are references to objects; they are not objects. So, you are testing whether std1 and std2 refer to the same object. This is fine, if it's what you want to do. But sometimes, what you want to check is whether the instance variables in the objects have the same values. To do that, you would need to ask whether "std1.test1 == std2.test1 && std1.test2 == std2.test2 && std1.test3 == std2.test3 && std1.name.equals(std2.name)".

I've remarked previously that *Strings* are objects, and I've shown the strings "Mary Jones" and "John Smith" as objects in the above illustration. (Strings are special objects, treated by Java in a special way, and I haven't attempted to show the actual internal structure of the *String* objects.) Since strings are objects, a variable of type *String* can only hold a reference to a string, not the string itself. This explains why using the == operator to test strings for equality is not a good idea. Suppose that greeting is a variable of type *String*, and that it refers to the string "Hello". Then would the test greeting == "Hello" be true? Well, maybe, maybe not. The variable greeting and the *String* literal "Hello" each refer to a string that contains the characters H-e-l-l-o. But the strings could still be different objects, that just happen to contain the same characters; in that case, greeting == "Hello" would be false. The function greeting.equals("Hello") tests whether greeting and "Hello" contain the same characters, which is almost certainly the question you want to ask. The expression greeting == "Hello" tests whether greeting and "Hello" contain the same characters stored in the same memory location. (Of course, a *String* variable such as greeting can also contain the special value null, and it would make sense to use the == operator to test whether "greeting == null".)

The fact that variables hold references to objects, not objects themselves, has a couple of other consequences that you should be aware of. They follow logically, if you just keep in mind the basic fact that the object is not stored in the variable. The object is somewhere else; the variable points to it.

Suppose that a variable that refers to an object is declared to be final. This means that the value stored in the variable can never be changed, once the variable has been initialized. The value stored in the variable is a reference to the object. So the variable will continue to refer to the same object as long as the variable exists. However, this does not prevent the data in the object from changing. The variable is final, not the object. It's perfectly legal to say

```
final Student stu = new Student();
stu.name = "John Doe";        // Change data in the object;
                              // The value stored in stu is not changed!
                              // It still refers to the same object.
```

Next, suppose that obj is a variable that refers to an object. Let's consider what happens when obj is passed as an actual parameter to a subroutine. The value of obj is assigned to a formal parameter in the subroutine, and the subroutine is executed. The subroutine has no power to change the value stored in the variable, obj. It only has a copy of that value. However, the value is a reference to an object. Since the subroutine has a reference to the object, it can change the data stored in the object. After the subroutine ends, obj still points to the same object, but the data stored in the object might have changed. Suppose x is a variable of type int and stu is a variable of type Student. Compare:

```
void dontChange(int z) {      void change(Student s)
    z = 42;                              s.name = "Fred";
}                                        }
The lines:    The lines:
x = 17;       stu.name = "Jane";
dontChange(x);        change(stu);
System.out.println(x);        System.out.println(stu.name);

output the value 17.  output the value "Fred".
The value of x is not  The value of stu is not
changed by the subroutine,    changed, but stu.name is changed. which is equivalent to
This is equivalent to
z = x;        s = stu;
z = 42;       s.name = "Fred";
```

5.1.3 Getters and Setters

When writing new classes, it's a good idea to pay attention to the issue of access control. Recall that making a member of a class public makes it accessible from anywhere, including from other classes. On the other hand, a private member can only be used in the class where it is defined.

In the opinion of many programmers, almost all member variables should be declared private. This gives you complete control over what can be done with the variable. Even if the variable itself is private, you can allow other classes to find out what its value is by providing a public *accessor method* that returns the value of the variable. For example, if your class contains a private member variable, title, of type *String*, you can provide a method

```
public String getTitle() {
    return title;
}
```

that returns the value of title. By convention, the name of an accessor method for a variable is obtained by capitalizing the name of variable and adding "get" in front of the name. So, for the variable title, we get an accessor method named "get" + "Title", or getTitle(). Because of this naming convention, accessor methods are more often referred to as *getter methods*. A getter method provides "read access" to a variable. (Sometimes for boolean variables, "is" is used in place of "get". For example, a getter for a boolean member variable named done might be called isDone().)

You might also want to allow "write access" to a private variable. That is, you might want to make it possible for other classes to specify a new value for the variable. This is done with a *setter method* . (If you don't like simple, Anglo-Saxon words, you can use the fancier term *mutator method* .) The name of a setter method should consist of "set" followed by a capitalized copy of the variable's name, and it should have a parameter with the same type as the variable. A setter method for the variable title could be written

```
public void setTitle( String newTitle ) {
    title = newTitle;
}
```

It is actually very common to provide both a getter and a setter method for a private member variable. Since this allows other classes both to see and to change the value of the variable, you might wonder why not just make the variable public? The reason is that getters and setters are not restricted to simply reading and writing the variable's value. In fact, they can take any action at all. For example, a getter method might keep track of the number of times that the variable has been accessed:

```
public String getTitle() {
    titleAccessCount++;        // Increment member variable titleAccessCount.
    return title;
}
```

and a setter method might check that the value that is being assigned to the variable is legal:

```
public void setTitle( String newTitle ) {
    if ( newTitle == null )     // Don't allow null strings as titles!
            title = "(Untitled)";       // Use an appropriate default value
    instead. else
            title = newTitle;
    }
```

Even if you can't think of any extra chores to do in a getter or setter method, you might change your mind in the future when you redesign and improve your class. If you've used a getter and setter from the beginning, you can make the modification to your class without affecting any of the classes that use your class. The private member variable is not part of the public interface of your class; only the public getter and setter methods are, and you are free to change their implementations without changing the public interface of your class. If you haven't used get and set from the beginning, you'll have to contact everyone who uses your class and tell them, "Sorry people, you'll have to track down every use that you've made of this variable and change your code to use my new get and set methods instead."

A couple of final notes: Some advanced aspects of Java rely on the naming convention for getter and setter methods, so it's a good idea to follow the convention rigorously. And though I've been talking about using getter and setter methods for a variable, you can define get and set methods even if there is no variable. A getter and/or setter method defines a *property* of the class, that might or might not correspond to a variable. For example, if a class includes a public void instance method with signature setValue(double), then the class has a "property" named value of type double, and it has this property whether or not the class has a member variable named value.

5.1.4 Arrays and Objects

Arrays are objects. Like *Strings* they are special objects, with their own unique syntax. An array type such as int[ ] or String[ ] is actually a class, and arrays are created using a special version of the new operator. As in the case for other object variables, an array variable can never hold an actual array—only a reference to an array object. The array object itself exists in the heap. It is possible for an array variable to hold the value null, which means there is no actual array.

For example, suppose that list is a variable of type int[ ]. If the value of list is null, then any attempt to access list.length or an array element list[i] would be an error and would cause an exception of type *NullPointerException*. If newlist is another variable of type int[ ], then the assignment statement

newlist = list;

only copies the reference value in list into newlist. If list is null, the result is that newlist will also be null. If list points to an array, the assignment statement does not make a copy of the array. It just sets newlist to refer to the same array as list. For example, the output of the following code segment

list = new int[3];

list[1]

= 17;

newlist = list; // newlist points to the same array as

list! newlist[1] = 42;

System.out.println(list[1]);

would be 42, not 17, since list[1] and newlist[1] are just different names for the same element in the array. All this is very natural, once you understand that arrays are objects and array variables hold pointers to arrays.

This fact also comes into play when an array is passed as a parameter to a subroutine. The value that is copied into the subroutine is a pointer to the array. The array is not copied. Since the subroutine has a reference to the original array, any changes that it makes to elements of the array are being made to the original and will persist after the subroutine returns.

Arrays are objects. They can also hold objects. The base type of an array can be a class. We have already seen this when we used arrays of type String[ ], but any class can be used as the base type. For example, suppose *Student* is the class defined earlier in this section. Then we can have arrays of type Student[ ]. For an array of type Student[ ], each element of the array is a variable of type *Student*. To store information about 30 students, we could use an array:

Student[] classlist; // Declare a variable of type Student[].

classlist = new Student[30]; // The variable now points

to an array.

The array has 30 elements, classlist[0], classlist[1], . . . classlist[29]. When the array is created, it is filled with the default initial value, which for an object type is null. So, although we have 30 array elements of type *Student*, we don't yet have any actual *Student* objects! All we have is 30 nulls. If we want student objects, we have to create them:

```
Student[] classlist;
classlist = new
Student[30];
for ( int i = 0; i < 30; i++ ) {
    classlist[i] = new Student();
}
```

Once we have done this, each classlist[i] points to an object of type *Student*. If we want to talk about the name of student number 3, we can use classlist[3].name. The average for student number i can be computed by calling classlist[i].getAverage(). You can do anything with classlist[i] that you could do with any other variable of type *Student*.

5.2 CONSTRUCTORS AND OBJECT INITIALIZATION

Object types in Java are very different from the primitive types. Simply declaring a variable whose type is given as a class does not automatically create an object of that class. Objects must be explicitly *constructed* . For the computer, the process of constructing an object means, first, finding some unused memory in the heap that can be used to hold the object and, second, filling in the object's instance variables. As a programmer, you don't care where in memory the object is stored, but you will usually want to exercise some control over what initial values are stored in a new object's instance variables. In many cases, you will also want to do more complicated initialization or bookkeeping every time an object is created.

5.2.1 Initializing Instance Variables

An instance variable can be assigned an initial value in its declaration, just like any other variable. For example, consider a class named *PairOfDice*. An object of this class will represent a pair of dice. It will contain two instance variables to represent the numbers showing on the dice and an instance method for rolling the dice:

```
public class PairOfDice {
    public int die1 = 3;        // Number showing on the first die.
    public int die2 = 4;        //      Number showing on the second die.
    public void roll() {
```

```
            // Roll the dice by setting each of the dice to be
            // a random number between 1 and 6.
        die1 = (int)(Math.random()*6) + 1;
        die2 = (int)(Math.random()*6) + 1;
    }
} // end class PairOfDice
```

The instance variables die1 and die2 are initialized to the values 3 and 4 respectively. These initializations are executed whenever a *PairOfDice* object is constructed. It's important to understand when and how this happens. There can be many *PairOfDice* objects. Each time one is created, it gets its own instance variables, and the assignments "die1 = 3" and "die2 = 4" are executed to fill in the values of those variables. To make this clearer, consider a variation of the *PairOfDice* class:

```
public class PairOfDice {
    public int die1 = (int)(Math.random()*6) + 1;
    public int die2 = (int)(Math.random()*6) + 1;
    public void roll() {
            die1 = (int)(Math.random()*6) + 1;
            die2 = (int)(Math.random()*6) + 1;
    }
} // end class PairOfDice
```

Here, every time a new *PairOfDice* is created, the dice are initialized to random values, as if a new pair of dice were being thrown onto the gaming table. Since the initialization is executed for each new object, a set of random initial values will be computed for each new pair of dice. Different pairs of dice can have different initial values. For initialization of static member variables, of course, the situation is quite different. There is only one copy of a static variable, and initialization of that variable is executed just once, when the class is first loaded.

If you don't provide any initial value for an instance variable, a default initial value is provided automatically. Instance variables of numerical type (int, double, etc.) are automatically initialized to zero if you provide no other values; boolean variables are initialized to false; and char variables, to the Unicode character with code number zero. An instance variable can also be a variable of object type. For such variables, the default initial value is null. (In particular, since Strings are objects, the default initial value for *String* variables is null.)

5.2.2 Constructors

Objects are created with the operator, new. For example, a program that wants to use a *PairOfDice* object could say:

```
PairOfDice dice;        // Declare a variable of type PairOfDice.
dice = new PairOfDice();        // Construct a new object and store a
                                //        reference to it in the variable.
```

In this example, "new PairOfDice()" is an expression that allocates memory for the object, initializes the object's instance variables, and then returns a reference to the object. This reference is the value of the expression, and that value is stored by the assignment statement in the variable, dice. So, after the assignment statement is executed, dice refers to the newly created object. Part of this expression, "PairOfDice()", looks like a subroutine call, and that is no accident. It is, in fact, a call to a special type of subroutine called a *constructor* . This might puzzle you, since there is no such subroutine in the class definition. However, every class has at least one constructor. If the programmer doesn't write a constructor definition in a class, then the system will provide a *default constructor* for that class. This default constructor does nothing beyond the basics: allocate memory and initialize instance variables. If you want more than that to happen when an object is created, you can include one or more constructors in the class definition.

The definition of a constructor looks much like the definition of any other subroutine, with three exceptions. A constructor does not have any return type (not even void). The name of the constructor must be the same as the name of the class in which it is defined. And the only modifiers that can be used on a constructor definition are the access modifiers public, private, and protected. (In particular, a constructor can't be declared static.)

However, a constructor does have a subroutine body of the usual form, a block of statements. There are no restrictions on what statements can be used. And a constructor can have a list of formal parameters. In fact, the ability to include parameters is one of the main reasons for using constructors. The parameters can provide data to be used in the construction of the object. For example, a constructor for the *PairOfDice* class could provide the values that are initially showing on the dice. Here is what the class would look like in that case:

```
public class PairOfDice {
    public int die1;  // Number showing on the first die.
    public int die2;  // Number showing on the second die.
    public PairOfDice(int val1, int val2) {
                // Constructor.  Creates a pair of dice that
```

```
                // are initially showing the values val1 and val2.
        die1 = val1;        // Assign specified values
        die2 = val2;        //         to the instance variables.
    }
    public void roll() {
                // Roll the dice by setting each of the dice to be
                // a random number between 1 and 6.
        die1 = (int)(Math.random()*6) + 1;
        die2 = (int)(Math.random()*6) + 1;
    }
} // end class PairOfDice
```

The constructor is declared as "public PairOfDice(int val1, int val2) ...", with no return type and with the same name as the name of the class. This is how the Java compiler recognizes a constructor. The constructor has two parameters, and values for these parameters must be provided when the constructor is called. For example, the expression "new PairOfDice(3,4)" would create a *PairOfDice* object in which the values of the instance variables die1 and die2 are initially 3 and 4. Of course, in a program, the value returned by the constructor should be used in some way, as in

```
PairOfDice dice;        // Declare a variable of type PairOfDice.
dice = new PairOfDice(1,1); // Let dice refer to a new PairOfDice
                            //         object that initially shows 1, 1.
```

Now that we've added a constructor to the *PairOfDice* class, we can no longer create an object by saying "new PairOfDice()"! The system provides a default constructor for a class only if the class definition does not already include a constructor. In this version of *PairOfDice*, there is only one constructor in the class, and it requires two actual parameters. However, this is not a big problem, since we can add a second constructor to the class, one that has no parameters. In fact, you can have as many different constructors as you want, as long as their signatures are different, that is, as long as they have different numbers or types of formal parameters. In the *PairOfDice* class, we might have a constructor with no parameters which produces a pair of dice showing random numbers:

```
public class PairOfDice {
    public int die1;  // Number showing on the first die.
    public int die2;  // Number showing on the second die.
```

```
    public PairOfDice() {
                    // Constructor.  Rolls the dice, so that they initially
                    // show some random values.
            roll();  // Call the roll() method to roll the dice.
    }
    public PairOfDice(int val1, int val2) {
                    // Constructor.  Creates a pair of dice that
                    // are initially showing the values val1 and val2.
            die1 = val1;      // Assign specified values
            die2 = val2;      //        to the instance variables.
    }
    public void roll() {
                        // Roll the dice by setting each of the dice to be
                        // a random number between 1 and 6.
            die1 = (int)(Math.random()*6) + 1;
            die2 = (int)(Math.random()*6) + 1;
    }
} // end class PairOfDice
```

Now we have the option of constructing a *PairOfDice* object either with "new PairOfDice()" or with "new PairOfDice(x,y)", where x and y are int-valued expressions.

This class, once it is written, can be used in any program that needs to work with one or more pairs of dice. None of those programs will ever have to use the obscure incantation "(int)(Math.random()*6)+1", because it's done inside the *PairOfDice* class. And the programmer, having once gotten the dice-rolling thing straight will never have to worry about it again. Here, for example, is a main program that uses the *PairOfDice* class to count how many times two pairs of dice are rolled before the two pairs come up showing the same value. This illustrates once again that you can create several instances of the same class:

```
public class RollTwoPairs {
    public static void main(String[] args) {
            PairOfDice firstDice;      // Refers to the first pair of dice.
            firstDice = new PairOfDice();
```

```
        PairOfDice secondDice; // Refers to the second pair of dice.
        secondDice = new PairOfDice();
        int countRolls;  // Counts how many times the two pairs of
                         //        dice have been rolled.
        int total1;      // Total showing on first pair of dice.
        int total2;      // Total showing on second pair of dice.
        countRolls = 0;
        do {     // Roll the two pairs of dice until totals are the same.
            firstDice.roll();  // Roll the first pair of dice.
            total1 = firstDice.die1 + firstDice.die2;      // Get total.
            System.out.println("First pair comes up   " + total1);
            secondDice.roll();          // Roll the second pair of dice.
            total2 = secondDice.die1 + secondDice.die2;          // Get total.
            System.out.println("Second pair comes up " + total2);
            countRolls++;      // Count this roll.
            System.out.println();      // Blank line.
        } while (total1 != total2);
        System.out.println("It took " + countRolls
                + " rolls until the totals were the same.");
    } // end main()
} // end class RollTwoPairs
```

Constructors are subroutines, but they are subroutines of a special type. They are certainly not instance methods, since they don't belong to objects. Since they are responsible for creating objects, they exist before any objects have been created. They are more like static member subroutines, but they are not and cannot be declared to be static. In fact, according to the Java language specification, they are technically not members of the class at all! In particular, constructors are not referred to as "methods."

Unlike other subroutines, a constructor can only be called using the new operator, in an expression that has the form

new (class-name) ((parameter-list))

where the (*parameter-list*) is possibly empty. I call this an expression because it computes and returns a value, namely a reference to the object that is constructed. Most often, you will store the returned reference in a variable, but it is also legal to use a constructor call in other ways, for example as a parameter in a subroutine call or as part of a more complex expression. Of course, if you don't save the reference in a variable, you won't have any way of referring to the object that was just created.

A constructor call is more complicated than an ordinary subroutine or function call. It is helpful to understand the exact steps that the computer goes through to execute a constructor call:

1. First, the computer gets a block of unused memory in the heap, large enough to hold an object of the specified type.
2. It initializes the instance variables of the object. If the declaration of an instance variable specifies an initial value, then that value is computed and stored in the instance variable. Otherwise, the default initial value is used.
3. The actual parameters in the constructor, if any, are evaluated, and the values are assigned to the formal parameters of the constructor.
4. The statements in the body of the constructor, if any, are executed.
5. A reference to the object is returned as the value of the constructor call.

The end result of this is that you have a reference to a newly constructed object.

For another example, let's rewrite the *Student* class that was used in Section 1. I'll add a constructor, and I'll also take the opportunity to make the instance variable, name, private.

```
public class Student {

    private String name;       // Student's name.

    public double test1, test2, test3;  // Grades on three tests.

    public Student(String theName) {

                    // Constructor for Student objects;

                    // provides a name for the Student.

                    // The name can't be null.

            if ( theName == null )

                    throw new IllegalArgumentException("name can't be null");

            name = theName;

    }

    public String getName() {

                    // Getter method for reading the value of the private

                    // instance variable, name. return name;
```

```
    }
    public double getAverage() {
                    // Compute average test grade.
                    return (test1 + test2 + test3) / 3;
          }
    }         // end of class Student
```

An object of type *Student* contains information about some particular student. The constructor in this class has a parameter of type *String*, which specifies the name of that student. Objects of type *Student* can be created with statements such as:

```
std = new Student("John Smith");
std1 = new Student("Mary Jones");
```

In the original version of this class, the value of name had to be assigned by a program after it created the object of type *Student*. There was no guarantee that the programmer would always remember to set the name properly. In the new version of the class, there is no way to create a *Student* object except by calling the constructor, and that constructor automatically sets the name. Furthermore, the constructor makes it impossible to have a student object whose name is null. The programmer's life is made easier, and whole hordes of frustrating bugs are squashed before they even have a chance to be born.

Another type of guarantee is provided by the private modifier. Since the instance variable, name, is private, there is no way for any part of the program outside the *Student* class to get at the name directly. The program sets the value of name, indirectly, when it calls the constructor. I've provided a getter function, getName(), that can be used from outside the class to find out the name of the student. But I haven't provided any setter method or other way to change the name. Once a student object is created, it keeps the same name as long as it exists.

Note that it would be legal, and good style, to declare the variable name to be "final" in this class. An instance variable can be final provided it is either assigned a value in its declaration or is assigned a value in every constructor in the class. It is illegal to assign a value to a final instance variable, except inside a constructor.

Let's take this example a little farther to illustrate one more aspect of classes: What happens when you mix static and non-static in the same class? In that case, it's legal for an instance method in the class to use static member variables or call static member subroutines. An object knows what class it belongs to, and it can refer to static members of that class. But there is only one copy of the static member, in the class itself. Effectively, all the objects share one copy of the static member.

As an example, consider a version of the *Student* class to which I've added an ID for each student and a static member called nextUniqueID. Although there is an ID variable in each student object, there is only one nextUniqueID variable.

```
public class Student {
    private String name;     // Student's name.
    public double test1, test2, test3;   // Grades on three tests.
    private int ID;   // Unique ID number for this student.
    private static int nextUniqueID = 0;
                    // keep track of next available unique ID number
    Student(String theName) {
                    // Constructor for Student objects; provides a name for the Student,
                    // and assigns the student a unique ID number.
        name = theName;
        nextUniqueID++;
        ID = nextUniqueID;
    }
    public String getName() {
                    // Getter method for reading the value of the private
                    // instance variable, name.
        return name;
    }
    public int getID() {
                    // Getter method for reading the value of ID.
        return ID;
    }
    public double getAverage() {
                    // Compute average test grade.
        return (test1 + test2 + test3) / 3;
    }
} // end of class Student
```

Since nextUniqueID is a static variable, the initialization "nextUniqueID = 0" is done only once, when the class is first loaded. Whenever a *Student* object is constructed and the constructor says "nextUniqueID++;", it's always the same static member variable that is being incremented. When the very first *Student* object is created, nextUniqueID becomes 1. When the second object is created, nextUniqueID becomes 2. After the third object, it becomes 3. And so on. The constructor stores the new value of nextUniqueID in the ID variable of the object that is being created. Of course, ID is an instance variable, so every object has its own individual ID variable. The class is constructed so that each student will automatically get a different value for its ID variable. Furthermore, the ID variable is private, so there is no way for this variable to be tampered with after the object has been created. You are guaranteed, just by the way the class is designed, that every student object will have its own permanent, unique identification number. Which is kind of cool if you think about it.

5.2.3 Garbage Collection

So far, this section has been about creating objects. What about destroying them? In Java, the destruction of objects takes place automatically.

An object exists in the heap, and it can be accessed only through variables that hold references to the object. What should be done with an object if there are no variables that refer to it? Such things can happen. Consider the following two statements (though in reality, you'd never do anything like this in consecutive statements!):

Student std = new Student("John Smith");

std = null;

In the first line, a reference to a newly created *Student* object is stored in the variable std. But in the next line, the value of std is changed, and the reference to the *Student* object is gone. In fact, there are now no references whatsoever to that object, in any variable. So there is no way for the program ever to use the object again! It might as well not exist. In fact, the memory occupied by the object should be reclaimed to be used for another purpose.

Java uses a procedure called *garbage collection* to reclaim memory occupied by objects that are no longer accessible to a program. It is the responsibility of the system, not the programmer, to keep track of which objects are "garbage." In the above example, it was very easy to see that the *Student* object had become garbage. Usually, it's much harder. If an object has been used for a while, there might be several references to the object stored in several variables. The object doesn't become garbage until all those references have been dropped.

In some other programming languages, it's the programmer's responsibility to delete the garbage. Unfortunately, keeping track of memory usage is very error-prone, and many serious program bugs are caused by such errors. A programmer might accidently delete an object even though there are still references to that object. This is called a *dangling pointer error* , and it leads to problems when the program tries to access an object that is no longer there. Another type of error is a *memory leak* , where a programmer neglects to delete objects that are no longer in use. This can lead to filling memory with objects that are completely inaccessible, and the program might run out of memory even though, in fact, large amounts of memory are being wasted.

Because Java uses garbage collection, such errors are simply impossible. Garbage collection is an old idea and has been used in some programming languages since the 1960s. You might wonder why all languages don't use garbage collection. In the past, it was considered too slow and wasteful. However, research into garbage collection techniques combined with the incredible speed of modern computers have combined to make garbage collection feasible. Programmers should rejoice.

5.3 PROGRAMMING WITH OBJECTS

There are several ways in which object-oriented concepts can be applied to the process of designing and writing programs. The broadest of these is *object-oriented analysis and design* which applies an object-oriented methodology to the earliest stages of program development, during which the overall design of a program is created. Here, the idea is to identify things in the problem domain that can be modeled as objects. On another level, object-oriented programming encourages programmers to produce *generalized software components* that can be used in a wide variety of programming projects.

Of course, for the most part, you will experience "generalized software components" by using the standard classes that come along with Java. We begin this section by looking at some built-in classes that are used for creating objects. At the end of the section, we will get back to generalities.

5.3.1 Some Built-in Classes

Although the focus of object-oriented programming is generally on the design and implementa- tion of new classes, it's important not to forget that the designers of Java have already provided a large number of reusable classes. Some of these classes are meant to be extended to produce new classes, while others can be used directly to create useful objects. A true mastery of Java requires familiarity with a large number of built-in classes—something that takes a lot of time and experience to develop. Let's take a moment to look at a few built-in classes that you might find useful.

A string can be built up from smaller pieces using the + operator, but this is not always efficient. If str is a *String* and ch is a character, then executing the command "str = str + ch;" involves creating a whole new string that is a copy of str, with the value of ch appended onto the end. Copying the string takes some time. Building up a long string letter by letter would require a surprising amount of processing. The class *StringBuilder* makes it possible to be efficient about building up a long string from a number of smaller pieces. To do this, you must make an object belonging to the *StringBuilder* class. For example:

StringBuilder builder = new StringBuilder();

(This statement both declares the variable builder and initializes it to refer to a newly created *StringBuilder* object. Combining declaration with initialization was covered and works for objects just as it does for primitive types.)

Like a *String*, a *StringBuilder* contains a sequence of characters. However, it is possible to add new characters onto the end of a StringBuilder without continually making copies of the data that it already contains. If x is a value of any type and builder is the variable defined above, then the command builder.append(x) will add x, converted into a string representation, onto the end of the data that was already in the builder. This can be done more efficiently than copying the data every time something is appended. A long string can be built up in a *StringBuilder* using a sequence of append() commands. When the string is complete, the function builder.toString() will return a copy of the string in the builder as an ordinary value of type *String*. The *StringBuilder* class is in the standard package java.lang, so you can use its simple name without importing it.

A number of useful classes are collected in the package java.util. For example, this package contains classes for working with collections of objects. We will study such collection classes extensively in Chapter 10. And we have already encountered java.util.Scanner. Another class in this package, java.util.Date, is used to represent times. When a Date object is constructed without parameters, the result represents the current date and time, so an easy way to display this information is:

System.out.println(new Date());

Of course, since it is in the package java.util, in order to use the Date class in your program, you must make it available by importing it with one of the statements "import java.util.Date;" or "import java.util.*;" at the beginning of your program.

I will also mention the class java.util.Random. An object belonging to this class is a *source* of random numbers (or, more precisely pseudorandom numbers). The standard function Math.random() uses one of these objects behind the scenes to generate its random numbers. An object of type Random can generate random integers, as well as random real numbers. If randGen is created with the command:

Random randGen = new Random();

and if N is a positive integer, then randGen.nextInt(N) generates a random integer in the range from 0 to N-1. For example, this makes it a little easier to roll a pair of dice. Instead of saying "die1 = (int)(6*Math.random())+1;", one can say "die1 = randGen.nextInt(6)+1;". (Since you also have to import the class java.util.Random and create the Random object, you might not agree that it is actually easier.) An object of type Random can also be used to generate so-called Gaussian distributed random real numbers.

Some of Java's standard classes are used in GUI programming. You will encounter many of them. Here, I will mention only the class *Color*, from the package javafx.scene.paint, so that I can use it in the next example. A *Color* object represents a color that can be used for drawing. You encountered color constants such as Color.RED. These constants are final static member variables in the *Color* class, and their values are objects of type *Color*. It is also possible to create new color objects. Class *Color* has a constructor new Color(r,g,b,a), which takes four double parameters to specify the red, green, and blue components of the color, plus an "alpha" component that says how transparent the color is. The parameters must be in the range 0.0 to 1.0. For example, a value of 0.0 for *r* means that the color contains no red, while a value of 1.0 means that the color contains the maximum possible amount of red. When you draw with a partially transparent color, the background shows through the color to some extent. A larger value of the fourth parameter gives a color that is less transparent and more opaque.

A *Color* object has only a few instance methods that you are likely to use. Mainly, there are functions like getRed() to get the individual color components of the color. There are no "setter" methods to change the color components. In fact, a *Color* is an *immutable* object, meaning that all of its instance variables are final and cannot be changed after the object is created. *Strings* are another example of immutable objects, and we will make some of our own later in this chapter.

The main point of all this, again, is that many problems have already been solved, and the solutions are available in Java's standard classes. If you are faced with a task that looks like it should be fairly common, it might be worth looking through a Java reference to see whether someone has already written a class that you can use.

5.3.2 The class "Object"

We have already seen that one of the major features of object-oriented programming is the ability to create subclasses of a class. The subclass inherits all the properties or behaviors of the class, but can modify and add to what it inherits. You'll learn how to create subclasses. What you don't know yet is that every class in Java (with just one exception) is a subclass of some other class. If you create a class and don't explicitly make it a subclass of some other class, then it automatically becomes a subclass of the special class named *Object*, in package java.lang. (*Object* is the one class that is not a subclass of any other class.)

Class *Object* defines several instance methods that are inherited by every other class. These methods can be used with any object whatsoever. I will mention two of them here. You will encounter more of them later in the book.

The method equals(obj) is defined in class *Object.* It takes one parameter, which can be any object. It is meant for testing whether two objects are "equal" but its definition gives obj1.equals(obj2) the same meaning as obj1 == obj2. That is, it tests whether obj1 and obj2 refer to the same object. The *String* class overrides this method to say that two *Strings* are equal if they contain the same sequence of characters, and it is common to similarly override equals() in a class to say that two objects belonging to that class are equal if they have the same contents. We see again that what it means for objects to be "equal" is not always clear. We will have more use for this method later.

The instance method toString() in class *Object* returns a value of type *String* that is supposed to be a string representation of the object. You've already used this method implicitly, any time you've printed out an object or concatenated an object onto a string. When you use an object in a context that requires a string, the object is automatically converted to type *String* by calling its toString() method.

The version of toString that is defined in *Object* just returns the name of the class that the object belongs to, concatenated with a code number called the *hash code* of the object; this is not very useful. When you create a class, you can write a new toString() method for it, which will replace the inherited version. For example, we might add the following method to any of the *PairOfDice* classes from the previous section:

```
/**
    Return a String representation of a pair of dice, where die1
    and die2 are instance variables containing the numbers that are
    showing on the two dice.
*/
    public String toString() {
        if (die1 == die2)
            return "double " + die1;
        else
            return die1 + " and " + die2;
    }
```

If dice refers to a *PairOfDice* object, then dice.toString() will return strings such as "3 and 6", "5 and 1", and "double 2", depending on the numbers showing on the dice. This method would be used automatically to convert dice to type *String* in a statement such as

```
System.out.println( "The dice came up " + dice );
```

so this statement might output, "The dice came up 5 and 1" or "The dice came up double 2". You'll see another example of a toString() method in the next section.

5.3.3 Writing and Using a Class

As an example of designing and using a new class, we will write an animation program, based on the same animation framework that was used. The animation shows a number of semi-transparent disks that grow in size as the animation plays. The disks have random colors and locations. When a disk gets too big, or sometimes just at random, the disk disappears and is replaced with a new disk at a random location. Here is a reduced-size screenshot from the program:

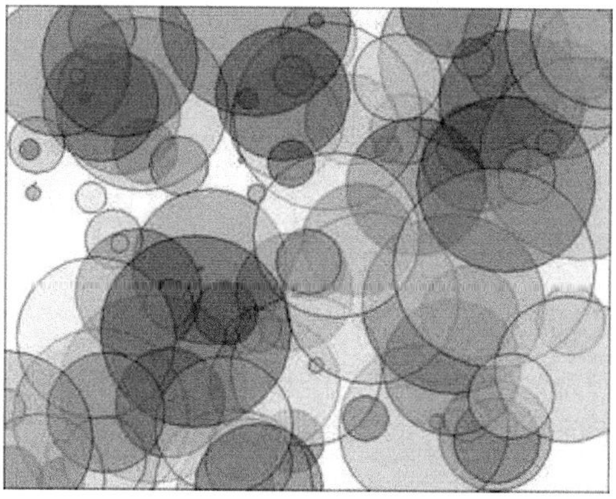

A disk in this program can be represented as an object. A disk has properties—color, location, and size—that can be instance variables in the object. As for instance methods, we need to think about what we might want to do with a disk. An obvious candidate is that we need to be able to draw it, so we can include an instance method draw(g), where g is a graphics context that will be used to do the drawing. The class can also include one or more constructors. A constructor initializes the object. It's not always clear what data should be provided as parameters to the constructor. In this case, as an example, the constructor's parameters specify the location and size for the circle, but the constructor makes up a color using random values for the red, green, and blue components. Here's the complete class:

```
import javafx.scene.paint.Color;

import javafx.scene.canvas.GraphicsContext;

/**

    A simple class that holds the size, color, and location of a colored disk,

    with a method for drawing the circle in a graphics context. The circle
```

```
    is drawn as a filled oval, with a black outline.
    */
public class CircleInfo {
    public int radius;          // The radius of the circle.
    public int x,y;    // The location of the center of the circle.
    public Color color;         // The color of the circle.
    /**
    Create a CircleInfo with a given location and radius and with a
    randomly selected, semi-transparent color.
    @param centerX          The x coordinate of the center.
    @param centerY          The y coordinate of the center.
    @param rad      The radius of the circle.
    */
public CircleInfo( int centerX, int centerY, int rad ) {
            x = centerX;
            y = centerY;
            radius = rad;
            double red = Math.random();
            double green = Math.random();
            double blue = Math.random();
            color = new Color( red,green,blue, 0.4 );
    }
    /**
    Draw the disk in graphics context g, with a black outline.
    */
public void draw( GraphicsContext g ) {
    g.setFill( color );
    g.fillOval( x - radius, y - radius, 2*radius, 2*radius );
    g.setStroke( Color.BLACK );
    g.strokeOval( x - radius, y - radius, 2*radius, 2*radius );
    }
}
```

It would probably be better style to write getters and setters for the instance variables, but to keep things simple, I made the variables public.

The main program for my animation is a class *GrowingCircleAnimation*. The program uses 100 disks, each one represented by an object of type *CircleInfo*. To make that manageable, the program uses an array of objects. The array variable is an instance variable in the class:

```
private CircleInfo[] circleData; // holds the data for all 100 circles
```

Note that it is not static. GUI programming generally uses objects rather than static variables and methods. Basically, this is because we can imagine having several *GrowingCircleAnimations* going on at the same time, each with its own array of disks. Each animation would be represented by an object, and each object will need to have its own circleData instance variable. If circleData were static, there would only be one array and all the animations would show exactly the same thing.

The array must be created and filled with data. The array is created using new CircleInfo[100], and then 100 objects of type *CircleInfo* are created to fill the array. The new objects are created with random locations and sizes. In the program, this is done before drawing the first frame of the animation. Here is the code, where width and height are the size of the drawing area:

```
circleData = new CircleInfo[100],        // create the array
for (int i = 0; i < circleData.length; i++) { // create the objects
    circleData[i] = new CircleInfo(
                    (int)(width*Math.random()),
                    (int)(height*Math.random()), (int
                    (100*Math.random()) );
        }
```

In each frame, the radius of the disk is increased and the disk is drawn using the code

```
circleData[i].radius++;
circleData[i].draw(g);
```

These statements look complicated, so let's unpack them. Now, circleData[i] is an element of the array circleData. That means that it is a variable of type *CircleInfo*. This variable refers to an object of type *CircleInfo*, which contains a public instance variable named radius. This means that circleData[i].radius is the full name for that variable. Since it is a variable of type int, we can use the ++ operator to increment its value. So the effect of circleData[i].radius++ is to increase the radius of the circle by one. The second line of code is similar, but in that statement, circleData[i].draw is an instance method in the *CircleInfo* object. The statement circleData[i].draw(g) calls that instance method with a parameter g that represents the graphics context that is being used for drawing.

The source code example GrowingCircleAnimation.java contains the full source code for the program, if you are interested. Since the program uses class *CircleInfo*, you will also need a copy of CircleInfo.java in order to compile and run the program.

5.3.4 Object-oriented Analysis and Design

Every programmer builds up a stock of techniques and expertise expressed as snippets of code that can be reused in new programs using the tried-and-true method of cut-and-paste: The old code is physically copied into the new program and then edited to customize it as necessary. The problem is that the editing is error-prone and time-consuming, and the whole enterprise is dependent on the programmer's ability to pull out that particular piece of code from last year's project that looks like it might be made to fit. (On the level of a corporation that wants to save money by not reinventing the wheel for each new project, just keeping track of all the old wheels becomes a major task.)

Well-designed classes are software components that can be reused without editing. A well- designed class is not carefully crafted to do a particular job in a particular program. Instead, it is crafted to model some particular type of object or a single coherent concept. Since objects and concepts can recur in many problems, a well-designed class is likely to be reusable without modification in a variety of projects.

Furthermore, in an object-oriented programming language, it is possible to make *subclasses* of an existing class. This makes classes even more reusable. If a class needs to be customized, a subclass can be created, and additions or modifications can be made in the subclass without making any changes to the original class. This can be done even if the programmer doesn't have access to the source code of the class and doesn't know any details of its internal, hidden implementation.

The *PairOfDice* class in the previous section is already an example of a generalized software component, although one that could certainly be improved. The class represents a single, coherent concept, "a pair of dice." The instance variables hold the data relevant to the state of the dice, that is, the number showing on each of the dice. The instance method represents the behavior of a pair of dice, that is, the ability to be rolled. This class would be reusable in many different programming projects.

On the other hand, the *Student* class from the previous section is not very reusable. It seems to be crafted to represent students in a particular course where the grade will be based on three tests. If there are more tests or quizzes or papers, it's useless. If there are two people in the class who have the same name, we are in trouble (one reason why numerical student ID's are often used). Admittedly, it's much more difficult to develop a general-purpose student class than a general-purpose pair-of-dice class. But this particular *Student* class is good only as an example in a programming textbook.

A large programming project goes through a number of stages, starting with *specification* of the problem to be solved, followed by *analysis* of the problem and *design* of a program to solve it. Then comes *coding* , in which the program's design is expressed in some actual programming language. This is followed by *testing* and *debugging* of the program. After that comes a long period of *maintenance*, which means fixing any new problems that are found in the program and modifying it to adapt it to changing requirements. Together, these stages form what is called the *software life cycle*. (In the real world, the ideal of consecutive stages is seldom if ever achieved. During the analysis stage, it might turn out that the specifications are incomplete or inconsistent. A problem found during testing requires at least a brief return to the coding stage. If the problem is serious enough, it might even require a new design. Maintenance usually involves redoing some of the work from previous stages)

Large, complex programming projects are only likely to succeed if a careful, systematic approach is adopted during all stages of the software life cycle. The systematic approach to programming, using accepted principles of good design, is called *software engineering* . The software engineer tries to efficiently construct programs that verifiably meet their specifications and that are easy to modify if necessary. There is a wide range of "methodologies" that can be applied to help in the systematic design of programs. (Most of these methodologies seem to involve drawing little boxes to represent program components, with labeled arrows to represent relationships among the boxes.)

We have been discussing object orientation in programming languages, which is relevant to the coding stage of program development. But there are also object-oriented methodologies for analysis and design. The question in this stage of the software life cycle is, How can one discover or invent the overall structure of a program? As an example of a rather simple object-oriented approach to analysis and design, consider this advice: Write down a description of the problem.

Underline all the nouns in that description. The nouns should be considered as candidates for becoming classes or objects in the program design. Similarly, underline all the verbs. These are candidates for methods. This is your starting point. Further analysis might uncover the need for more classes and methods, and it might reveal that subclassing can be used to take advantage of similarities among classes.

This is perhaps a bit simple-minded. (This is not a software engineering textbook.) But the idea is clear and the general approach can be effective: Analyze the problem to discover the concepts that are involved, and create classes to represent those concepts. The design should arise from the problem itself, and you should end up with a program whose structure reflects the structure of the problem in a natural way.

Chapter 6 BASIC GUI PROGRAMMING: AN INTRODUCTION

Contemporary computer users anticipate engaging with their devices through a graphical user interface (GUI), and Java is capable of developing advanced GUI applications.

GUI programs contrast with conventional "straight-through" programs discussed in the initial chapters of this book. A significant distinction is that GUI applications are event-driven. User activities, such as clicking a button or pushing a key, generate events to which the program must reply promptly.

Event-driven programming is founded on the competencies acquired in the initial five chapters of this work. It is essential to compose the methods that react to events. Within those methods, you are engaging in the programming-in-the-small techniques discussed in Chapters 2 and 3. Objects are ubiquitous in GUI programming. Events constitute objects. Colors and typography constitute objects. Graphical user interface components, including buttons and menus, are classified as objects. Events are managed using instance methods within objects. In Java, GUI programming is a form of object-oriented programming. The objective of this chapter is primarily to provide you with expertise in utilizing a large-scale object-oriented API.

This chapter serves as an introduction to JavaFX, encompassing the fundamental aspects of GUI programming with sufficient detail to develop engaging applications. Chapter 13 will further explore JavaFX, including further details and advanced approaches; nonetheless, a comprehensive examination of JavaFX would necessitate a full book.

Be aware that JavaFX is not included in the Java Development Kit distribution. Refer to Section 2.6 for instructions for acquiring JavaFX and compiling and executing programs that utilize it. This edition of the textbook addresses GUI programming utilizing the JavaFX toolkit. An alternate edition addresses the Swing GUI toolkit rather than JavaFX. Swing is a standard component of Java, hence necessitating no further downloads or configuration. The Swing edition is available at https://math.hws.edu/javanotes9-swing. The sole substantial variations between the two editions are seen in this chapter and Chapter 13.

6.1 A BASIC JAVAFX APPLICATION

The command-line programs that you have learned how to write would seem very alien to most computer users. The style of interaction where the user and the computer take turns typing strings of text seems like something out of the early days of computing, although it was only in the mid 1980s that home computers with graphical user interfaces started to become available. Today, most people interact with their computers exclusively through a GUI. A GUI program offers a much richer type of user interface, where the user uses a mouse and keyboard (or other input devices) to interact with GUI components such as windows, menus, buttons, check boxes, text input boxes, scroll bars, and so on.

This section introduces some of the basic ideas of programming with JavaFX by looking at a very simple GUI application. ("Application" is the preferred term for "program" in this context.) The application simply displays a window containing a message and three buttons. Here's what the window looks like when it first opens:

Clicking "Say Hello" will get the computer to tell you, "Hello World!". Clicking "Say Goodbye" will change the text of the message to "Goodbye". Clicking the "Quit" button will end the application, which can also be ended by clicking the window's close box.

6.1.1 JavaFX Applications

A JavaFX program (or "application") is represented by an object of type *Application*, which is defined in the package javafx.application. *Application* is an abstract class, which defines, among other things, one abstract instance method, named start(). To create a JavaFX program, you need to create a class that extends *Application* and provides a definition for the start() method.

The class that you write to create a JavaFX application also typically includes a main() method that simply "launches" the application:

```
public static void main(String[] args) {
    launch();
}
```

(The call to launch() can be replace by launch(args) for an application that uses command- line arguments (Subsection 4.3.6), but the parameter is optional for all of the examples in this book.) When this main() routine is executed, the launch() method creates a new thread, called the *JavaFX application thread* . Recall from Section 1.2 that a thread can execute a sequence of instructions that can be run in parallel with other threads. It is important that anything that affects the GUI be done on the JavaFX application thread. That will be pretty much automatic for the things that we do in this chapter, but it's something that will become important when we cover threads in Chapter 12 and write some GUI programs that use several threads. The launch() method then creates the object that represents the application; that object is an instance of the class that contains the call to the launch() method. The start() method of that object is then called on the JavaFX application thread, and it is the responsibility of that start() method to set up the GUI and open a window on the screen.

Here, then is our first JavaFX application. We will spend the rest of this section discussing

it:

```
import javafx.application.Application;
import javafx.scene.Scene;
import javafx.stage.Stage;
import javafx.application.Platform;
import javafx.scene.layout.BorderPane;
import javafx.scene.layout.HBox;
import javafx.geometry.Pos;
import javafx.scene.control.Label;
import javafx.scene.control.Button;
import javafx.scene.text.Font;
public class HelloWorldFX extends Application {
    public void start(Stage stage) {
            Label message = new Label("First FX Application!")
            message.setFont( new Font(40) );
            Button helloButton = new Button("Say Hello");
            helloButton.setOnAction( evt -> message.setText("Hello World!") );
            Button goodbyeButton = new Button("Say Goodbye");
            goodbyeButton.setOnAction( evt -> message.setText("Goodbye!!") );
            Button quitButton = new Button("Quit");
```

```
            quitButton.setOnAction( evt -> Platform.exit() );

            HBox buttonBar = new HBox( 20, helloButton, goodbyeButton, quitButton );
            buttonBar.setAlignment(Pos.CENTER);
            BorderPane root = new BorderPane();
            root.setCenter(message);
            root.setBottom(buttonBar);

            Scene scene = new Scene(root, 450, 200);
            stage.setScene(scene);
            stage.setTitle("JavaFX  Test");
            stage.show();
    } // end start();

    public static void main(String[] args) {
            launch(); // Run this Application.
    }
} // end class HelloWorldFX
```

The first thing that you will notice is the large number of imports at the start of the program, all from subpackages of the javafx package. A typical JavaFX program uses many classes from such packages. When I discuss a JavaFX class for the first time, I will usually mention the package that it comes from. But in any case, you can look up the class in the JavaFX API documentation. As I write this, the documentation for JavaFX 17 can be be found at https://openjfx.io/javadoc/17/.

The *HelloWorldFX* program contains a main method to launch the application, and it contains the required start() method. Of course, we will often add other methods to our application classes, to be called by start(). There are also a couple other methods in *Application* that can be overridden. In particular, there is an init(), that will be called by the system before start(), and a stop() method that is called by the system when the application is shutting down. These two methods are defined in class *Application* to do nothing. A programmer can redefine init() to do some initialization and stop() to do cleanup. However, we will rarely if ever need them. Any initialization that we need can be done in start().

6.1.2 Stage, Scene, and SceneGraph

The start() method has a parameter of type *Stage*, from package javafx.stage. A *Stage* object represents a window on the computer's screen. The stage that is passed as a parameter to start() is constructed by the system. It represents the main window of a program, and is often referred to as the "primary stage." A program can create other windows by constructing new objects of type *Stage*.

A window is an area on the screen that can be filled with content. It can contain GUI components such as menus, buttons, and text input boxes, as well as drawing areas like those used in the graphical programs from Section 3.9. Although the primary stage is created before start() is called, the window does not have any content, and it is not yet visible on the screen.

The start() method is responsible for adding content to the window and making it visible.

The very last line of start() in the *HelloWorldFX* program, stage.show(), is what makes the window visible. The rest of the method creates content, adds the content to the window, and sets various configuration options for the content and for the window itself. For example, the line

stage.setTitle("JavaFX Test");

sets the text that will appear in the title bar at the top of the window.

A stage shows a *scene*, which fills its content area and serves as a container for the GUI components in the window. A scene is represented by an object of type *Scene*. In the sample program, the statement sets the scene that will be displayed in the content area of the stage.

stage.setScene(scene);

A scene can be filled with things called GUI *components*, such as buttons and menu bars. Each component is represented by an object belonging to a JavaFX class. For example, a push button such as the "Say Hello" button in the sample program, is represented by an object belonging to the class *Button*, from the package javafx.scene.control. Some components, such as the object buttonBar of type *HBox*, are *containers*. A container represents a region in the window that can contain other components, including other containers. So, a window contains GUI components, inside containers, which can be inside bigger containers, each represented by an object. All of these objects make up something called the *scene graph* for the window. The scene graph shows the containment relationships among all the components in the scene. For the sample program, the scene graph looks like this:

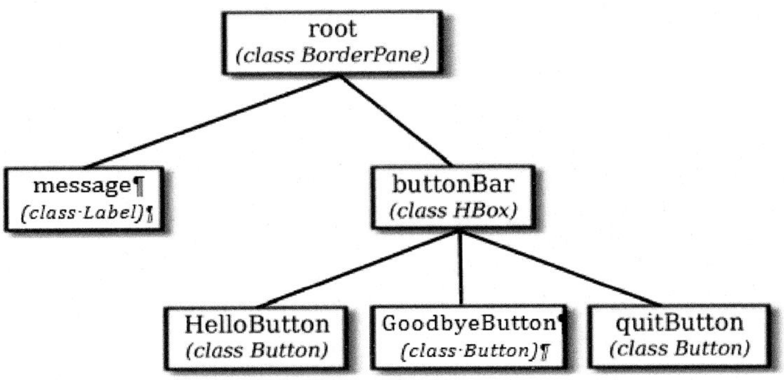

Note that this is not a class hierarchy. It does not show the relationships among the classes of the objects in the program; rather, it is a containment hierarchy that shows how the components are contained within other components on the screen. In this scene graph, root and buttonBar are containers while message and the three buttons are simple components.

A scene contains a single "root" component, which is a container that contains all of the other components in the scene. In the sample program, the root component is named root (although of course that is not required), and the root of the scene is set when the *Scene* object is constructed:

Scene scene = new Scene(root, 450, 200);

The numbers in this constructor specify the width and the height of the scene, in pixels. The numbers can be omitted, in which case the size will be computed based on the contents of the scene.

6.1.3 Nodes and Layout

Objects that can be part of a scene graph are referred to as nodes. Scene graph nodes must belong to one of the subclasses of *javafx.scene.Node*. Scene graph objects that can act as containers must belong to one of the subclasses of javafx.scene. Parent, which is a subclass of *Node*. The nodes that are contained in a parent are called *children* of that node. The root node in a scene graph must be a *Parent*.

The buttons in *HelloWorldFX* are represented by objects of type *Button*. The constructor that is used to create the button objects specifies the text that is displayed on the button. Similarly, message is a node of type *Label*, from package javafx.scene.control, whose purpose is simply to passively display a *String*. One of the properties of a *Label* object is a font, which specifies the size and style of the characters in the displayed string. The font for the text is set by calling the label's setFont() method. The *Font* constructor that is used in the sample program, new Font(40), takes a parameter that specifies the size of the font.

Containers are *Nodes* which can have other nodes as children. The act of arranging a container's children on the screen is referred to as *layout*. Layout means setting the size and location of the components inside the container. While it is possible for a program to set the sizes and locations directly, it is more commonly done automatically by the container. Different containers implement different layout policies. For example, an *HBox* is a container that simply arranges the components that it contains in a horizontal row. In the constructor

HBox buttonBar = new HBox(20, helloButton, goodbyeButton, quitButton);

the first parameter specifies the size of a gap that the *HBox* will place between its children, and the remaining parameters are nodes to be added as children of the container.

A *BorderPane* is a container that implements a completely different layout policy. A *BorderPane* can contain up to five components, one in the center of the pane and up to four more placed at the top, at the bottom, to the left, and to the right of the center. In the sample program, the root of the scene is a *BorderPane* and components are added in the pane's center and bottom positions with the statements

root.setCenter(message);

root.setBottom(buttonBar);

Layout is configurable by a large number of options. The sample program has only one example of this,

buttonBar.setAlignment(Pos.CENTER);

This command centers the buttons within the *HBox*; without it, they would be shoved over to the left edge of the window. *Pos*, short for "position," is an enumerated type. JavaFX uses many enumerated types for specifying various options.

6.1.4 Events and Event Handlers

In addition to setting up the physical layout of the window, the start() method configures *event handling* . In *HelloWorldFX*, an event occurs when the user clicks one of the buttons. The application must be configured to respond to, or "handle," these events. Handling an event involves two objects. The event itself is represented by an object that holds information about the event. For a button click, the event is of type *ActionEvent*, and the information that it carries is the button that was clicked. The second object is of type *EventHandler*, a functional interface that defines a method handle(evt), where the parameter, evt, is the event object. To program a response to an event, you can create a class that implements the *EventHandler* interface and provides a definition for the handle() method. However, since *EventHandler* is a functional interface, the handler can alternatively be specified as a lambda expression (see Section 4.5). Lambda expressions are very commonly used in JavaFX for writing event handlers, among other uses. For example, the lambda expression

evt -> message.setText("Hello World!")

represents an event handler that responds to an event by changing the text of the message to read "Hello World!". The parameter, evt, is the *ActionEvent* object that represents the event. In this case, the parameter is not used in the response in any way, but it still has to be there to satisfy the syntax of the lambda expression: Since the function in the *EventHandler* interface has a parameter, the lambda expression must have a parameter to match the interface.

In addition to writing the event handler, you also have to *register* the handler with the object that will produce the event. In this case, the object is helloButton, and the handler is registered by calling the button's setOnAction() method:

helloButton.setOnAction(evt -> message.setText("Hello World!"));

Handlers for each of the other two buttons are set up in a similar way. Remember that in each case, there is an object that generates the event in response to a user action, an object that represents the event, and an event handler that contains the code that is executed in response to the event. This diagram summarizes how it all works:

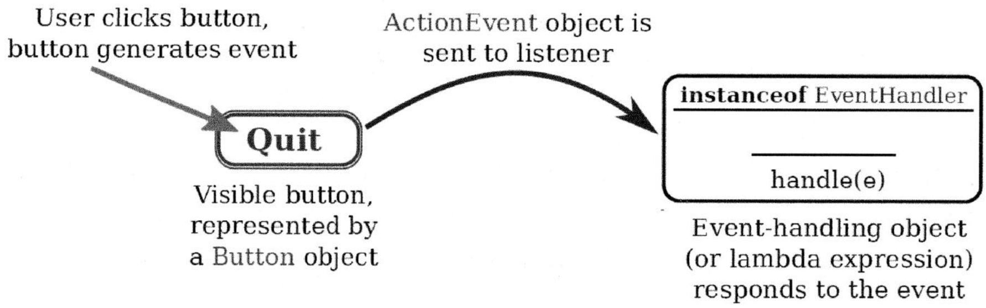

About all that still remains to be explained in the sample program is the response to a click on the "Quit" button: Platform.exit(). The static exit() method in the *Platform* class is the preferred way to programmatically end a JavaFX program. It is preferred to System.exit() because it cleanly shuts down the application thread and gives it an opportunity to clean up by calling the application's stop() method before terminating.

This section has been only a brief overview of JavaFX applications, but it has introduced many of the fundamental concepts. We will cover all of this in much greater detail in the following sections.

6.2 SOME BASIC CLASSES

In this section, we will look at some basic classes, including classes representing colors, fonts, and images. We will see how these classes are used in the *GraphicsContext* API, which you already encountered in a preliminary way in Section 3.9, but they are also useful in other parts of JavaFX. There is also a brief introduction to *CSS style sheets*, which can be used to control many aspects of the visual appearance of GUI components.

6.2.1 Color and Paint

Computer color uses an *RGB color system* . That is, a color on a computer screen is specified by three numbers, called *color components*, giving the level of red, green, and blue in the color. A color is represented by an object of type *Color*, from package javafx.scene.paint. In JavaFX, each color component is a double value in the range 0.0 to 1.0. A *Color* object also has a fourth component in the range 0.0 to 1.0, referred as the *alpha color component*, which is generally used to represent the transparency or opaqueness of the color when it is used for drawing. When a fully opaque color (alpha component equal to 1.0) is used for drawing, the drawing color completely replaces the current color of the drawing surface. When a fully transparent color (alpha component equal to 0.0) is used for drawing, it has no effect at all. When the alpha component is between 0.0 and 1.0, the drawing color is combined with the current color to give the new color of the drawing surface, as if the original contents of the drawing surface were being viewed through colored, translucent glass. A *Color* object can be constructed by giving its red, green, blue, and alpha components; for example,

Color myColor = new Color(r, g, b, a);

where r, g, b, and a are in the range 0.0 to 1.0. However, the *Color* class also has a number of static methods for making color objects. Static methods whose job is to create objects are sometimes called *factory methods*. So instead of using the constructor, you could also say

Color myColor = Color.color(r, g, b, a);

and in the common case of a fully opaque color, with *a* equal to 1.0, you can use

Color myColor = Color.color(r, g, b);

These static factory methods are preferable to the constructor because they have the option of reusing color objects. For example, two calls to Color.color(0.2,0.3,1.0) might return the same *Color* object. This is OK because color objects are immutable; that is, there is no way to change a color after it has been constructed. So there is really no reason to use two different objects to represent the same color.

Your computer screen probably uses "32-bit color," which means that the color of each pixel is actually represented using just 8 bits for each of the four color components. Eight bits can represent the 256 integers in the range 0 to 255, so computer colors have traditionally been specified using integer color components in the range 0 to 255. The *Color* class has the following static method for making colors in this way:

Color.rgb(r, g, b)

where r, g, and b are integers in the range 0 to 255. There is also Color.rgb(r,g,b,a) where r, g, and b are ints in the range 0 to 255, and a is a double in the range 0.0 to 1.0.

An alternative to RGB is the *HSB color system*. In the HSB system, a color is specified by three numbers called the *hue*, the *saturation*, and the *brightness*. The hue is the basic color, ranging from red through orange through all the other colors of the rainbow. The brightness is pretty much what it sounds like. A fully saturated color is a pure color tone. Decreasing the saturation is like mixing white or gray paint into the pure color. In JavaFX, the hue is given by a double value in the range 0.0 to 360.0, while saturation and brightness are double values in the range 0.0 to 1.0. (The hue value is given in degrees, were the colors are seen as laid out along a circle, with both 0.0 and 360.0 representing pure red.) The *Color* class has static methods Color.hsb(h,s,b) and Color.hsb(h,s,b,a) for making HSB colors. For example, to make a color with a random hue that is as bright and as saturated as possible, you could use:

*Color randomColor = Color.hsb(360*Math.random(), 1.0, 1.0);*

The RGB system and the HSB system are just different ways of describing the same set of colors. It is possible to translate between one system and the other. The best way to understand the color systems is to experiment with them. The sample program SimpleColorChooser.java lets you do that. You won't understand the source code at this time, but you can run it to play with color selection or to find RGB or HSB values for the color that want.

The *Color* class also contains a large number of constants representing colors, such as Color.RED, Color.BLACK, Color.LIGHTGRAY, and Color.GOLDENROD. It might be worth mentioning that Color.GREEN is the fairly dark green color given by Color.rgb(0,128,0); the constant representing Color.rgb(0,255,0) is Color.LIME. There is also Color.TRANSPARENT, which represents a fully transparent color, with all RGBA color components equal to zero.

Given a *Color*, c, you can find out the values of the various color components by calling functions such as c.getRed(), c.getHue(), and c.getOpacity(). These methods return double values in the range 0.0 to 1.0, except for c.getHue(), which returns a double in the range 0.0 to 360.0.

Color is a subclass of another class, *Paint*, which represents the more general idea of "something that can be used to fill and to stroke shapes." In addition to colors, there are image paints and gradient paints. I will not use these more general paints in this chapter, but they will be covered in Subsection 13.2.2. For now, you should just know that when a method has a parameter of type *Paint*, you can use a *Color*.

6.2.2 Fonts

A *font* represents a particular size and style of text. The same character will appear different in different fonts. In JavaFX, a font is represented by an object of type *Font*, from the package javafx.scene.text. Although the *Font* defines a couple of constructors, the best way to make a font object is with one of the static factory methods from that class.

A font has a name, which is a string that specifies a font family such as "Times New Roman." A given family can have variations such as a bold or an italic version of the font. And a font has a size, which is specified in "points," where a point should really be 1/72 inch but might in practice be equal to the size of a pixel. The most general function for making fonts can specify all of these options:

Font myFont = Font.font(family, weight, posture, size);

If the system can't match the requested font properties exactly, it will return the font that it thinks best matches the parameters. Here, family is a *String* that should specify a font family that is available to the program. Unfortunately, there is no set of fonts that is required to be available. "Times New Roman," "Arial," and "Verdana" are likely to work. (These are fonts that were created by Microsoft and released for free use; they are installed on many systems.) You can pass null as the familyName to use the default font family.

Font "weight" is given as an enumerated type value from the enum *FontWeight.* It will usually be either FontWeight.BOLD or FontWeight.NORMAL, although there are a few other values such as FontWeight.EXTRA BOLD. Similarly, font "posture" is one of the constants FontPosture.ITALIC or FontPosture.REGULAR. Both *FontWeight* and *FontPosture* are from package javafx.scene.text.

The *Font* class has several other static functions for making fonts, which specify only a subset of the four properties family, weight, posture, and size. These include: Font.font(size), Font.font(family), Font.font(family,weight,size), and a few others. The missing properties will have default values, which can depend on the computer where the program is running. The static function Font.getDefault() returns a font that has default values for all the properties. You can call Font.getDefault().getSize() to find the default point size. (It's 13.0 on my computer, but might be different on yours.) Here are a few examples of making fonts:

Font font1 = Font.font(40);

Font font2 = Font.font("Times New Roman", FontWeight.BOLD, 24);

Font font3 = Font.font(null, FontWeight.BOLD, FontPosture.ITALIC, 14);

6.2.3 Image

The term "image" refers to something like a photograph or drawing—anything that can be represented by a rectangular grid of colored pixels. Images are often stored in files. JavaFX makes it easy to load an image from a file so that it can be displayed by a program. An image is represented by an object of type *Image*, from package javafx.scene.image. The constructor

new Image(path)

is used to load an image from an image file. The path parameter is a string that specifies the location of the file. The location can be very general, such as an image on the Internet or on the user's computer, but for now I'm interested in images from *resource files.* A resource is something that is part of a program but is not code. Resources can include things like sounds, data files, and fonts, as well as images. The system can load resources for a program from the same places where it looks for the program's .class files. For a resource file in the program's top- level directory, the path to the file is simply the name of the file. If the file is in a subdirectory of the main directory, then the path includes the subdirectory name. For example, the path "images/cards.png" refers to a file named "cards.png" inside a subdirectory named "images," and "resources/sounds/beep.aiff" refers to a file named "beep. aiff" inside a directory named "sounds" that is in turn inside a directory named "resources."

There are many kinds of image files, which store the image data in a variety of formats. For JavaFX *Image* objects, you can use image files whose names end with .gif, .jpeg (or .jpg), .png, and .bmp. So, for example, if "cards.png" is a file in the top-level program directory, you can create the image object

Image cards = new Image("cards.png");

The image can then be displayed in a *GraphicsContext,* as we will soon see. There will be other uses for images later in this chapter.

6.2.4 Canvas and GraphicsContext

The screen of a computer is a grid of little squares called *pixels.* The color of each pixel can be set individually, and drawing on the screen just means setting the colors of individual pixels. Every visible GUI component is drawn by coloring pixels, and every component has a coordinate system that maps (x,y) coordinates to points within the component. Most components draw themselves, but there is one JavaFX component on which you can draw anything you want by calling the appropriate methods. Such "drawing surface" components are of type *Canvas,* in package javafx.scene.canvas. A *Canvas* is a *Node* and so can be part of a scene graph. (However, it is not a *Parent,* so it cannot act as a container for other nodes and it cannot be the root of a scene graph. This means that even when a canvas is the only thing that you want to show in a window, it must still be placed into a container that will serve as the root of the scene graph.)

A *Canvas* appears on the screen as a rectangle made up of pixels. A position in the rectangle is specified by a pair of coordinates, (x,y). The upper left corner has coordinates (0,0). The x coordinate increases from left to right, and the y coordinate increases from top to bottom. The illustration shows a 20-pixel by 12-pixel canvas (with very large pixels). A small line, rectangle, and oval are shown as they would be drawn by coloring individual pixels:

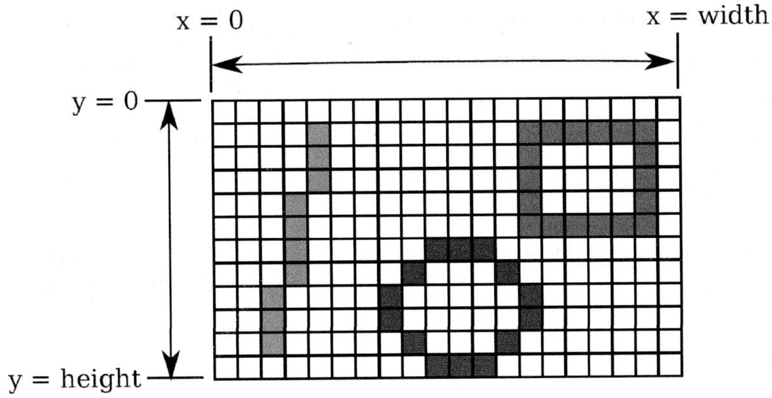

Note that, properly speaking, the coordinates don't belong to the pixels but to the grid lines between them, and coordinates can, in fact, be numbers of type double and can refer to points inside a pixel. For example, the center of the top left pixel in a canvas has coordinates (0.5,0.5). In fact, all drawing is done using coordinates of type double.

The width and height of a *Canvas* can be specified in the constructor that is used to create the canvas object. For example, to create a tiny 20-by-12 canvas:

Canvas canvas = new Canvas(20,12)

You can query the size of a canvas by calling canvas.getWidth() and canvas. getHeight(), which return values of type double. Canvasses are usually meant to be non-resizable, but the size can be changed if necessary by calling canvas. setWidth(w) and canvas.setHeight(h).

When a canvas is first created, it is filled with "transparent black," that is, with a color that has all RGBA components set to zero. This makes the canvas transparent: You will see whatever lies behind the canvas in the scene.

In order to draw on a canvas, you need an object of type *GraphicsContext*. Every *Canvas* has an associated *GraphicsContext*; different *GraphicsContexts* draw on different *Canvases*. You can get the graphics context for a *Canvas*, canvas, by calling canvas. getGraphicsContext2D(). For any given *Canvas*, this method will always return the same *GraphicsContext* object. Section 3.9 discussed some of the things that can be done with a graphics context. In particular, you learned that a shape can be stroked and, if it has an interior, it can also be filled. Methods in *GraphicsContext*, g, that can be used for drawing include the following, where all numeric parameters are of type double:

- g.strokeRect(x,y,w,h) and g.fillRect(x,y,w,h) – Draw a rectangle with top left corner at (x,y), with width w and with height h. If w or h is less than or equal to zero, nothing is drawn.

- g.clearRect(x,y,w,h) — Fill the same rectangle with a fully transparent color, so that whatever lies behind the rectangle will be visible through the canvas. Note that this is not the same as calling g.fillRect(x,y,w,h) with a transparent fill color; doing that has no effect at all on the contents of the rectangle.
- g.strokeOval(x,y,w,h) and g.fillOval(x,y,w,h) — Draw an oval that just fits inside the rectangle with top left corner at (x,y), with width w and with height h.
- g.strokeRoundRect(x,y,w,h,rh,rv) and g.fillRoundRect(x,y,w,h,rh,rv) — Draw a rectangle with rounded corners. The rectangle has top left corner at (x,y), with width w and with height h. A quarter oval is cut off each corner, where the horizontal radius of the oval is rh and its vertical radius is rv.
- g.strokeText(str,x,y) and g.fillText(str,x,y) — Draw the text of the *String* str. The point (x,y) is the left end of the baseline of the text. (A string is drawn on top of its baseline, with descenders such as the tail of a "y" extending below the baseline.) The string can contain multiple lines separated by newline ('\n') characters; (x,y) then gives the baseline of the first line of the string. Note that stroking text means drawing just the outlines of the characters.
- g.strokePolygon(xcoords,ycoords,n) and g.fillPolygon(xcoords,ycoords,n) — Draw a polygon, consisting of line segments connecting a sequence of points. The number of points is given by the third parameter, n. The first two parameters are arrays of type double[ ] containing the coordinates of the points. An extra line segment is automatically added to connect the last point back to the first. That is, the polygon connects the points (xcoords[0],ycoords[0]), (xcoords[1],ycoords[1]), . . . , (xcoords[n-1],ycoords[n-1]), (xcoords[0],ycoords[0]).
- g.strokeLine(x1,y1,x2,y2) — Draws a line from (x1,y1) to (x2,y2). (It's no use trying to fill a line, since it has no interior.)

The *GraphicsContext* object, g has a number of properties that affect drawing. When anything is drawn using g, the current values of the relevant properties are used. This means that changing the value of a property does not affect anything that has already been drawn; the change only applies to things drawn in the future. Each property has a setter method and a getter method. One of the properties is the *Paint* that is used for filling (which in this chapter will always be a *Color*); this property can be set by calling g.setFill(paint), and you can get its current value by calling g.getFill(). Similarly, the *Paint* that is used for stroking can be set and get using g.setStroke(paint) and g.getStroke(), and the width of strokes can be set and get using g.setLineWidth(w) and g.getLineWidth(), where w is of type double.

And you can set and get the font that will be used for drawing text with g.setFont(font) and g.getFont().

Note that stroking a shape is like dragging the center of a pen along the outline of the shape. The size of the pen is given by the linewidth property. The stroke that is drawn extends on both sides of the actual path of the pen by an amount equal to half of the linewidth. For example, if you draw a horizontal line of width 1 with endpoints (100,100) and (300,100), half of the stroke lies above the geometric line and half lies below it. The computer might show this by blending the color of the stroke color with the current color. If you want the stroke to nicely cover complete pixels, you should actually use (100.5,100.5) and (300.5,100.5) as the coordinates of the endpoints of the line. (Whenever you draw something, you might find that for pixels that are only partially covered, the drawing color is blended with the current color instead of replacing it. This is done to decrease the jagged appearance of shapes that are made out of whole pixels, like the line and oval in the above illustration. This is known as *antialiasing* .)

It is also possible to draw an image onto a canvas, where the image is represented by an object of type *Image*. There are several methods for drawing images:

g.drawImage(image,x,y) — Draws the image with its upper left corner at (x,y), using the actual size of the image.

- g.drawImage(image,x,y,w,h) — Draws the image in the rectangle with upper left corner at (x,y), with width w, and with height h. The image is stretched or shrunk to fit that rectangle if necessary.
- g.drawImage(image, sx,sy,sw,sh, dx,dy,dh,dw) — Draws the contents of a specified "source" rectangle in the image to a specified "destination" rectangle on the canvas. This method lets you draw just part of an image. The source rectangle has upper left corner at (sx,sy), width sw, and height sh. The last four parameters specify the destination rectangle in a similar way.

It's time for a couple of actual examples. First, an example that draws some text using a variety of fonts. The program draws multiple copies of the string "Hello JavaFX" using random fonts and locations. The text is filled with random colors and stroked with a thin black stroke:

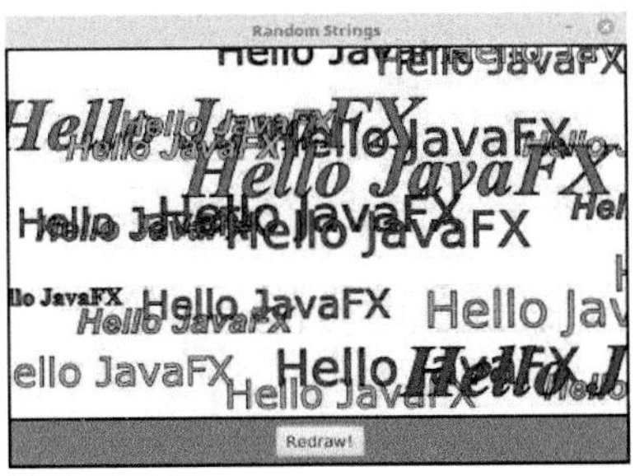

The program uses five fonts, which are created in the start() method using several different static factory methods from the *Font* class:

```
font1 = Font.font("Times New Roman", FontWeight.BOLD, 20);
font2 = Font.font("Arial", FontWeight.BOLD, FontPosture.ITALIC, 28);
font3 = Font.font("Verdana", 32);
font4 = Font.font(40);
font5 = Font.font("Times New Roman",FontWeight.BOLD,FontPosture.ITALIC,60);
```

The program defines a draw() method that completely redraws the content of a canvas. It is called when the canvas is first created, and it is also called when the user clicks the "Redraw" button. The method first fills the canvas with a white background, which erases the previous contents of the canvas. It then fills and strokes 25 copies of "Hello JavaFX", using a random fill color, a random position for the text, and a randomly selected font for each copy:

```
private void draw() {
    GraphicsContext g = canvas.getGraphicsContext2D();
    double width = canvas.getWidth();
    double height = canvas.getHeight();
    g.setFill( Color.WHITE ); // fill with white background
    g.fillRect(0, 0, width, height);
    for (int i = 0; i < 25; i++) {
        // Draw one string.     First, set the font to be one of the five
        // available fonts, at random.
        int fontNum = (int)(5*Math.random()) + 1;
        switch (fontNum) {
            case 1 -> g.setFont(font1);
            case 2 -> g.setFont(font2);
            case 3 -> g.setFont(font3);
            case 4 -> g.setFont(font4);
            case 5 -> g.setFont(font5);
        } // end switch
        // Set the color to a bright, saturated color, with random hue.
        double hue = 360*Math.random();
        g.setFill( Color.hsb(hue, 1.0, 1.0) );
        // Select the position of the string, at random.
```

```
            double x,y;
            x = -50 + Math.random()*(width+40);
            y = Math.random()*(height+20);
            // Draw the message.
            g.fillText("Hello JavaFX",x,y);
            // Also stroke the outline of the strings with black.
            g.setStroke(Color.BLACK);
            g.strokeText("Hello JavaFX",x,y);
        } // end for
    } // end draw()
```

You can find the full source code for the program in RandomStrings.java.

The second sample program is similar, but instead of drawing random strings, it draws five playing cards dealt at random from a deck:

The deck and cards are represented using the *Deck* and *Card* classes from Section 5.4. The card images come from the file cards.png, which is a resource file for the program. The file contains a single image that contains images of all the cards, arranged in rows and columns. Here it is, shown at reduced size:

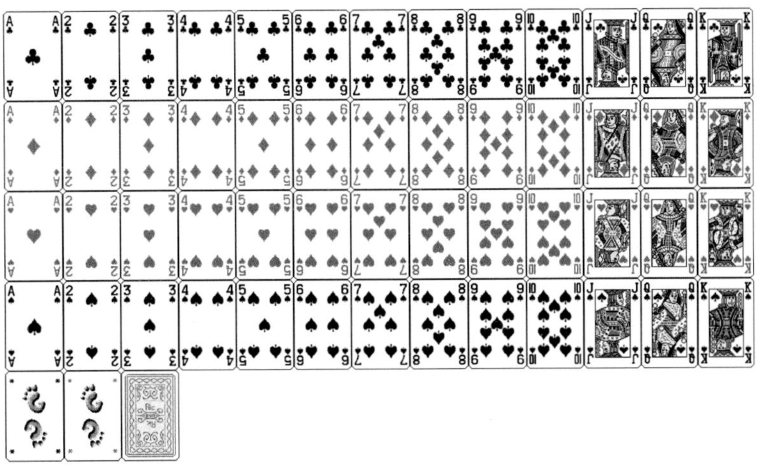

(This image is from the Gnome desktop project, http://www.gnome.org.) The image file is loaded into the program in the start() method simply by saying

```
cardImages = new Image("cards.png");
```

where cardImages is an instance variable of type *Image*. Suppose that we want to draw the card from row number R and column number C in a *GraphicsContext* g (where both rows and columns are numbered starting at zero). Each card in the image is 79 pixels by 123 pixels, so the card that we want has its top left corner at (79*C,123*R). If we want to place the card on the canvas with its top left corner at (x,y), we can use the third drawImage() method given above, which specifies a source rectangle in the image and a destination rectangle on the canvas:

```
g.drawImage( cardImages, 79*C,123*R,79,123, x,y,79,123 );
```

In the program, the card that we want to draw is given by a variable card of type *Card*. The row and column in the image are determined by the suit and value of the card, which are given by card.getSuit() and *card.getValue()*. The values returned by these functions have to be manipulated a little to get the correct row and column numbers, and the position of the card on the canvas is calculated to leave a 20-pixel gap between one card and the next. Here is the *draw()* method from the program, which deals five random cards from a deck and draws them:

```
private void draw() {
    GraphicsContext g = canvas.getGraphicsContext2D();
    Deck deck = new Deck();
    deck.shuffle();
    double sx,sy;     // top left corner of source rect for card in cardImages
    double dx,dy;     // corner of destination rect for card in the canvas
    for (int i = 0; i < 5; i++) {
            Card card = deck.dealCard();
            System.out.println(card); // for testing
            sx = 79 * (card.getValue()-1);
            sy = 123 * (3 - card.getSuit());
            dx = 20 + (79+20) * i;
            dy = 20;
            g.drawImage( cardImages, sx,sy,79,123, dx,dy,79,123 );
    }
} // end draw()
```

For the complete program, see RandomCards.java.

6.2.5 A Bit of CSS

JavaFX makes it possible to control the style—that is, the visual appearance—of components in a GUI using *CSS* (Cascading Style Sheets). CSS is one of several languages that are used to make web pages. It can control things like colors, fonts, and borders of elements of a web page. It has been adapted to play a similar role in other contexts, such as JavaFX. I do not intend to cover CSS in any detail, and anything that can be done with CSS can also be done with Java code. However, there are some things that are just easier to do with CSS; I will cover a few of them in this short section and will use them in my programs. For people who already know CSS, a guide to its use in JavaFX is available as I write this at

https://openjfx.io/javadoc/17/javafx.graphics/javafx/scene/doc-files/cssref.html

A CSS *style rule* consists of a property and a value for that property. For example, CSS can be used to place a border around many kinds of GUI components. A border has properties with names such as -fx-border-color and -fx-border-width. (All JavaFX CSS properties have names that begin with "-fx-" to distinguish them from regular CSS properties.) A value for -fx-border-color can be a color name such as red or lightblue, among other formats. One color format that I will use takes the form #RRGGBB, where R, G, and B stand for hexadecimal digits. A two-digit hexadecimal number can represent numbers from 0 to 255. The RR, GG, and BB in #RRGGBB represent the red, green, and blue components of a color, each in the range 0 to 255. For example, #FF0000 represents pure red, and #004444 represents a dark blue-green.

For the border width, the value can be a single size, such as 3px or 0.2cm. The syntax is a number followed by a unit of measure, with no space between them. Here, "px" stands for "pixels," and 3px means 3 pixels. When a width is given by a single size, the size applies to all four sides of the border. Alternatively, four sizes can be given, separated by spaces, specifying the border width on the top, right, bottom, and left, in that order. For example, a thick, blue border could be specified as

-fx-border-color: blue; -fx-border-width: 5px

and for a dark red border that is thicker on the top than on the other sides, you can use

-fx-border-color: #550000; -fx-border-width: 3px 1px 1px 1px

When several CSS rules are used together, they should be separated by semicolons.

The background color of a component can be set using -fx-background-color as the property name. The value is the same sort of color specification that would be used with -fx-border-color.

And the CSS property -fx-padding represents space that is left between the content of a component and its edge (or border if there is one). Like border width, padding can be specified as either a single size or a list of four sizes. For example: -fx-padding: 8px.

You can apply a style to a component using its setStyle() method, whose parameter is a *String* containing one or more CSS style rules. For example, suppose message is a *Label*. By default, labels have no padding or border. They can be added with a command such as

message.setStyle(
"-fx-padding: 5px; -fx-border-color: black; -fx-border-width: 1px");

You can set the font for a component that displays text using the -fx-font property. The value for this property specifies the size and font family for the font, and can optionally be modified by a weight ("bold"), or by a style ("italic"), or both. Some examples:

-fx-font: 30pt "Times New Roman";

-fx-font: bold italic 18pt serif;

-fx-font: bold 42pt monospace;

Note that if the font family name contains spaces, it must be enclosed in quotes. The font families in the last two examples, "serif" and "monospace", are so-called generic family names that specify a certain style of font. Other generic names include "sans-serif", "cursive", and "fantasy". The characters in a serif font have short lines as decorations such as at the top and bottom of an upper case "I". A "sans-serif" font lacks these decorations. The characters in a "monospace" font all have the same width. Monospace fonts are good for drawing characters that are meant to line up in columns.

Many other properties can be set using CSS, but I will not cover them here. I will use CSS only for borders, padding, background colors, and fonts.

Setting the style for many components can be tedious. A *CSS style sheet* can be used to apply style to all components of a given type as well as to individual components and sets of components. A style sheet is a file, usually with a name ending with .css. I will not discuss the syntax, but here is a style sheet that will apply some style rules to all *Labels* and *Buttons*:

```
Button {
    -fx-font: bold 16pt "Times New Roman";
    -fx-text-fill: darkblue;
}
```

```
Label {
    -fx-font: 15pt sans-serif;
    -fx-padding: 7px;
    -fx-border-color: darkred;
    -fx-border-width: 2px;
    -fx-text-fill: darkred;
    -fx-background-color: pink;
}
```

A style sheet file, just like an image file, can be a resource for a program. That is, it can be stored in the same place as the .class files for the program. Suppose that a style sheet named "mystyle.css" is in the program's top-level directory. You can then apply the style to all components in a scene with the statement

```
scene.getStylesheets().add("mystyle.css");
```

A *Scene* can have several style sheets, and style sheets can also be added to individual containers.

6.3 BASIC EVENTS

Events are central to programming for a graphical user interface. A GUI program doesn't have a main() routine that outlines what will happen when the program is run, in a step-by-step process from beginning to end. Instead, the program must be prepared to respond to various kinds of events that can happen at unpredictable times and in an order that the program doesn't control. The most basic kinds of events are generated by the mouse and keyboard. The user can press any key on the keyboard, move the mouse, or press a button on the mouse. The user can do any of these things at any time, and the computer has to respond appropriately.

In Java, events are represented by objects. When an event occurs, the system collects all the information relevant to the event and constructs an object to contain that information. Different types of events are represented by objects belonging to different classes. For example, when the user presses one of the buttons on a mouse, an object belonging to a class called *MouseEvent* is constructed. The object contains information such as the target of the event (that is, the component on which the user clicked), the (x,y) coordinates of the point in the component where the click occurred, which modifier keys (such as the shift key) are being held down, and which button on the mouse was pressed. When the user presses a key on the keyboard, on the other hand, it is a *KeyEvent* object that is created, containing information relevant to an event generated by using the keyboard. After the event object is constructed, it can be passed as a parameter to a designated method. That method is called an *event handler* for the event. In JavaFX, event handlers are often written as lambda expressions. By writing an event handler, the programmer says what should happen when the event occurs.

As a Java programmer, you get a fairly high-level view of events. There is a lot of processing that goes on between the time that the user presses a key or moves the mouse and the time that a method in your program is called to respond to the event. Fortunately, you don't need to know much about that processing. But you should understand this much: Even though you didn't write it, there is a routine running somewhere that executes a loop of the form

while the program is still running:

Wait for the next event to occur

Handle the event

This loop is called an *event loop*. Every GUI program has an event loop. In Java, you don't have to write the loop. It's part of "the system." If you write a GUI program in some other language, you might have to provide a main routine that runs the event loop. In this section, we'll look at handling mouse and key events in Java, and we'll cover the framework for handling events in general. We will also see how to make an animation.

6.3.1 Event Handling

For an event to have any effect, a program must detect the event and react to it. In order to detect an event, the program must "listen" for it. Listening for events is something that is done by an *event listener* , which contains an event handler method that can respond to the event. An event listener is defined by an interface that specifies the event handling methods that it contains. Listeners for different kinds of events are defined by different interfaces. In most cases, the interface is a functional interface, defining a single event handler method; in that case, the listener can be given by a lambda expression.

For many kinds of events in JavaFX, listeners are defined by a functional interface named *EventHandler*, which defines the method handle(event). The parameter to this method, event, is the event object that contains information about the event. When you provide a definition for handle(), you write the code that will be executed to handle the event.

(*EventHandler* is actually a parameterized type, something that we have not encountered before and will not encounter officially until Section 7.3. Basically, all this really means is that *EventHandler* really defines many different types, with names like *Even- tHandler<MouseEvent>*, *EventHandler<KeyEvent>*, and *EventHandler<ActionEvent>*. The type *EventHandler<MouseEvent>* defines a handle(event) method in which the event is of type *MouseEvent*, the type *EventHandler<KeyEvent>* defines a handle(event) method in which the event is of type *KeyEvent*, and so on. Fortunately, you don't need to understand parameterized types in this chapter; you only need to know that the event object that you use when handling an event will have the appropriate type for that event. For example, when handling a mouse event, the event object is of type *MouseEvent*.)

Many events in JavaFX are associated with GUI components. For example, when the user presses a button on the mouse, the associated component is the one that contains the mouse cursor when the button is pressed. This object is called the *target* of the event. In order to respond to the event, you need to register a listener either with the target of the event or with some other object that knows about the event. For example, lets look again at this statement from HelloWorldFX.java, our first GUI program from Section 6.1:

helloButton.setOnAction(evt -> message.setText("Hello World!"));

Here, helloButton is an object of type *Button*. When the user clicks on the button, an event of type *ActionEvent* is generated. The target of that event is helloButton. The method helloButton.setOnAction() registers an event listener that will receive notification of any *ActionEvents* from the button. The listener in this case is defined by a lambda expression. In the lambda expression, the parameter, evt, is the *ActionEvent* object, and the code in the lambda expression is what happens in response to the event. Most event handling in this chapter will be set up in a similar way.

For key events and some mouse events, it's not just the event target that gets a chance to respond to the event. For example, suppose that you press a mouse button over a *Canvas* that is inside a *BorderPane* that is in turn inside a *Scene*. The target of the mouse event is the *Canvas* but the *BorderPane* and the *Scene* also have a chance to respond to the event. That is, you can register a mouse event listener on any or all of these objects to respond to the event. The object that the listener is registered with is called the *source* of the event. The event object parameter, evt, in an event handler method has both a source, given by evt.getSource(), and a target, given by evt.getTarget(); often they are the same, but they don't have to be. Note that the same event can be sent to several handlers. A handler can "consume" an event, by calling evt.consume(), to stop it from being sent to any additional handlers. For example, when you are typing in a text input box, the input box consumes the key events that you generate by typing, so that the scene doesn't get a chance to handle them.

(Actually, it's more complicated than that. For key events and some kinds of mouse events, the event first travels down through the scene and then through scene graph nodes that contain the event target; this is called the "event filtering" or "bubble down" phase of event processing. After reaching the target, the event travels back up through the scene graph and finally to the scene; this is the "event handling" or "bubble up" phase. The event can be consumed at any point along the way, and if that happens, the process stops. None of this is used in this chapter, but for more information, see the documentation for the addEventFilter() and addEventHandler() methods in the *Scene* and *Node* classes.)

Most of this section is concerned with mouse and key events. It is important to understand that many GUI programs do not need to deal with such events directly. Instead, you work with GUI components that are already programmed to handle mouse and key events on their own. For example, when the user clicks a *Button*, it is the button that listens for mouse events and responds to them. When the button detects that it has been clicked, it generates an *ActionEvent*. When you write an application that uses buttons, you program responses to *ActionEvents*, not to mouse events. Similarly, when the user types in a text input box, it is the input box that listens for key events and responds to them. Nevertheless, at base, it's mouse and keyboard events that drive the action in a program. It's useful to understand them—and you can do some interesting things by processing them directly.

6.3.2 Mouse Events

A mouse event is represented by an object of type *MouseEvent*. (In fact, mouse events can actually be generated by other input devices, such as a trackpad or touch screen; events from these devices are translated by the system into *MouseEvents*.) That class, and all of the classes related to mouse and key events, can be found in package javafx.scene.input. As the user manipulates the mouse, several kinds of event are generated. For example, clicking a mouse button generates three events, a "mouse pressed" event, a "mouse released" event, and a "mouse clicked" event. Simply moving the mouse generates a sequence of events as the mouse cursor moves from point to point on the screen. To respond to mouse events on a component, you can register listeners with that component. You can register a separate listener for each kind of mouse event on a component c using instance methods such as c.setOnMousePressed(handler) and c.setOnMouseMoved(handler). The parameter is a mouse event handler, generally given as a lambda expression. Suppose, for example, that canvas is a component of type *canvas*, and that you would like a method, redraw(), to be called when the user clicks the canvas. You can make that happen by saying

```
canvas.setOnMousePressed( evt -> redraw() );
```

Generally, you would put this statement in the start() method of an *Application*, while setting up the GUI for the program. Mouse clicks on the canvas could be also be handled by the scene or by any scene graph node that contains the canvas, directly or indirectly, but it is much more usual for the target of a mouse event to handle the event.

Mouse event types include: MouseEntered, generated when the mouse cursor moves from outside a component into the component; MouseExited, generated when the mouse cursor moves out of a component; MousePressed, generated when the user presses one of the buttons on the mouse; MouseReleased, generated when the user releases one of the buttons on the mouse; MouseClicked, generated after a mouse released event if the user pressed and released the mouse button on the same component; MouseDragged, generated when the user moves the mouse while holding down a mouse button; and MouseMoved, generated when the user moves the mouse without holding down a button.

The target of a MouseDragged, MouseReleased, or MouseClicked event is the same component where the mouse button was pressed, even if the mouse has moved outside of that component. The target of a MousePressed or MouseMoved event is the component that contains the mouse cursor when the event occurs. And for MouseEntered and MouseExited, the target is the component that is being entered or exited.

Often, when a mouse event occurs, you want to know the location of the mouse cursor. This information is available from the *MouseEvent* parameter in the event-handling method, which contains instance methods that return information about the event. If evt is the parameter, then you can find out the coordinates of the mouse cursor by calling evt.getX() and evt.getY(). These methods return values of type double that give the x and y coordinates where the mouse cursor was positioned at the time when the event occurred. The coordinates are expressed in the coordinate system of the source of the event, where the top left corner of the component is (0,0). (The source is the component on which the event listener is registered; this is not necessarily the same as the event target, but it usually is.)

The user can hold down certain *modifier keys* while using the mouse. The possible modifier keys include: the Shift key, the Control key, the Alt key (called the Option key on the Mac), and the Meta key (called the Command or Apple key on the Mac). Not every computer has a Meta key. You might want to respond to a mouse event differently when the user is holding down a modifier key. The boolean-valued instance methods evt.isShiftDown(), evt.isControlDown(), evt.isAltDown(), and evt.isMetaDown() can be called to test whether the modifier keys are pressed.

You might also want to have different responses depending on whether the user presses the left mouse button, the middle mouse button, or the right mouse button.For events triggered by a mouse button, you can determine which button was pressed or released by calling evt.getButton(), which returns one of the enumerated type constants MouseButton.PRIMARY, MouseButton.MIDDLE, or MouseButton. SECONDARY. Generally, the left mouse button is the primary button and the right mouse button is secondary. For events such as mouseEntered and mouseExited that are not triggered by buttons, evt.getButton() returns MouseButton.NONE. The user can hold down several mouse buttons at the same time. If you want to know which mouse buttons are actually down at the time of an event, you can use the boolean-valued functions evt.isPrimaryButtonDown(), evt.isMiddleButtonDown(), and evt.isSecondaryButtonDown().

As a simple example, suppose that when the user clicks a *Canvas*, canvas, you would like to draw a red rectangle at the point where the user clicked. But if the shift key is down, you want to draw a blue oval instead. An event handler to do that can be defined as:

```
canvas.setOnMousePressed( evt -> {
    GraphicsContext g = canvas.getGraphicsContext2D();
    if ( evt.isShiftDown() ) {
            g.setFill( Color.BLUE );
            g.fillOval( evt.getX() - 30, evt.getY() - 15, 60, 30 )
    }
    else {
            g.setFill( Color.RED );
            g.fillRect( evt.getX() - 30, evt.getY() - 15, 60, 30 );
    }
} );
```

To get a better idea of how mouse events work, you should try the sample program SimpleTrackMouse.java. This program responds to any of the seven different kinds of mouse events by displaying the coordinates of the mouse, the type of event, and a list of the modifier keys and buttons that are down. You can experiment with the program to see what happens as you do various things with the mouse. I also encourage you to read the source code.

6.3.3 Dragging

A drag gesture occurs when the user moves the mouse while holding down one of the buttons on the mouse. It is interesting to look at what a program needs to do in order to respond to dragging operations. The drag gesture starts when the user presses a mouse button, it continues while the mouse is dragged, and it ends when the user releases the button. This means that the programming for the response to one dragging gesture must be spread out over the three event handlers, one for MousePressed, one for MouseDragged, and one for MouseReleased! Furthermore, the MouseDragged handler can be called many times as the mouse moves. To keep track of what is going on between one method call and the next, you need to set up some instance variables. In many applications, for example, in order to process a MouseDragged event, you need to remember the previous coordinates of the mouse. You can store this information in two instance variables prevX and prevY of type double. It can also be useful to save the starting coordinates, where the original MousePressed event occurred, in instance variables. And I suggest having a boolean variable, dragging, which is set to true while a dragging gesture is being processed. This is necessary because in many applications, not every MousePressed event starts a dragging operation to which you want to respond. Also, if the user presses a second mouse button without releasing the first, there will be two MousePressed events before the MouseReleased event; usually, you don't want the second MousePressed to start a new drag operation. The event-handling methods can use the value of dragging to check whether a drag operation is actually in progress. Often, I will write instance methods to handle the events, which in outline look something like this:

```
private double startX, startY; // Point where original mouse press occurred.
private double prevX, prevY; // Most recently processed mouse coords.
private boolean dragging;      // Set to true when dragging is in progress.
. . . // other instance variables for use in dragging
public void mousePressed(MouseEvent evt) {
    if (dragging) {
            // The user pressed a second mouse button before releasing the first.
            // Ignore the second button press.
            return;
    }
if ( (we-want-to-start-dragging ) ) {
    dragging = true;
    startX = evt.getX();        // Remember starting position.
    startY = evt.getY();
    prevX = startX;  // Remember most recent coords.
    prevY = startY;
            .
            . // Other processing.
            .
    }
}
```

```
public void mouseDragged(MouseEvent evt) {
    if ( dragging == false )    // First, check if we are
            return; //          processing a dragging gesture.
    int x = evt.getX(); // Current position of Mouse.
    int y = evt.getY();
            .
            .       // Process a mouse movement from (prevX, prevY) to (x,y).
            .
    prevX = x;      // Remember the current position for the next call.
    prevY = y;
}
public void mouseReleased(MouseEvent evt) {
    if ( dragging == false )    // First, check if we are
            return;         //      processing a dragging gesture.
    dragging = false; // We are done dragging.
    .
    .       // Other processing and clean-up.
    .
}
```

I will then install event handlers on the relevant component that simply call these methods:

```
c.setOnMousePressed( e -> mousePressed(e) );
c.setOnMouseDragged( e -> mouseDragged(e) );
c.setOnMouseReleased( e -> mouseReleased(e) );
```

Note that the event handlers in these statements simply call another method in the same class, and that method has the same parameter as the event handler. That means that it's possible to write the lambda expressions as method references. The methods that are called are instance methods in the object "this", so the method references would have names like this::mousePressed, and the event handlers could be installed using

```
c.setOnMousePressed( this::mousePressed );
c.setOnMouseDragged( this::mouseDragged );
c.setOnMouseReleased( this::mouseReleased );
```

As an example, let's look at a typical use of dragging: allowing the user to sketch a curve by dragging the mouse. This example also shows many other features of graphics and mouse processing. In the program, you can draw a curve by dragging the mouse on a large white drawing area, and you can select a color for drawing by clicking on one of several colored rectangles to the right of the drawing area. The complete source code can be found in SimplePaint.java. Here is a picture of the program window after some drawing has been done:

I will discuss a few aspects of the source code here, but I encourage you to read it carefully in its entirety. There are lots of informative comments in the source code.

In this program, all drawing is done on a single canvas that fills the entire window. The program is designed to work for any reasonable canvas size, that is, unless the canvas is too small. This means that coordinates are computed in terms of the actual width and height of the canvas. (The width and height are obtained by calling canvas.getWidth() and canvas.getHeight().) This makes things quite a bit harder than they would be if we assumed some particular fixed size for the canvas. Let's look at some of these computations in detail. For example, the large white drawing area extends from y = 3 to y = height - 3 vertically and from x = 3 to x = width - 56 horizontally. These numbers are needed in order to interpret the meaning of a mouse click. They take into account a gray border around the canvas and the color palette along the right edge of the canvas. The gray border is 3 pixels wide. The colored rectangles are 50 pixels wide. Together with the 3-pixel border around the canvas and a 3-pixel divider between the drawing area and the colored rectangles, this adds up to put the right edge of the drawing area 56 pixels from the right edge of the canvas.

A white square labeled "CLEAR" occupies the region beneath the colored rectangles on the right edge of the canvas. Allowing for this region, we can figure out how much vertical space is available for the seven colored rectangles, and then divide that space by 7 to get the vertical space available for each rectangle. This quantity is represented by a variable, colorSpace. Out of this space, 3 pixels are used as spacing between the rectangles, so the height of each rectangle is colorSpacing - 3. The top of the N-th rectangle is located (N*colorSpacing + 3) pixels down from the top of the canvas, assuming that we count the rectangles starting with zero. This is because there are N rectangles above the N-th rectangle, each of which uses colorSpace pixels. The extra 3 is for the border at the top of the canvas. After all that, we can write down the command for drawing the N-th rectangle:

*g.fillRect(width - 53, N*colorSpace + 3, 50, colorSpace - 3);*

That was not easy! But it shows the kind of careful thinking and precision graphics that are sometimes necessary to get good results.

The mouse in this program is used to do three different things: Select a color, clear the drawing, and draw a curve. Only the third of these involves dragging, so not every mouse click will start a dragging operation. The mousePressed() method has to look at the (x,y) coordinates where the mouse was clicked and decide how to respond. If the user clicked on the CLEAR rectangle, the drawing area is cleared by calling a clearAndDrawPalette() method that redraws the entire canvas. If the user clicked somewhere in the strip of colored rectangles, the corresponding color is selected for drawing. This involves computing which color the user clicked on, which is done by dividing the y coordinate by colorSpacing. Finally, if the user clicked on the drawing area, a drag operation is initiated. In this case, a boolean variable, dragging, is set to true so that the mouseDragged and mouseReleased methods will know that a curve is being drawn. The code for this follows the general form given above. The actual drawing of the curve is done in the mouseDragged() method, which draws a line from the previous location of the mouse to its current location. Some effort is required to make sure that the line does not extend beyond the white drawing area of the canvas. This is not automatic, since as far as the computer is concerned, the border and the color bar are part of the canvas. If the user drags the mouse outside the white drawing area while drawing a curve, the mouseDragged() routine changes the x and y coordinates to make them lie within the drawing area.

6.3.4 Main Events

In Java, user actions become events in a program, with a GUI component as the target of the event. When the user presses a button on the mouse, the component that contains the mouse cursor is the target of the event. But what about keyboard events? When the user presses a key, what component is the target of the *KeyEvent* that is generated?

A GUI uses the idea of *input focus* to determine the target of keyboard events. At any given time, just one interface element on the screen can have the input focus, and that is where keyboard events are directed. If the interface element happens to be a JavaFX component, then the information about the keyboard event becomes an object of type *KeyEvent*, and it is delivered to any key event handlers that are listening for KeyEvents associated with that component. Note that because of the way key events are processed, the *Scene* object in the window that contains the focused component also gets a chance to handle a key event. If there is no other focused component in the window, then the scene itself will be the target for key events. In my sample programs, I will usually add key event handlers to the scene object.

A program generally gives some visual feedback to the user about which component has the input focus. For example, if the component is a text-input box, the feedback is usually in the form of a blinking text cursor. Another possible visual clue is to draw a brightly colored border around the edge of a component when it has the input focus. You might see that on a button that has focus. When a button has focus, pressing the space bar is equivalent to clicking the button.

If comp is any component, and you would like it to have the input focus, you can call comp.requestFocus(). In a typical user interface, the user can choose to give the focus to a component by clicking on that component with the mouse. And pressing the tab key will often move the focus from one component to another. This is handled automatically by the components involved, without any programming on your part. However, some components do not automatically request the input focus when the user clicks on them. That includes, for example, a *Canvas*. Such a component can still receive the input focus if its requestFocus() is called. However, you can't automatically move the focus to that component with the tab key. To enable that, you can call comp.setFocusTraversable(true). And you can test whether a component is focused by calling comp.isFocused().

The focused component is contained in—or sometimes is itself—a window. That window is said to be the "focused" or "active" window. It is usually the front window on the screen. In JavaFX a *Stage* object is a window. You can call stage.requestFocus() to request that the window be moved to the front of the screen and become the active window. And you can call stage.isFocused() to test whether the window is active.

Java makes a careful distinction between *the keys that you press* and *the characters that you type*. There are lots of keys on a keyboard: letter keys, number keys, modifier keys such as Control and Shift, arrow keys, page up and page down keys, keypad keys, function keys, and so on. In some cases, such as the shift key, pressing a key does not type a character. On the other hand, typing a character sometimes involves pressing several keys. For example, to type an uppercase "A", you have to press the Shift key and then press the A key before releasing the Shift key. On my MacOS computer, I can type an accented e, by holding down the Option key, pressing the E key, releasing the Option key, and pressing E again. Only one character was typed, but I had to perform three key-presses and I had to release a key at the right time.

In JavaFX, there are three types of key event: KeyPressed, which is generated when the user depresses any key on the keyboard; KeyReleased, which is generated when the user releases a key that had been pressed; and KeyTyped, which is generated when the user types a character, possibly using a series of key presses and key releases. Note that one user action, such as pressing the E key, can be responsible for two events, a keyPressed event and a keyTyped event. Typing an upper case "A" can generate two keyPressed events, two keyReleased events, and one keyTyped event.

Usually, it is better to think in terms of two separate streams of events, one consisting of keyPressed and keyReleased events and the other consisting of keyTyped events. For some applications, you want to monitor the first stream; for other applications, you want to monitor the second one. Of course, the information in the keyTyped stream could be extracted from the keyPressed/keyReleased stream, but it would be difficult (and also system-dependent to some extent). Some user actions, such as pressing the Shift key, can only be detected as keyPressed events. I used to have a computer solitaire game that highlighted every card that could be moved, when I held down the Shift key. You can do something like that in Java by highlighting the cards when the Shift key is pressed and removing the highlight when the Shift key is released.

There is one more complication. When you hold down a key on the keyboard, that key might *auto-repeat*. This means that it will generate multiple KeyPressed events with just one KeyReleased at the end of the sequence. It can also generate multiple KeyTyped events. For the most part, this will not affect your programming, but you should not expect every KeyPressed event to have a corresponding KeyReleased event.

Each key on the keyboard has a code that identifies it. In JavaFX, key codes are represented by enumerated type constants from the enum *KeyCode*. When an event handler for a KeyPressed or KeyReleased event is called, the parameter, evt, contains the code of the key that was pressed or released. The code can be obtained by calling the function evt.getCode(). For example, when the user presses the shift key, this function will return the value KeyCode.SHIFT. You can find all the codes in the documentation for *KeyCode*, but names for most keys are easy to guess. Letter keys have names like KeyCode.A and KeyCode.Q. The arrow keys are named KeyCode.LEFT, KeyCode.RIGHT, KeyCode.UP, and KeyCode.DOWN. The space bar is KeyCode.SPACE. And function keys have names like KeyCode.F7.

In the case of a KeyTyped event, you want to know which character was typed. This information can be obtained by calling the function evt.getCharacter(). This function returns a value of type String that contains the character that was typed.

As a first example, you can check out the sample program KeyboardEventDemo.java. This program draws a small square on a canvas. The user can move the square left, right, up, and down by pressing arrow keys. This is implemented in a method

private void keyPressed(KeyEvent evt)

that is called by an event handler for KeyPressed events. The handler is installed on the *Scene* object in the start() method with the statement

scene.setOnKeyPressed(e -> keyPressed(e));

In the keyPressed() method, the value of evt.getCode() is checked. If it's one of the arrow keys that was pressed, the canvas is redrawn to show the square in a different position.

The program also installs handlers for KeyReleased and KeyTyped events in a similar way. To give the KeyTyped handler something to do, it changes the color of the square when the user types "r", "g", "b", or "k". I encourage you to run the program and to read the entire source code.

6.3.5 AnimationTimer

There is another kind of basic event that I would like to introduce before turning to a more interesting example; that is, events that are used to drive an animation. The events in this case happen in the background, and you don't have to register a listener to respond to them. However, you do need to write a method that will be called by the system when the events occur.

A computer animation is just a sequence of still images, presented to the user one after the other. If the time between images is short, and if the change from one image to another is not too great, then the user perceives continuous motion. In JavaFX, you can program an animation using an object of type *AnimationTimer* from package javafx.animation. An *AnimationTimer*, animator, has a method animator.start() that you can call to start the animation running or to restart it if it has been paused. It has the method animator.stop() to pause the animation. It also has a method handle(time), but handle() is not a method that you call; it's one that you need to write to say what happens in the animation. The system will call your handle() method once for each frame of the animation. Its job is to do whatever is necessary to implement each frame.

The handle() method will be called on the JavaFX application thread, which means that you can do things like draw on a canvas or manipulate a GUI component. However, whatever you do should not take very long, since JavaFX animations are meant to run at at least 60 frames per second, which means handle() should ideally take less than 1/60 second to run.

AnimationTimer itself is an abstract class, and handle() is an abstract method. This means that to make an animation, you need to write a subclass of *AnimationTimer* and provide a definition for the handle() method. Suppose, for example, that you simply want to call a draw() method for each frame. This could be done as follows, using an anonymous subclass of *AnimationTimer*:

```
AnimationTimer animator = new AnimationTimer() {
    public void handle( long time ) {
            draw();
    }
};
```

Then, to get the animation started, you would need to call animator.start(). This could all be done in an application's start() method.

The parameter, time, gives the current time, measured as the number of nanoseconds since some arbitrary time in the past (the same arbitrary time that is used by System.nanoTime()). You can use time in the calculations that you do for the frame, as a way of making each frame different from the next. Another option is to use a frame number that increases by one each time a frame is drawn, but you should keep in mind that the rate at which handle() is called can vary, and the time between frames is not guaranteed to be 1/60 second.

6.2.6 State Machines

We are ready to look at a program that uses animation and key events to implement a simple game. The program uses an *AnimationTimer* to drive the animation, and it uses a number of instance variables to keep track of the current state of the game. The idea of "state" is an important one.

The information stored in an object's instance variables is said to represent the *state* of that object. When one of the object's methods is called, the action taken by the object can depend on its state. (Or, in the terminology we have been using, the definition of the method can look at the instance variables to decide what to do.) Furthermore, the state can change. (That is, the definition of the method can assign new values to the instance variables.) In computer science, there is the idea of a *state machine*, which is just something that has a state and can change state in response to events or inputs. The response of a state machine to an event depends on what state it's in when the event occurs. An object is a kind of state machine. Sometimes, this point of view can be very useful in designing classes.

The state machine point of view can be especially useful in the type of event-oriented programming that is required by graphical user interfaces. When designing a GUI program, you can ask yourself: What information about state do I need to keep track of? What events can change the state of the program? How will my response to a given event depend on the current state? Should the appearance of the GUI be changed to reflect a change in state? How should the state be taken into account when drawing the content of a canvas? All this is an alternative to the top-down, step-wise-refinement style of program design, which does not apply to the overall design of an event-oriented program.

In the *KeyboardEventDemo* program, discussed above, the state of the program is recorded in instance variables such as squareColor, squareLeft, and squareTop, which record the color and position of the colored square. These state variables are used in a draw() method that draws the square on a canvas. Their values are changed in the key-event-handling methods.

In the rest of this section, we'll look at another example, where the state plays an even bigger role. In this example, the user plays a simple arcade-style game by pressing the arrow keys. The program is defined in the source code file SubKiller. java. As usual, it would be a good idea to compile and run the program as well as read the full source code. Here is a picture:

The entire application window is filled by a canvas. The program shows a black "submarine" near the bottom of the canvas. The submarine moves erratically back and forth near the bottom of the window. Near the top, there is a blue "boat." You can move this boat back and forth by pressing the left and right arrow keys. Attached to the boat is a red "bomb" (or "depth charge"). You can drop the bomb by hitting the down arrow key. The objective is to blow up the submarine by hitting it with the bomb. If the bomb falls off the bottom of the screen, you get a new one. If the submarine explodes, a new sub is created and you get a new bomb. Try it! Make sure to hit the sub at least once, so you can see the explosion.

Let's think about how this game can be programmed. First of all, since we are doing object- oriented programming, I decided to represent the boat, the depth charge, and the submarine as objects. Each of these objects is defined by a separate nested class inside the main application class, and each object has its own state which is represented by the instance variables in the corresponding class. I use variables boat, bomb, and sub to refer to the boat, bomb, and submarine objects.

Now, what constitutes the "state" of the program? That is, what things change from time to time and affect the appearance or behavior of the program? Of course, the state includes the positions of the boat, submarine, and bomb, so those objects have instance variables to store the positions. Anything else, possibly less obvious? Well, sometimes the bomb is falling, and sometimes it's not. That is a difference in state. Since there are two possibilities, I represent this aspect of the state with a boolean variable in the bomb object, bomb.isFalling. Sometimes the submarine is moving left and sometimes it is moving right. The difference is represented by another boolean variable, sub.isMovingLeft. Sometimes, the sub is exploding. This is also part of the state, and it is represented by a boolean variable, sub.isExploding. However, the explosions require a little more thought. An explosion is something that takes place over a series of frames. While an explosion is in progress, the sub looks different in each frame, as the size of the explosion increases. Also, I need to know when the explosion is over so that I can go back to moving and drawing the sub as usual. So, I use an integer variable, sub.explosionFrameNumber to record how many frames have been drawn since the explosion started; the value of this variable is used only when an explosion is in progress.

How and when do the values of these state variables change? Some of them seem to change on their own: For example, as the sub moves left and right, the state variables that specify its position change. Of course, these variables are changing because of an animation, and that animation is driven by an *AnimationTimer*. Each time the animator's handle() method is called, some of the state variables have to change to get ready to draw next frame of the animation. The changes are made in the handle() method before redrawing the canvas. The boat, bomb, and sub objects each contain an updateForNextFrame() method that updates the state variables of the object to get ready for the next frame of the animation. The handle() method calls these methods with the statements

boat.updateForNewFrame();

bomb.updateForNewFrame();

sub.updateForNewFrame();

There are several state variables that change in these update methods, in addition to the position of the sub: If the bomb is falling, then its y-coordinate increases from one frame to the next. If the bomb hits the sub, then the isExploding variable of the sub changes to true, and the isFalling variable of the bomb becomes false. The isFalling variable also becomes false when the bomb falls off the bottom of the screen. If the sub is exploding, then its explosionFrameNumber increases by one in each frame, and if it has reached a certain value, the explosion ends and isExploding is reset to false. At random times, the sub switches between moving to the left and moving to the right. Its direction of motion is recorded in the sub's isMovingLeft variable. The sub's updateForNewFrame() method includes the following lines to change the value of isMovingLeft at random times:

```
if ( Math.random() < 0.02 ) {
    isMovingLeft = ! isMovingLeft;
}
```

There is a 1 in 50 chance that Math.random() will be less than 0.02, so the statement "isMovingLeft = ! isMovingLeft" is executed in one out of every fifty frames, on average. The effect of this statement is to reverse the value of isMovingLeft, from false to true or from true to false. That is, the direction of motion of the sub is reversed.

In addition to changes in state that take place from one frame to the next, a few state variables change when the user presses certain keys. In the program, this is checked in a handler for KeyPressed events. If the user presses the left or right arrow key, the position of the boat is changed. If the user presses the down arrow key, the bomb changes from not-falling to falling. The handler is a long lambda expression that is registered with the scene in the application's start() method:

```
scene.setOnKeyPressed( evt -> {
        // The key listener responds to keyPressed events on the canvas.
        // The left- and right-arrow keys move the boat while down-arrow
        // releases the bomb.
    KeyCode code = evt.getCode();    // Which key was pressed?
    if (code == KeyCode.LEFT) {
        boat.centerX -= 15;
    }
    else if (code == KeyCode.RIGHT) {
        boat.centerX += 15;
    }
    else if (code == KeyCode.DOWN) {
        if ( bomb.isFalling == false )
```

```
            bomb.isFalling = true;
        }
    });
```

Note that it's not necessary to redraw the canvas in this method, since this canvas shows an animation that is constantly being redrawn anyway. Any changes in the state will become visible to the user as soon as the next frame is drawn. At some point in the program, I have to make sure that the user does not move the boat off the screen. I could have done this in the key event handler, but I chose to check for this in another routine, in the boat object, since it seems natural to let the boat object be responsible for keeping itself on the screen.

I encourage you to read the source code in SubKiller.java. Although a few points are tricky, you should with some effort be able to read and understand the entire program. Try to understand the program in terms of state machines. Note how the state of each of the three objects in the program changes in response to events from the timer and from the user.

While it's not at all sophisticated as arcade games go, the SubKiller game does use some interesting programming. And it nicely illustrates how to apply state-machine thinking in event-oriented programming.

6.3.7 Observable Values

There is one more kind of basic event that plays an important role in JavaFX: events that are generated when an *observable value* is modified. There is an example in the SubKiller program. A *Stage*, stage, has a property of type *ObservableBooleanValue* that tells whether or not stage is currently the focused window. You can access the property by calling stage.focusedProperty(). When the value of an *ObservableBooleanProperty* changes, an event is generated. You can register a *ChangeListener* with the property, containing an event handler method that will be called when the event occurs. The handler method in this case has three parameters: the observable property that generated the event, the previous value of the property, and the new value. For an *ObservableBooleanValue*, the old and new values are of type boolean. There are other observable value types, such as *ObservableIntegerValue*, *ObservableStringValue*, and *ObservableObjectValue*.

When I first wrote SubKiller, the animation would continue to run even when the SubKiller window was not the focused window, which I found annoying when I was trying to work in another window. I decided to pause the animation when the window loses the input focus and to restart it when the window regains focus. When the window loses or gains focus, the value of the observable boolean property stage.focusedProperty() changes. To react to that change, I added a change listener to the property, which stops the animation when the value of the property changes to false and starts the animation when the value changes to true. So, I added this code to the start() method:

```
stage.focusedProperty().addListener( (obj,oldVal,newVal) -> {
                // This listener turns the animation off when this program's
                // window does not have the input focus.
        if (newVal) { // The window has gained focus.
                timer.start();
        }
        else {  // The window has lost focus.
                timer.stop();
        }
        draw(); // Redraw canvas. (Appearance changes depending on focus.)
    });
```

The addListener() method of an observable property registers a change listener with the property. Note that the lambda expression for the event handler takes three parameters. The only one that I need here is newVal which represents the current value of the stage's focused property. The draw() method draws draws some things differently, depending on whether the stage is focused. It tests for that calling stage.isFocused().

JavaFX GUI components have many observable properties, of various types. For example, the text on a *Button* is a property of type *ObservableStringProperty*, and the width and the height of a canvas are values of type *ObservableDoubleProperty*. We will encounter more examples in the next section.

INDEX